PRAISE FOR *RED HOT CITY*

"The most thorough assessment of the political economy of Atlanta's urban and regional growth and development in over twenty years."

—LARRY KEATING, Professor Emeritus, School of City and Regional Planning, Georgia Tech University

"The scholarship and writing are excellent. Dan Immergluck is a first-hand participant in many of the debates described in the book as well as an international expert on housing."

—EDWARD G. GOETZ, Professor of Urban and Regional Planning, University of Minnesota

"Immergluck forces the reader to look at the raw and painful history of racist land use practices and their effect on vulnerable people and places in Metro Atlanta. Under the guise of 'Smart Growth' and 'New Urbanism,' government, corporate, and affluent interests have worked collectively to use fear, greed, and public policy as covert weapons of mass inequity. As opposed to serving as a beacon of light for inclusive growth, Immergluck makes us accept the ugly truth. The history and current condition of Atlanta and its suburbs must be studied as a cautionary tale of what happens when a region becomes too busy to care about its most vulnerable residents. One question stayed with me after reading *Red Hot City*: What if?"

—NATHANIEL SMITH, President and Chief Equity Officer, Partnership for Southern Equity

"Immergluck's *Red Hot City* skillfully captures the nuanced and historically embedded complexities concerning politics, race, urban development and divestment, racialized displacement and inequalities, growing ethnic diversity, unprecedented growth, and the evolution of creative entrepreneurship in the Atlanta region. *Red Hot City* also provides a clear picture of the linkages and the borderlines between Atlanta the city—one of the nation's most prominent Black Meccas—and its sprawling, increasingly diverse metropolitan area, ninth largest in the country and growing."

—DEIRDRE OAKLEY, Georgia State University

"Steeped in the promise of the American Dream—life, liberty, and the pursuit of happiness—Immergluck offers a glimpse of Atlanta's reality with this shining example of scholarship as a solution to one of the city's most glaring problems. He shifts the narrative of civil and human rights from the more highbrow discussions of Atlanta's civil rights lore, bringing it down to the lived experiences through trends and tensions of home ownership, public housing, and/or the lack thereof."

—MAURICE J. HOBSON, author of *The Legend of the Black Mecca: Politics and Class in the Making of Modern Atlanta*

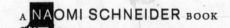

RED HOT CITY

The publisher and the University of California Press Foundation gratefully acknowledge the generous support of the George Gund Foundation Imprint in African American Studies.

The publisher and the University of California Press Foundation also gratefully acknowledge the generous support of the Lawrence Grauman, Jr. Fund.

RED HOT CITY

Housing, Race, and Exclusion in
Twenty-First Century Atlanta

||||||||||||||||||||||||||||||||||||||||||||||||||||||||||||||||||||||||||||||||||||||||||||||||||||||

DAN IMMERGLUCK

UNIVERSITY OF CALIFORNIA PRESS

University of California Press
Oakland, California

Library of Congress Cataloging-in-Publication Data

Names: Immergluck, Daniel, author.
Title: Red hot city : housing, race, and exclusion in twenty-first-century
    Atlanta / Dan Immergluck.
Description: Oakland, California : University of California Press, [2022] |
    Includes bibliographical references and index.
Identifiers: LCCN 2022003725 (print) | LCCN 2022003726 (ebook) |
    ISBN 9780520387638 (cloth) | ISBN 9780520387645 (paperback) |
    ISBN 9780520387652 (ebook)
Subjects: LCSH: Discrimination in housing—Georgia—Atlanta—History—20th
    century. | Discrimination in housing—Georgia—Atlanta—History—21st
    century. | Housing policy--Georgia--Atlanta.
Classification: LCC HD7288.76.U52 A85 2022 (print) | LCC HD7288.76.U52
    (ebook) | DDC 363.5/1097582310904—dc23/eng/20220607
LC record available at https://lccn.loc.gov/2022003725
LC ebook record available at https://lccn.loc.gov/2022003726

Manufactured in the United States of America

31 30 29 28 27 26 25 24 23 22
10 9 8 7 6 5 4 3 2 1

Contents

Preface

THIS BOOK IS PARTLY the product of decades of working in and studying urban places that had suffered from histories of racialized disinvestment, wealth extraction, predatory finance, and hostile public policy. Before becoming an academic, I spent over a decade working in community development and advocating against predatory finance and for responsible reinvestment. As an academic, I have continued to do research and policy-oriented work about places, including many Black neighborhoods, where disinvestment, population loss, and property abandonment persist.

Coming to Atlanta in 2005, I saw the familiar effects of disinvestment, predatory finance, and wealth extraction in many Black neighborhoods. Yet, I also quickly began to appreciate a set of more complicated, fast-moving trends occurring in the city. I noticed home prices rising rapidly in certain parts of town, especially around an area slated for a major, publicly financed redevelopment project called "the

Beltline." I noticed speculators buying up numerous parcels. Affordable housing advocates voiced concerns over displacement and gentrification. I began to educate myself on the city's history, read about emergent gentrification in the wake of the 1996 Olympics and public housing demolitions, and obtained a copy of a 2001 report by a citywide gentrification task force. While I certainly had seen gentrification while working in Chicago in the 1990s, the relative scale of speculation and property value increases that I saw in Atlanta were more widespread. Moreover, these changes were not just contained to certain parts of town adjacent to previously gentrified neighborhoods as I had often seen in Chicago.

As the subprime crisis began in 2007, I saw the devastation it wreaked on families and neighborhoods in both the city and suburbs, especially in Black neighborhoods. I had seen the damage that subprime lending had done before in the late 1990s in Chicago. So, knowing the greater scale of the 2000s subprime boom, the magnitude of damage in the late 2000s and early 2010s did not come as a surprise. Then, as real estate markets came roaring back after the crisis, especially in the city and around the Beltline, the unevenness of the recovery was striking. I had seen the Beltline's effects on speculation and land values before the crash. As real estate capital once again began flowing into the city, the patterns quickly reemerged, although at a grander scale and accompanied by more physical redevelopment.

Sometime around the early 2010s, I began thinking more about all that policymakers could do, but weren't doing, to "reset" Atlanta's development trajectory in a way that might generate inclusive, diverse spaces in which lower-income, primarily Black families could benefit more from growth instead of communities simply being recast as places intended for much different populations. Did the fate of neighborhoods that had experienced serious population loss and disinvestment in the 1970s and 1980s have only two paths, either continuing the one they were on or switching to one of rampant, racialized gentrification and displacement? Did policymakers and planners face a choice only between maintaining the status quo or retrofitting formerly cast-off neighborhoods into ones for whiter and more affluent populations, places where lower-income and more diverse families would be unlikely to afford? Wasn't it the job of policymakers and planners to advocate for a third way, one of responsible reinvestment providing for improvements in residents' lives and housing options, instead of focusing on glitzy "transformative" redevelopment projects that result in dramatic increases in rents?

As the redevelopment of the city and region resumed and accelerated following the foreclosure crisis, I continued to think about the decisions being made, and not made, that shaped the trajectory of the region and that were leading to a new era of geographically reshaped, but still heavily racialized and exclusionary. The initial policy design and planning of the Beltline, even after strong warnings, was one that mostly ignored the impact that the project would likely have on housing affordability. When the subprime crisis hit and land values plummeted, an opportunity presented itself to hit a sort of reset button. Local and state government, and philanthropic actors, could have acquired and banked land to establish significant amounts of long-term affordable housing in neighborhoods that would experience rapid increases in land values in just a few years. In the suburbs, large numbers of foreclosed homes flowed into the hands of investors, including many smaller ones, but also new, larger Wall Street-backed firms that federal policymakers encouraged to move into the single-family rental industry. The minimal federal resources provided to state and local governments were often ineffectively deployed. More importantly, the level of the response at all levels of government was woefully inadequate to create an equitable recovery.

This book is an effort to tell the story of the choices that have contributed to and shaped the racially and economically exclusionary patterns of development in the region over the last twenty-five years. It is critical to recognize that these were policy choices and not the result of some magical free market. Cities are, of course, shaped partly by markets. But markets are heavily shaped and constructed by politics, institutions, racial discrimination, and policy choices.

This book would not have been possible without the support of so many people, not all of whom I can mention here. I begin with all the wonderful scholars who have written books on Atlanta. It is an important place to study, and it is a privilege to build upon these authors' work. I must mention at least some of these scholars because I relied on their work so much in gaining a more robust understanding of Atlanta's development in the twentieth century. They include Carlton Basmajian, Ronald Bayor, Tomiko Brown-Nagin, Maurice Hobson, Alton Hornsby, Jr., Larry Keating, Kevin Kruse, Lee Ann Lands, Gary Pomerantz, Akira Drake Rodriguez, Charles Rutheiser, and Clarence Stone.

I also want to thank the many local journalists in Atlanta who worked over the years to shine a light on the many decisions of policymakers, planners, and developers that shaped the region. I cannot mention them all here, but you will see their names in the endnotes.

I have had the pleasure to teach and advise hundreds of students over the last seventeen years in Atlanta at Georgia State and Georgia Tech. They are too numerous to name, of course, but I have learned so much from them, and this learning continues. In the last few years, I have bounced ideas that were brewing in my head off of them as I prepared to write this book, and those discussions were extremely helpful in clarifying my thinking. I want to especially thank Austin Harrison for giving the entire manuscript a close read and providing thoughtful comments.

Several advocates and scholars with expertise and knowledge about many of the topics in the book were gracious enough to read drafts of various sections of the book. Some read smaller excerpts, while others read several chapters or the entire book. All were incredibly generous with their time. Of course, their reading and comments strengthened the book, but I remain the only person responsible for any errors and all opinions expressed in the manuscript. These readers include Julian Bene, David Couchman, Ed Goetz, Larry Keating, Marion Liou, Kate Little, Melanie Noble-Couchman, and Sara Patenaude.

The folks at the University of California Press were very helpful, especially Naomi Schneider and Summer Farah. I appreciated their understanding of my goals for the book and their appreciation of my aim to write for a larger audience than some scholarly books aim to reach. I am honored that Naomi has chosen the put the book under the "A Naomi Schneider" imprint.

I owe so much to my immediate and extended family. I worked far too hard during the time I developed and wrote the book. Kate and Anna both showed great support for me doing the project. And what can I say about Lilly? For over thirty years, she has provided so much support, in so many ways, especially during some more challenging times in recent years. She has been a true, invaluable partner.

Finally, I expect that this book may be perceived by some—including perhaps some who may not bother to read it—as a simple condemnation of Atlanta. It is not. It is a wish, a call, for a better Atlanta, a more compassionate Atlanta. It is a call for Atlanta—and cities like Atlanta—to change their fundamental approach to developing their futures in ways that prioritize the interests of those who have been most adversely affected by patterns of racial and economic exclusion.

Abbreviations

ABI	Atlanta Beltline, Inc.
ACP	Atlanta Committee for Progress
ADU	accessory dwelling unit
AHA	Atlanta Housing Authority (later known as "Atlanta Housing")
AHC	Atlanta Housing Council
AHAND	Atlanta Housing Association of Neighborhood-based Developers
AJC	*Atlanta Journal-Constitution*
ALT	Atlanta Land Trust
ALTC	Atlanta Land Trust Collaborative
AMI	(metropolitan) area median income
AMRPC	Atlanta Metropolitan Regional Planning Commission
ANDP	Atlanta Neighborhood Development Partnership

ARC	Atlanta Regional Commission
ASF	American Securitization Forum
BAHTF	Beltline Affordable Housing Trust Fund
CBA	community benefits agreement
CCCS	Consumer Credit Counseling Services
CFD	contract-for-deed
CLT	community land trust
CODA	Corporation for Olympic Development in Atlanta
DAFC	Development Authority of Fulton County
DCA	(Georgia) Department of Community Affairs
FDIC	Federal Deposit Insurance Corporation
FHA	Federal Housing Administration
FHFA	Federal Housing Finance Agency
GFLA	Georgia Fair Lending Act
GRTA	Georgia Regional Transportation Agency
GSU	Georgia State University
HAMP	Home Affordable Modification Program
HDP	(Atlanta Legal Aid's) Home Defense Project
HERA	Housing and Economic Recovery Act
HHF	Hardest Hit Fund
IZ	inclusionary zoning
LIHTC	Low-Income Housing Tax Credit
MARTA	Metropolitan Atlanta Rapid Transit Authority
MPC	Metropolitan Planning Commission
MSA	metropolitan statistical area
NFMC	National Foreclosure Mitigation Counseling (program)
NPU	Neighborhood Planning Unit
NSP	Neighborhood Stabilization Program
OTP	outside the perimeter
PCM	Ponce City Market
REO	real-estate-owned

SFR   single-family rental
TAD   tax allocation district
TFCBC Turner Field Community Benefits Coalition
WECC   West End Cooperative Corporation

INTRODUCTION

IN THE FALL OF 2020, Atlanta was all over the national news. It was the place that made Georgia the only blue state in the South, helped seal the election for Joe Biden, and put the U.S. Senate in Democratic hands. It is the capital of the South, still laying claim to being the "Black Mecca," as tens of thousands of Black households move to the region each year, while also developing into a multiethnic metropolis. In terms of urban form, the area is simultaneously a preeminent example of both suburban sprawl and twenty-first-century gentrification.

A growth-above-all development ethos permeates the region and is rooted in the city's twentieth-century expansion. Like some other booming Sunbelt metros, Atlanta has combined a continuing reliance on public-private partnerships and a state and regional planning and policy regime that excessively caters to capital, often at the expense of its poorer residents, who are predominantly Black and Latinx. As the city proper has become a hot commodity in the real

Map 1. The Atlanta metropolitan region

estate arena and is no longer majority-Black, the region has inverted the late-twentieth-century poor-in-the-core urban model to one where less-affluent families face exclusion from the central city and more-affluent suburbs and are pushed out to lower-income, sometimes quite distant suburbs, usually farther from mass transit, large public hospitals, and other essential services.

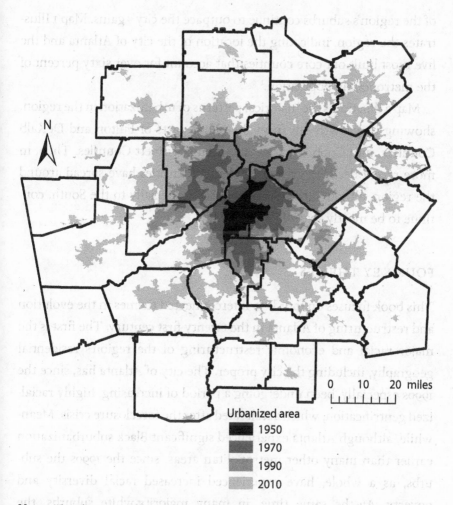

Urbanized area
■ 1950
■ 1970
■ 1990
■ 2010

0   10   20 miles

Map 2. The urbanization of the Atlanta region, 1950 to 2010

At this writing, the Atlanta metropolitan area is the ninth largest in the country and likely to climb into the eighth spot in the not-too-distant future. The metro grew from 4.1 million people in 2000 to just over 6 million by 2019. The city of Atlanta comprises less than a tenth of the region's population and, while its population has been increasing since 1990, and especially since 2010, the growth and spatial expansion of the region's suburbs continue to outpace the city's gains. Map 1 Illus-trates the region, indicating the location of the city of Atlanta and the five most built-out core counties that account for over sixty percent of the metropolitan population.[1]

Map 2 illustrates the historical patterns of urbanization in the region, showing its growth out from the oldest parts of Fulton and DeKalb Counties, into Cobb, Clayton, and then Gwinnett Counties. Then, in more recent decades, greater residential densities have spread around the region, although the fringe counties, especially to the South, con-tinue to be mostly sparsely populated.

FOUR KEY THEMES

This book focuses on four key, interconnected themes in the evolution and restructuring of Atlanta in the twenty-first century. The first is the major racial and economic restructuring of the region's residential geography, including the city proper. The city of Atlanta has, since the 1990s especially, been undergoing a period of increasing, highly racial-ized gentrification, which accelerated after the foreclosure crisis. Mean-while, although Atlanta experienced significant Black suburbanization earlier than many other metropolitan areas, since the 1990s the sub-urbs, as a whole, have experienced increased racial diversity and poverty. At the same time, in many majority-white suburbs, the encroaching racial and economic diversity, which has included grow-ing Latinx and Asian as well as Black populations, has been met with significant resistance and deliberate efforts to maintain whiteness and economic exclusivity. Lower-income families, mostly households of color, have faced racialized displacement and exclusion not just from the gentrifying city but also from the more affluent suburbs in the region. These suburbs have done this not just through the traditional tools of exclusionary zoning or building codes but also through large-scale redevelopment projects aimed at parts of their communities from which they have cleared away "tired" older apartment buildings and replaced them with new housing and commercial development that caters to a more affluent and, often, whiter population. Both in the city and the suburbs, racial and economic residential change has not simply been the unintended outcome of growing wealth in the region. Rather, these patterns of exclusion are key results of decisions made continually and repeatedly by policymakers and planners at the local and state level.

A second theme of the book is the failure of the city of Atlanta to capture a significant share of a tremendous growth in local land values. Local governments could have channeled a substantial portion of such growth into providing long-term, affordable housing for its less-affluent Black residents. Generating large increases in property and land wealth through processes that leave much of it severely under-taxed and unavailable to benefit ordinary residents makes little sense. Moreover, places like Atlanta need to create sustainable funding streams to provide affordable, stable housing for existing and prospective lower-income residents. A focus only on the direct displacement of "legacy" residents is understandable because such families have often lived through periods of disinvestment, wealth extraction, and decline, only to find that they can no longer afford to live in a place when it is redeveloped. But eventually, the number of legacy residents will decline, even if direct displacement is minimized. Suppose local actors pay no attention to the long-term provision of affordable housing options in places experiencing strong gentrifying pressures. In such a case, they would become places of racial and economic exclusion, reproducing segregation in different parts of the region. Reshuffling poverty out to remote suburban areas can leave lower-income families worse off than when they lived closer to public transit, major public hospitals, and other critical services.

A third theme of the book is the critical role of state government in constraining and enabling how development and redevelopment occur and whether the interests of those most vulnerable to exclusion and displacement are given serious consideration. Though it has become an increasingly blue region, Atlanta still has to operate in what is still effectively a red state, at least when it comes to state politics and policy. Moreover, even if the state legislature fell under the control of Democrats someday, it is unclear how much this would affect the policy environment for housing and real estate development. Georgia is a strong property-rights state where landlords and mortgage lenders benefit from a legal regime that gives them most of what they want and provides few protections for renters. The topic of "local control" is a highly normative one. When it comes to providing local governments with the power to exclude affordable housing through exclusionary zoning or building codes, local control usually prevails. But local authority does not extend to allowing local governments to provide for stronger tenant protections, rent control, or fair housing ordinances in their communities. The state legislature has been quick to preempt such measures.

The final theme of the book, and its key overarching narrative, concerns the political economy of urban change and the presence of inflection points. These are periods during which particularly consequential policy decisions are made that have a disproportionate impact on the trajectories of a place and have direct and long-lasting implications for racial and economic exclusion. The forces reshaping the city and its suburbs, including those that displace and exclude, are not the product of anonymous, impersonal, "free markets." Rather, these forces are generated through a political economy of actors working towards redeveloping space that houses less-affluent, racially diverse populations and works to remake places for a more desirable residential base and the businesses accompanying them. Highly organized and deliberate planning studies and processes, together with the force and subsidy provided by publicly financed redevelopment, are brought to bear. Of course, there are many smaller, atomistic transactions that also play a role, but the projects that move markets, like the Atlanta Beltline, or the "revitalization" of Sandy Springs' North End, are the results of political choices and processes and are executed through extensive, often multi-year planning exercises. These projects get funded by general obliga-tion bonds, tax increment financing districts, and other financial schemes from the "public-private partnership" toolbox. Urban regimes or suburban redevelopment machines are called into action or formed to gather political support for these projects, often through a network of elected officials, homeowner associations, and real estate firms and consultants. The focus of this book is not on contributing to the now long-running debates over whether biracial urban regimes, growth machines, or homevoter power are the most influential force at play in shaping the city and its suburbs. They have all contributed to the restructuring of, and exclusion within, the region.

In Atlanta's case, there were several key inflection points since the 1990s, times at which institutions and actors made decisions that fur-thered a trajectory of racial and economic exclusion, instead of ones that could have provided a more inclusive path in which lower-income people of color were not relegated, with little apparent consideration, to some other, less attractive location. An early inflection point was the period around the 1996 Olympics. Various decisions were made that effectively set the stage for long-term gentrification and exclusion in the city, focusing primarily on making the city more attractive to a more affluent set of prospective citizens. Another inflection point occurred in the city with the early planning and design of the Atlanta Beltline. This project concentrated speculation and housing demand in a corridor encircling the city's core, leading to strong increases in gen-trification. Instead of securing a substantial amount of land for devel-oping affordable housing early in the process, the city and the Beltline organization chose instead to prioritize a quick rollout of parks and trails, which themselves fueled further housing demand. The period during and after the foreclosure crisis presented another inflection point. Land values plummeted and vacancies mounted across the region, while insufficient efforts were made to secure housing stock and land to provide a sizable base of long-term affordable housing as some bulwark against the coming wave of gentrification and rising rents. Instead, in the city and in many suburbs, a great deal of low-cost property flowed into the hands of speculators and investors.

Some have argued, and will continue to argue, that Atlanta's leaders have made mostly good policy choices in shaping the city's and the region's trajectories. For example, in a boosterish history of the city in the latter decades of the twentieth century, a former local columnist argued that the corporate-led white-Black governing regime had repeatedly picked "the right fork in the road."[2] If a city's or region's primary goals are simply to grow its population and land values, such claims could be argued to have merit. If, however, cities and regions are judged more on the welfare of their less-powerful and less-affluent residents, arguments that leaders in the region have made mostly good choices become much harder to accept.

ATLANTA AS A PARADIGMATIC CASE FOR GROWING, GENTRIFYING CITIES

The significant changes that have occurred in Atlanta and how policymakers, real estate market actors, and others have fueled and shaped these changes make Atlanta a paradigmatic case for regions undergoing profound transformation and investment pressures, i.e., emerging hot-market metros. Lessons from Atlanta's last twenty-five years are helpful in considering what could happen to other cities that are undergoing—or might be vulnerable to undergoing—similar regional housing market pressures within a context of weak state and local policy environments that tend not to give much attention to the welfare of lower-income families and households of color. Atlanta provides a case of a region experiencing very strong growth pressures with little policy attention aimed at capturing the benefits of that growth for the region's working-class residents or for protecting lower-income households from racial and class exclusion and housing market instability.

While each metropolitan area is unique, and rarely do different regions exhibit very similar trajectories over long periods, a significant number of metros, especially in the South, have experienced changes in recent decades that resemble Atlanta's in some important ways. However, few cities have undergone quite as much transformation.[3] At least five other large metros have experienced changes similar to Atlanta over the last two decades, for example, Tampa, Richmond, Nashville, Austin, and Denver. All have seen significant growth in their metropolitan populations, with all but one (Denver) experiencing growth of more than thirty percent from 2000 to 2019, with Austin leading the pack at seventy-eight percent. These metros experienced growth in their central cities as well, with Austin experiencing the most significant growth at almost fifty percent. Richmond, Nashville, Tampa, and Denver experienced growth of between seventeen and thirty-one percent over the nineteen years, a similar order of magnitude to the city of Atlanta's twenty-two percent growth.

These regions have also exhibited several signs of gentrification, although usually not to the degree that Atlanta has. All saw some increase in the ratio of the city's median family income compared to its corresponding suburbs, although none of the others have yet reached the point where the central city's median income now exceeds the suburbs', which is now the case in Atlanta. These cities also saw declines from 2000 to 2019 in non-college-educated populations, who are often the most vulnerable to exclusion and displacement. These declines ranged from ten percentage points in Richmond to nineteen percentage points in Denver, although none were as substantial as Atlanta's twenty-two percentage-point decline. These metros also experienced a significant suburbanization of poverty. The ratio of the city-to-suburban poverty rates increased by at least sixteen percent in all six metros. The median increase was about thirty percent, with the largest increases in Richmond and Atlanta, at forty-five percent and forty-one percent, respectively.

Atlanta also provides a cautionary tale for cities that have not yet experienced strong, measurable gentrification pressures but that could, in the not-too-distant future, be vulnerable to such pressures and the same kinds of exclusionary trajectories that Atlanta has seen over the last three decades. In fact, Atlanta policymakers persisted in acting as if the city would remain starved of higher-income residents and jobs for a long time. They focused primarily on trying to attract higher-income residents without preparing for the potential "turnaround" that was to arrive relatively swiftly as the twenty-first century arrived. More critically, their policies actively supported and encouraged "clearing the way" for investment aimed at a new race and class of Atlanta resident. If cities want to take a different path, one that maintains space for existing and future lower-income residents, they need to act early if they seek to maintain diversity and minimize racial and economic exclusion. The later they begin to react to such changes, the more it will be an attempt to catch a gentrifying tiger by the tail.

Even though other cities have been experiencing some of the same types of pressures as Atlanta, it is not accurate to suggest that Atlanta is narrowly representative of some larger cohort, even among this growing and gentrifying group of cities. The city itself has been ranked by two different reports since 2015 as among the five fastest-gentrifying cities in the country, and the data used in both of these studies did not account for continuing, robust gentrification in the later 2010s.[4] The region is also distinct in its substantial Black population, second only in total magnitude to the New York metro. As a share of the metropolitan population, Atlanta is the nation's leading large Black metro, with about thirty-five percent of the population being Black. At the same time, the region is increasingly multiethnic with Latinx and Asian residents now accounting for about twenty percent of the population.

THE STRUCTURE OF THE BOOK

The book is organized into five main chapters and a conclusion. Chapter 1 brings the reader up to speed on the history of residential development in Atlanta, from its founding before the civil war to the end of the twentieth century. I draw on a remarkable breadth and depth of scholarship, including a trove of wonderful books that each tend to focus on a different period or aspect of the city's growth and change during the twentieth century. The chapter pays particular attention to the political economy and governance of the city and how that impacted residential change, including the well-known Atlanta urban regime politics described by authors such as Clarence Stone, Tomiko Brown-Nagin, Alton Hornsby, Larry Keating, Maurice Hobson, and others.

Chapter 2 examines the largest redevelopment project in the Atlanta region, and arguably one of the most "transformative" projects in the country in the last twenty years, the Atlanta Beltline. The chapter delves into the political economy of the key planning and policy decisions at various stages of the project, especially as they relate to housing affordability, gentrification, and displacement.

Chapter 3 focuses on racialized gentrification and exclusion in the city of Atlanta since the 1990s and the forces that contributed to these patterns. It explores what I term the "dysfunctional public finance" of the city of Atlanta, in which the land values in the city skyrocketed after the foreclosure crisis while the city's coffers did not capture much of this growth due to excessive subsidies given to corporations and developers and a systematic under-taxation of larger commercial real estate. City leaders made grandiose campaign pledges to spend hundreds of millions on affordable housing but later complained that the funding was just not there to deliver it.

Chapter 4 describes the impact of the subprime and foreclosure crisis of the late 2000s and early 2010s on the region, and the responses to the crisis. It identifies failures at all levels of government and the opportunities that were missed to secure more land and homes for affordable housing purposes. Instead, hundreds of thousands of housing units flowed from homeowners, including many Black and Latinx homeowners, to private investors over this period.

Chapter 5 examines developments and changes in the suburbs over this time, including the growing overall diversity of the suburbs, including larger Black, Latinx, and Asian populations, while a group of more-affluent, whiter suburbs tried to resist this encroaching diversity as much as possible. The chapter describes some of the more exclusionary activities of wealthier suburbs, including large-scale displace-and-replace redevelopment projects that resulted in significant racial and economic exclusion. It also discusses housing precarity along Buford Highway, an important corridor of immigrant businesses and residents.

The book's conclusion ties together many of the lessons from these chapters. It ends with discussing what recent political trends could mean for the development trajectory of, and continued exclusion in, the region. It also calls for avoiding a "market-inevitability" fatalism which suggests that nothing can be done to redirect or alter the sorts of trajectories described in the book. It reminds the reader that the events and consequences described are not simply the result of apolitical, atomistic market forces. They are shaped heavily by institutional actors and processes. The city is a politically constructed space whose conditions and trends reflect many key policy decisions over time. No single decision is likely to reverse the exclusion continually experienced by those facing the worst housing precarity. But how major redevelopment projects get done, how they are financed, and the rules under which real estate markets operate are all policy choices, and these choices can and do make a difference.

1

BUILDING THE RACIALLY SEGREGATED SOUTHERN CAPITAL

IN 1837, AFTER THE MUSCOGEE and Cherokee had been violently expelled from much of northern Georgia, a settlement known as Terminus developed where downtown Atlanta is today. After a short-lived stint beginning in 1843 as Marthasville, the town was renamed again in 1847 to Atlanta and incorporated as a municipality.[1] Far from being something out of stereotypical southern cotillion life, Rutheiser describes Atlanta, in its early years, as a "rough and rowdy frontier town possessed of far more saloons and bawdy houses than churches and reputable establishments."[2] The city developed around the nexus of three railroads, the Western and Atlantic, the Georgia, and the Macon and Western. Once the Western and Atlantic crossed the Appalachian Mountains, one could travel through the city to any other place of importance in the South, leading to Atlanta being called the "Gate City," as it was a gateway to the rest of the South.

The city grew rapidly after the Civil War, with white and Black families migrating to it in large numbers. Much of the land in the city was rapidly scooped up by land speculators, some of whom were associated with the railroads, such as Richard Peters and George Adair. By the late 1860s, the two had acquired the Atlanta Street Railway Company and were quick to direct horse-car transit lines towards their property holdings to help them gain value.[3] Adair and Peters worked hand-in-glove with mayors, council members, and other politicians to ensure a business- and capital-friendly government, including garnering state aid to railroads and manufacturers and noncompetitive contracts with their streetcar lines.[4] Atlanta became the headquarters of many federal government operations for Georgia and sometimes beyond, including the military government of Georgia, the Freedmen's Bureau, and other organizations. In just six years, from 1860 to 1866, its population doubled, and in 1867 Atlanta became the state capital, which it remains to this day.[5]

Atlanta was the home of the "New South" movement, most frequently associated with publisher and orator Henry Grady. Grady and his supporters promoted the concept of a more industrialized South that would turn its back on the backward, rural dominance of the Old South and compete for jobs and industry with northern cities. Yet, as Maurice Hobson has argued, "Grady's New South idea did little to displace the Old South's hegemonic order of white supremacy . . . whites fine-tuned those traditions to create the New South."[6]

By the last decade of the nineteenth century, Atlanta had become home to six prominent Black institutions of higher education: Atlanta University, Morehouse College, Spellman College, Clark University, Morris Brown College, and Gammon Theological Seminary. This made Atlanta an intellectual powerhouse of Black America. The arrival of W. E. B. Du Bois at Atlanta University in 1897 sort of sealed the deal on Atlanta's critical place in Black intellectual history.[7]

The city of Atlanta has always had a substantial Black population, which increased dramatically from twenty percent in 1860 to forty-six percent in 1870.[8] As the city continued to grow, white in-migration and growth outpaced Black growth until the 1920s. By 1910, the city's total population hit just under 90,000 and, by 1920, reached 200,000, with the Black proportion dropping to about thirty-two percent. But as farm mechanization and the Great Depression hit, Black people poured into Atlanta. By 1950, 121,000 (thirty-seven percent) of the city proper's 331,000 residents were Black.[9]

In the last decades of the nineteenth century, Atlanta developed first around its Union Depot, with factories, warehouses, and stores located relatively close together in pre-zoning, walking-city fashion. But in short order, residential neighborhoods developed around the old core city, with middle-class white neighborhoods situated on higher ground, especially north of downtown. In contrast, working-class white and Black families were relegated more to lower-lying, flood-prone areas.[10]

At the turn of the twentieth century, the parks movement took hold in Atlanta, with developer-turned-parks commissioner Joel Hurt leading the way. Hurt, who came from the railroad and banking industries, was the developer of Inman Park and the owner of the streetcar system that created much of its value. Hurt also owned and operated forced-labor camps that leased prisoners from the state, exploiting hundreds of convicts under brutal conditions.[11] The "park-neighborhood" became the model for Atlanta, with curvilinear streets and parks as their centerpiece. This was, as historian Lee Ann Lands suggests, Atlanta's contribution to the City Beautiful movement.[12] But this housing was aimed at the white middle-class and more affluent and, especially, at homeowners. Speculators buying property to house renters were what today would be called in-fill developers, purchasing enough land to build two or three houses, or perhaps a block of homes, to develop and rent out. They often did not have the financing or wealth of developers such as Hurt to build entire neighborhoods. The job growth in the city meant that there was an intense housing shortage, so employers also got into the housing development business, sometimes building entire neighborhoods and sometimes simply shoehorning housing in between their factories and warehouses.

By the turn of the century, some well-established Black neighborhoods had developed, including on the city's west, south, and east sides. But significant in-fill development dampened the level of racial segregation in many working-class communities. In these places, there was substantial "checkerboard," street-by-street, or even some building-by-building segregation, in which individual properties were rented only to Black people or only to white people. Lee Ann Lands has described this housing as "raced more than classed," in that property owners assigned rental homes to white and Black people separately and advertised them accordingly.[13]

Some have argued that southern cities, especially in the late-nineteenth and early-twentieth centuries, didn't need to spatially segregate Black from white people as much as northern cities did because the strong systems of social control, including Jim Crow violence, made residential segregation less necessary.[14] They point to lower neighborhood-level racial segregation measures for southern cities as compared to northern ones. At the scale of relatively large "neighborhoods," this is generally correct. In 1890 in Atlanta, for example, at the "ward" level, a fairly large geographic scale at which to measure segregation, the dissimilarity index for Atlanta was only 0.18 (on a scale of 0.0 to 1.0, with 1.0 equating to complete segregation), compared to an average of 0.45 the same year for nine northern cities.[15] But segregation indices are sensitive to the geographic scale at which they are measured, and recent research has shed more light on how southern cities tended to exhibit segregation at a finer geographic level.[16]

John Logan and Matthew Martinez have shown that, when measured at smaller geographic levels, well below the geographic scale of a census tract, southern cities before the turn of the twentieth century tended to be quite segregated. Sometimes the segregation occurred at different spatial scales in different parts of the same city.[17] They found some predominantly Black neighborhoods in many of the ten southern cities they examined, which included Atlanta, but also a large amount of finer-grained segregation at the level of streets, blocks, and buildings. This is consistent with the notion that Atlanta had both segregated Black neighborhoods and segregated streets or buildings in different parts of the city during this period.

When looking at smaller geographic scales, likes streets and buildings, Atlanta's segregation was more pronounced in 1880 than it seemed when looking only at a larger, neighborhood level. Logan and Martinez found that at the census "enumeration district" level—effectively a larger neighborhood area—the dissimilarity index in 1880 in Atlanta was only 0.29. All ten of the cities never exceeded 0.46.[18] However, as they measured segregation at the block-face level (one side of a street, from one intersection to the next), the index reached 0.65, suggesting a high level of segregation. At the building level, segregation was even more intense at 0.87, a degree that would be classified as "hypersegregated" today. Detailed maps of these data show that while there were streets where both white and Black buildings were located, there were also many streets where either white or Black buildings dominated the street. And there were some parts of town, including on the west, south, and near northeast sides, where there were relatively significant concentrations of Black-occupied properties. Over time, racial segregation spread over larger areas in Atlanta so that the dissimilarity index at the larger, neighborhood-scale reached 0.44 by 1930, up from 0.29 in 1880, but was still significantly lower than for nine comparison northern cities (0.67). While it is fair to say that census tracts or similarly sized neighborhood areas in southern cities were generally less segregated than in northern cities, at the street level segregation was quite strong in the south, and over time grew to be more of a problem at the neighborhood level.

Of course, housing was not the only locus of segregation. White people had dominant control over public spaces as well as retail and service establishments. In 1891, state law legally segregated streetcars and railroads. The reaction by Black Atlantans was not passive. The law was met with a Black boycott of the streetcars.[19] To Black residents of the city, streetcar segregation was a step backward in a world where Black people already had far fewer rights.

The 1906 Atlanta anti-Black massacre was a formative accelerant to larger-scale segregation, leading to calls for more explicitly state-designated racial exclusion. The roots of the massacre are often attributed to the racist 1906 contest for governor between Hoke Smith and Clark Howell, who seemed to compete for who could out-race-bait the other. White voters were told that giving Black men the vote would pave the way for them to have their way with white women.[20] Local newspapers fueled the racist hatred with fabricated accounts of rape. On the evening of September 22, newspapers issued extra additions falsely reporting four assaults on white women by Black men had occurred that day. Anti-Black violence erupted, setting off three days of rioting by thousands of white men and boys, during which they killed at least 25 Black Atlantans and damaged hundreds of homes and businesses. The massacre precipitated both white and Black flight from some neighborhoods and led to greater fear among Black residents, making them more hesitant to consider moving into white areas. It also gave advocates of forced segregation a backdrop that they could later use to justify government-backed tools for furthering racial exclusion, including racial zoning.[21]

RACIAL ZONING, RESTRICTIVE COVENANTS, ANTI-BLACK VIOLENCE, AND BLACK-LED REAL ESTATE DEVELOPMENT

In 1913, the city of Atlanta passed its first racial segregation ordinance, patterned after Baltimore's 1910 law. The law stipulated that Black families could not reside in homes previously occupied by whites or next to white residences. After the ordinance was struck down in 1915 by the state supreme court, the city adopted another law, in 1916, that prevented Black residents from living in a block with a white majority. However, in 1917, the U.S. Supreme Court overturned Louisville's racial zoning ordinance, and the city of Atlanta did not aggressively enforce its own law.[22]

The pressure for racial segregation among white residents and leaders of the city was intense, however, and white homeowners and their politicians worked with national networks of planners to push for racial zoning in Atlanta. Many planners in Atlanta and elsewhere viewed comprehensive land-use zoning as a tool for racial exclusion. The city brought in Robert Whitten, a nationally prominent purveyor of "modern" comprehensive zoning practices. By adopting its 1922 racial zoning ordinance, the city portrayed housing Black families and housing white families as different property uses and therefore legitimate domain for comprehensive zoning. There would be white single-family zones and Black single-family zones, for example. The ordinance was justified partly as an attempt to reduce the likelihood of racial violence.[23]

When the 1922 ordinance was struck down as unconstitutional by the state supreme court, planners and elected officials were not deterred. Borrowing from an ordinance passed in Richmond, Virginia, in 1929, the City Council passed a law prohibiting citizens from living on a street where most residents were of a race with which the citizen was forbidden to intermarry.[24] The courts generally struck down this and other explicitly racially restrictive housing laws. However, the city had already firmly established a system of class-based zoning in its 1922 comprehensive zoning system, and this class-based zoning effectively survived the courts' stripping out its racially explicit components. Its architect, Whitten, was a firm believer in the segregation of different types of housing stock and the damaging effects of multifamily housing. As early as 1920, he argued that the "erection of a single apartment house in a block is almost certain to mean a radical change in the residential population," and concluded that "our civilization is at stake" in the need to create a zoning system that enabled the segregation of housing types.[25]

So, class-based zoning became a legally defensible tool of racial exclusion. When the Black middle class was quite small, it would be generally effective, at least in excluding Black people from middle- and upper-income neighborhoods. Of course, other tools of racial exclusion, including the fear of violent response by white residents, Black neighborhood removal, and other forms of housing discrimination, accompanied the land-use framework as an enforcer of residential segregation and were likely more critical to segregating Black and white working-class residents from each other.

Predating land-use zoning, restrictive covenants were a key tool to developing the early exclusive nineteenth-century residential subdivisions such as Inman Park and Druid Hills, preventing future landowners from building smaller homes or apartment buildings. These covenants could be used to set minimum lot sizes or even minimum price points of neighborhood homes. But in Inman Park and Druid Hills, these covenants were not explicitly racial. That is, they did not expressly prohibit homeowners from selling to Black buyers. Class-exclusionary restrictions were sufficient to serve this purpose, at least at the time. However, when the auto-oriented Ansley Park neighborhood was developed shortly after the turn of the century, the developer, Edwin Ansley, specifically included racially restrictive covenants in the deeds. After Atlanta's formal racial zoning was eventually overturned and, especially after the Federal Housing Administration endorsed their use in its developer financing, restrictive covenants became essential tools of segregation in the city and suburbs.[26]

While the violent response to Black families moving into white neighborhoods in the middle part of the twentieth century is sometimes more associated with northern cities dealing with racial transition, such threats were ever-present in Atlanta. The Ku Klux Klan located its national headquarters on Peachtree Street. In 1946, the Columbians, a fascist group, formed and wore brown shirts with lightning-bolt patches on their arms. In the mid-1940s, when the courts struck down the white Democratic primary and the poll tax ended, the NAACP organized a successful voting drive. By the summer of 1946, 100,000 Black Georgians had registered to vote. This quick rise in Black electoral power was a driving force in the creation of the Columbians.[27]

The presence of the Klan, the Columbians, and other racist organizations served to maintain a continuous threat of violent response to Black families thinking about moving into white parts of town. Columbians were often residents of neighborhoods transitioning from white to Black occupancy and explicitly recruited on the notion of defending one's community from Black infiltration. In their headquarters, they mapped out where white areas were being threatened with Black encroachment, and Columbian "troops" patrolled "threatened" streets with blackjacks and pistols. Despite racial zoning having long been ruled illegal, the Columbians posted signs saying "White Community" with their well-recognized logo prominently featured.[28] Another organization, the West End Cooperative Corporation (WECC), spun off from the local Ku Klux Klan. However, the WECC portrayed themselves less as paramilitary fascists or hooded racist thugs than, as Kevin Kruse describes, "honest homeowners confronted with a 'social problem.'"[29]

Given potentially violent reprisals and the severe shortages of housing that affected Black families, many Black leaders were not inclined to push for housing in white neighborhoods as their priority. Rather, much of the Black leadership pursued a different strategy—the creation of new Black neighborhoods in undeveloped areas as a primary way for reducing overcrowding and improving the quality of the housing stock for Black Atlantans. Black families had often been confined to neighborhoods with deteriorating and overcrowded housing.

In addition to the city being a national leader in Black higher education, with its six Black colleges and universities, the city also became known in the earlier decades of the twentieth century as a center of Black enterprise, including in finance, insurance, and real estate. Katherine Hankins and Steve Holloway argue that, while some cities like Chicago and New York had many Black entrepreneurs, and others like Tuskegee had Black colleges, no other city had the concentration of both Black entrepreneurs and Black colleges.[30] Moreover, the entrepreneurs in Atlanta were heavily involved in finance and real estate. Alonzo Herndon founded the Atlanta Life Insurance Company in 1905, and by the 1940s the company had approximately 1,500 employees. In real estate development, a key early pioneer was Heman Perry, who had founded Standard Life Insurance in 1911. He expanded into other businesses, including establishing a bank, the Citizens Trust Company, a laundry, a pharmacy, and a real estate brokerage. In the 1910s and early 1920s, Perry purchased land on the west side near Atlanta University to build homes and make mortgages to Black homebuyers.[31] He developed Washington Park, sometimes called Atlanta's first Black suburb.

The establishment of Black-owned insurance companies, development firms, and banks meant that Black Atlantans had at least some access to homeownership during a period of redlining and race-based discrimination in mortgage lending by both private lenders and the Federal Housing Administration.[32] The strong, violent hostility against Black people buying or renting homes in white neighborhoods, especially as the city became more segregated and the Black population grew in the 1930s and 1940s, left Black people with few options but to push for new development in peripheral areas of the city, and outside of it, to build new, Black neighborhoods. Without federal or local policymakers giving explicit attention to the rights of Black people to live where they wanted and protecting such choices, the expansion of segregation was perceived by many to be the only viable option to improve housing conditions.

Former college football coach and homebuilder Walter Aiken worked with the Federal Housing Administration (FHA) in the mid-1930s to develop a Black model home on the city's west side as part of the larger "Colored Better Housing Campaign."[33] Aiken was one of the first builders in Georgia to utilize FHA programs to help finance his developments. By the postwar period, he had become known as the most prominent Black homebuilder in the country, having built both single- and multifamily housing, particularly on the west side of the city.[34] While some Black developers were able to receive some limited support from the FHA, it paled in comparison to the aid provided to the developers of white suburbs. By 1947, over ninety percent of new development in the region, much of it insured by the FHA, was targeted to white owners and renters.[35]

"NEGOTIATED" RACIAL TRANSITION AND ANNEXING WHITENESS

By 1940, the city of Atlanta's population had grown to over 300,000, and the Black population had risen to thirty-seven percent, up from thirty-one percent in 1920.[36] Before World War II, in part because the Great Migration was not complete, many southern cities often had sizeable Black populations.[37] Southern white people were confronted with earlier racial change and a potential challenge to citywide electoral power much earlier in the century than were white people in other parts of the country. As Black people gained voting rights, often in fits and starts, this threatened white political hegemony and urban regimes.

The increased population density of the city by 1940, together with successful efforts to contain Black residents in particular neighborhoods, led to increased levels of residential segregation at the neighborhood level. Black Atlantans were increasingly constrained to neighborhoods on parts of the west, south, and east sides, although a secondary pattern

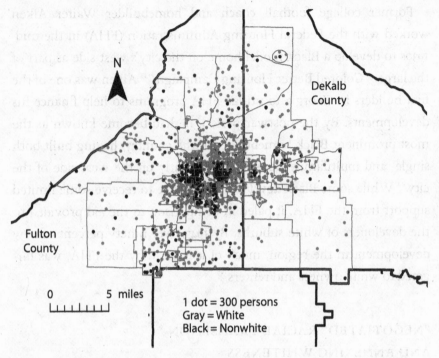

Map 3. The segregation of Black Atlantans in 1940.

Note: Data are only available for census tracts defined in 1940. Dots do not represent the precise location of persons but only the mix of residents in the census tracts (indicated by finer boundary lines).Data source: National Historical Geographic Information System.

of very small Black enclaves emerged in predominantly white areas. (See Map 3[38].)

Most new residential development in the 1940s was located outside the city limits, and while some early Black close-in suburbs were built outside the old, pre-1952 city borders, the bulk of suburban development was for white families. Metro Atlanta gained over 131,000 white residents over this decade, with 119,000 located outside city limits. The Black population grew by just over 22,000 over this decade, with just 5,600 outside the city. Moreover, the city proper became more segregated, with the Black population surging on the west and southwest sides of the city.[39]

Segregation was supported not just by the now well-known forces of FHA and bank redlining and exclusionary zoning but also by the deliberate, state-sanctioned biracial negotiations and planning for the location of expanded Black neighborhoods. While the city of Atlanta could no longer enforce its illegal racial zoning ordinance, it explicitly practiced a heavily racialized process of neighborhood development planning during the middle of the twentieth century.

In 1937, William Hartsfield was elected mayor of Atlanta and, after a brief interruption in 1941 and 1942, remained in office until 1962. Hartsfield served during some of the greatest periods of growth in the city proper, with white and Black families competing for land and housing. Hartsfield eventually built what Clarence Stone and others have called the Atlanta urban regime, a partnership between the white corporate elite and the growing Black power structure, led by Black ministers, Black politicians, and some Black businessmen. Despite this biracial partnership, many observers have argued that this regime, extending well beyond the Hartsfield era, did little to support the livelihoods or fortunes of most Black families in the city, who remained constrained to low-wage jobs, inadequate housing, and growing levels of segregation.[40]

The Atlanta urban regime involved a governance approach called the "Atlanta Style" by Alton Hornsby, Jr., and Tomiko Brown-Nagin. The Atlanta Style, nowadays often colloquially called the "Atlanta Way," was an approach that involved negotiation between the key parties of the urban regime, the white-led power-structure, backed by the city's white corporate elite, and the Black community power-structure. Hartsfield served as a broker between the two parties to the regime, a chief mediator of sorts and shaper of the negotiations, but not a boss or machine leader. The extent to which the traditional white-Black corporate-led Atlanta regime has persisted is a complex question, one to which this book will return.

The regime's approach to racial change in Atlanta's neighborhoods was an outgrowth of the larger Atlanta Style. Black leadership in the city, which by now had joined as junior partners in a coalition with the white corporate elite, argued not for the ability for Black residents to move into white neighborhoods but rather for the ability to develop new Black sub-divisions and apartment developments. In 1946, the Atlanta Urban League formed the Temporary Coordinating Committee on Housing, from which came the Atlanta Housing Council (AHC) in 1947. The AHC iden-tified six proposed expansion areas for Black residential development to the west, south, and north of the city near existing Black neighborhoods. The city and the Metropolitan Planning Commission (MPC), the region's planning organization, endorsed the expansion plan. The AHC plan relied heavily on Black-owned financial firms, including Atlanta Life Insurance, Citizens Trust, and Mutual Federal Savings and Loan, to pro-vide the mortgages for Black families to purchase homes in these areas.[41]

Black leadership was becoming more aggressive in demanding vot-ing rights and access to public accommodations. In the housing arena, however, many Black leaders were more focused on negotiating areas of segregated Black expansion, resulting in new Black neighborhoods, rather than opening up white neighborhoods to desegregation and geographically broader housing options. This strategy was at least partly due to the fear of anti-Black violence and the view that more dis-persed housing options were simply not feasible. The focus was on the development and provision of more housing in the context of severe housing shortages and the poor housing quality faced by Black fami-lies. Calls for open housing, which grew in the 1950s in northern cities, were viewed as unrealistic by many Black leaders in Atlanta. The aim was more housing for Black families wherever it might be built, espe-cially more new housing. However, some Black organizations, includ-ing the Black Empire Real Estate Board and some NAACP officials, argued for pushing against the segregated constraints of negotiated Black expansion areas, but they were not the strongest voices.[42]

Planners, including the city and the MPC, were fully engaged part-ners in planning the expansion of Black neighborhoods in a sanctioned, segregated fashion. Robert Stuart, the head of the MPC, argued to the U.S. Civil Rights Commission in 1959 that race "has a way of confusing the housing market picture" and that "race-mixing" in housing markets hurt both Black and white families.[43]

In April 1959, Mayor Hartsfield testified before the U.S. Civil Rights Commission at an Atlanta field hearing, describing the city's process of negotiated racial transition. In such negotiations, the Westside Mutual Development Committee would help manage neighborhood transitions from white to Black through "voluntary agreements." Of course, Hartsfield failed to point out that one party to these negotiations had far more options and power than the other, and some Black commenters at the hearing struggled with the question of whether the gains in more and decent housing outweighed the perpetuation of segregation. Moreover, the Black real estate board president suggested that the custom of "voluntary negotiations" was, in reality, backed up by "mob violence and the bombing of the homes of Negroes moving into white neighborhoods."[44]

As metro Atlanta grew, and especially as whites moved into white, exclusionary suburban spaces—often supported by FHA-financed developers and FHA home loans—white leaders "chased the suburbs," as Lee Anna Lands has written.[45] Until 1950, the city had continually annexed small parts of the suburbs, starting in 1866, then again in 1889, and many more times until 1925. In the 1930s and 1940s, annexations slowed.[46] In 1944, the Supreme Court Smith vs. Allright decision meant the end to the exclusion of Black voters from the Democratic primary. This threatened the viability of the white political leadership in the city, especially as the white population was becoming increasingly suburbanized. As a result, Hartsfield repeatedly argued that the city should annex upscale, predominantly white, more affluent suburbs such as Buckhead into the city, and this was aimed at maintaining the dominant position of the white-led urban regime.[47] But until 1950, his attempts to annex large parts of the suburbs failed.

In 1950, the mayor proposed the ambitious "Plan of Improvement," which called for a major expansion of the city via the annexation of primarily white suburban communities. This time, the effort was successful,

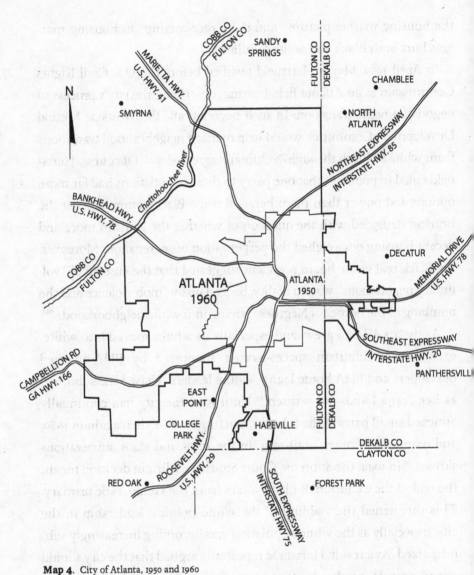

Map 4. City of Atlanta, 1950 and 1960

Map by Atlanta Metropolitan Planning Commission, Atlpp0005_22, Planning Atlanta City Planning Maps Collection, Georgia State University.

Figure 1. Mayor Hartsfield swears in new members of City Council after the 1952 annexation

From: Atlanta Journal-Constitution Photographic Archive, AJCP142-026C, Georgia State University.

and the city's land area expanded dramatically, from 37 to 118 square miles in 1952. Map 4 shows the city's expansion from 1950 to 1960, driven predominantly by this single annexation.[48] One effect of the annexation was to increase the number of white members on the City Council. (See Figure 1.[49])

While Hartsfield saw annexation as reducing the electoral power of the Black vote, thus protecting his electability, he and others also viewed it as preserving the white-Black urban regime.[50] He argued that protecting this regime was better than the alternative for the city's Black population, given that the regime had come to support Black voting rights and the federal government had not yet supported improving them in the South. The deal, it seemed, was to accept, strengthen, and preserve white-led governance in the city to avoid harsher, more Jim-Crow-like governance by someone like the aggressively racist Lester Maddox.

URBAN RENEWAL, HIGHWAYS, AND BLACK NEIGHBORHOOD REMOVAL

Beginning with the 1949 Housing Act, the federal government provided significant funding for urban renewal projects that often involved "slum clearance," which usually meant demolishing Black residential neighborhoods and their replacement with commercial projects and public facilities.[51] Urban renewal programs generally ran through the early 1970s. Researchers at the University of Richmond have identified, from federal records, that at least 4,000 families were displaced by federally funded urban renewal projects in Atlanta, with eighty-nine percent of those being Black families.[52] However, the displacement numbers for many projects appear to be missing, so the real figure could be substantially higher. Projects tended to be in Black neighborhoods such as the West End, Butler Street, Bedford Pine, and Buttermilk Bottoms. Larry Keating has argued that, after being publicly targeted for renewal programs well ahead of the actual redevelopments, Black neighborhoods would often enter a phase of decline, including falling property values, disinvestment by private and public sector organizations, and the exodus of many residents who were able to leave.[53] Therefore, formal, recorded counts of displaced residents could be large underestimates of the number of the people who were effectively displaced by urban renewal.

Even before federal urban renewal and expressway programs, the Atlanta urban regime supported or orchestrated the use of public housing and highway development to provide a pretext for "slum clearance." Techwood Homes, one of the first public housing developments in the country, was initially proposed as a slum-clearance project by developer Charles Palmer before the advent of federal public housing programs. Palmer had his eye on the slums of Techwood Flats because he had to drive by the eyesore on the way to his office and because he owned nearby office buildings. Palmer asked, "why such an untended abscess should fester between the lovely campus of our proudest school and the office buildings in the heart of our city?"[54] He had organized plans for the demolition of the Flats and the building of new housing just at the time when federal programs for public housing were created and, with some political maneuvering by Palmer, Techwood Homes became one of the first public housing projects funded under the New Deal, as a segregated-white development.

Similarly, even before the advent of the interstate highway system, Atlanta's corporate elite successfully advocated for highway construction in and near the central business district that displaced a significant portion of residents, many of whom were Black.[55] The 1946 Lochner Report, prepared for the city of Atlanta and Fulton County, laid out plans for expanding state highways in ways that led to them running through many Black neighborhoods. In 1960, the city's Bureau of Planning recommended that the construction of Interstate 20, running east and west, be used as a boundary between Black and white neighborhoods, and it certainly functioned like that for some time, especially on the east side of the city.[56]

A substantial portion of racially exclusionary activity in Atlanta was orchestrated without the help of the federal government. Larry Keating has described the city's extensive activities in eliminating Black residential clusters, especially in the 1940s and 1950s. One example is the "back-alley dwelling law" of 1955, which targeted for removal Black homes in the alleys of affluent, otherwise-white neighborhoods. These homes had traditionally been residences for Black domestic workers employed in nearby white homes. But with the Brown vs. Board of Education ruling in 1954, the prospect of integrated schools prompted affluent white homeowners and city officials to work to accelerate the process of Black residential expulsion from majority-white neighborhoods. In 247 blocks, in what is now the Midtown neighborhood, more than half of the blocks had some Black residents, and most of the residences occupied by Black people were those accessible from alleys.[57] The new law prohibited the repair and improvement of these residences. Combined with the closing of many of the alleys, the law resulted in expelling many of these Black households, and the neighborhood became almost entirely white.

WHITE FLIGHT, WHITE AVOIDANCE, AND RECONSTRUCTING SEGREGATION IN THE SUBURBS

While neighborhoods became more segregated in the broad middle of the twentieth century, the de jure segregation of schools, public spaces, and lunch counters was waning. Working-class whites protested their loss of legal supremacy in the late 1950s, but the courts, upper-income whites (who were well insulated from potential Black neighbors by their affluent single-family homes, exclusionary zoning, private schools, and private clubs), and the corporatist urban regime were too much for them. Their response was to flee the city. The principal "beneficiaries" of white flight were the surrounding counties. In 1970, Gwinnett County was ninety-five percent white, Cobb was ninety-six percent white, and North Fulton was ninety-nine percent white.[58]

But the growth in white suburbanites during the postwar period was not primarily due to white flight from the city. More of the growth of white suburbs was due to avoidance of the city by white families moving into the region, racial steering by the real estate industry, and federal, state, and local policies that subsidized and supported the development of new, often exclusionary suburbs. The metro region grew and, as white families moved into the region, they increasingly ended up in predominantly white suburbs. During the 1960s, for example, while the city saw the exodus of approximately 60,000 white residents, Cobb, Gwinnett, and North Fulton counties gained more than 153,000 white residents.[59] White families moving to the region tended to bypass the city proper. Therefore, the city experienced a substantial loss in white population due to both white flight and because whites avoided, and were steered away from, the city. The region's growth was really a *direct* suburbanization of the region, at least when it came to the influx of white households.

From 1940 to 1980, almost all counties in the Atlanta region experienced significant growth in their white populations, with the core suburban counties of DeKalb, Cobb, Gwinnett, and Clayton seeing the largest amount of change, ranging from a net increase in white residents of 128,000 in Clayton to 266,000 in DeKalb. However, the central county of Fulton saw relatively modest growth in its white population of just 6,700. Most of the suburban growth was not due to white flight, however, but to families moving into the region from other parts of the country.[60]

After 1970, white flight and white avoidance were occurring not just in the city of Atlanta. In 1970, DeKalb County was eighty-six percent white, but by 1980, as the Black population increased from 57,000 to 130,000, the white population declined by about five percent from 1970, and whites made up just over seventy percent of the population.[61] By 1990, DeKalb's population was just fifty-two percent white, with forty-two percent of the population being Black and about six percent Latinx or Asian. By 2000, DeKalb became a majority-Black and increasingly diverse county, with white people comprising less than one-third of the population, Black residents constituting about fifty-four percent, Latinx residents comprising about eight percent, and Asians about four percent. By 2000, the white population of DeKalb had declined forty percent from its 1970 level. The county had become starkly segregated internally, however. Primarily middle- and high-income white people were located on the north side of the county, while middle and working-class Black families were located mostly in the southern portion. Latinx and Asian populations had begun to cluster along the Buford Highway corridor running through the northern part of the county in the suburbs such as Chamblee and Doraville, just north of I-85. In 2000, the majority-Black county elected its first Black chief executive, and Black elected officials from the county gained power in the county commission and the state legislative delegation.

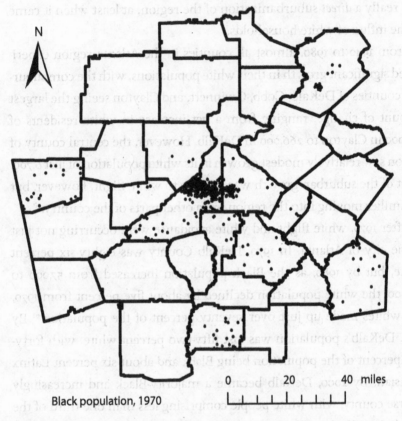

N

0   20   40 miles

Black population, 1970

Map 5. Black suburbanization, 1970 to 2000

Data source: US Decennial Census data in 2010 census tract boundaries via Socialexplorer.com. Dots do not indicate the precise location of the address, but just the neighborhood location.

Black suburbanization accelerated in the 1970s and 1980s. The percentage of the suburban population that was Black increased from six to twenty percent over this period, with more than fifty percent of Black married couples with children moving out of the city.[62] The suburbanization of Black families—both those relocating from the city and those relocating from other regions—generally continued during the 1990s, fueled by nascent gentrification, public housing redevelopment, and rising housing costs in many parts of the city. Map 5 illustrates the growth of the Black population in metropolitan Atlanta from 1970 to 2000, a

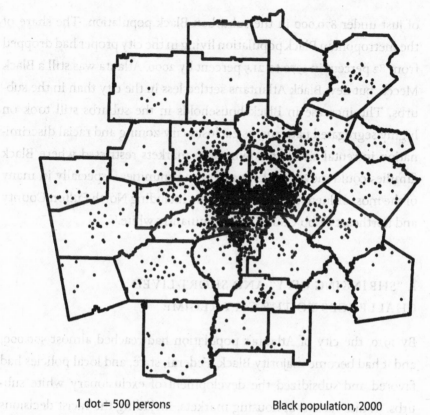

1 dot = 500 persons   Black population, 2000

period during which the region—and many other sunbelt metros—grew dramatically. Black families, many moving from different parts of the country, increased significantly in the southern parts of Fulton and DeKalb counties and, to a lesser extent, in the southern parts of Cobb County and the eastern parts of Gwinnett County.

The Black population in the city was almost the same in 2000 as it was in 1970, at 254,000, while the white population in the city had declined drastically, by over 111,000. All of the net growth in the metropolitan Black population had occurred outside the city, with an increase of just under 870,000 in the suburban Black population. The share of the metropolitan Black population living in the city proper had dropped from 82 percent in 1970 to 21.5 percent by 2000. Atlanta was still a Black Mecca, but new Black Atlantans settled less in the city than in the suburbs. The increase in Black households in the suburbs still took on highly segregated patterns, as exclusionary zoning and racial discrimination in rental and homeownership markets restricted where Black families could move and kept many communities, especially in many of the most affluent parts of the region, including North Fulton County and northeast Cobb County, predominantly white.[63]

A "SHRINKING CITY" AND SHORT-LIVED CHALLENGES TO THE CITY REGIME

By 1970, the city of Atlanta's population had reached almost 500,000, and it had become majority-Black. Federal, state, and local policies had favored and subsidized the development of exclusionary white suburbs. White racism in housing markets, including the racist decisions of homebuyers, renters, landlords, developers, and financial institutions, drove the booming suburbs as the primary destination of those moving into the region, including predominantly white middle-income families, during the broad middle part of the twentieth century.

The 1970s and 1980s were a period of economic decline in the city proper. The city's population declined by 14.5 percent during the 1970s, from 497,000 to 425,000 and, by 1990, had dropped over 20 percent from its 1970 level down to 394,000.[64] The poverty rate increased from 19.8 percent in 1970 to 27.5 percent in 1980, remaining at roughly that rate in 1990. The estimated ratio of the median family income in the city to that in the suburbs was 0.80 in 1970, but by 1980 the proportion had fallen to 0.62, and then to 0.59 in 1990. Middle-income whites were leaving the city, and both middle-income white and Black people moving into the region were moving predominantly to the suburbs. By 1990, the city was 30.3 percent white, down from 48.6 percent in 1970.

Over this same period, jobs and the commercial tax base increasingly shifted away from downtown Atlanta and towards other parts of the region, especially outside the city proper. Large "edge city" commercial and residential clusters formed in the suburbs, especially in the "northern arc" bounded by I-85 to the east and I-75 to the west, which market researchers in the region often referred to as the "favored quarter." These new developments included eastern Cobb County, Roswell and Alpharetta in north Fulton County, and the north perimeter at the junction of I-285 and state route 400. Within the city, jobs also shifted north to Buckhead and eventually to Midtown starting in the 1990s. More than two-thirds of office space in the region was in the Atlanta central business district in 1966. By 1999, the share had dropped to under fourteen percent.[65] Job sprawl accelerated residential sprawl and created a region that was no longer centered around the city of Atlanta. In fact, by the end of the twentieth century, the metro had become not a polycentric region with a few dominant job centers, but effectively an amorphous mishmash of jobs and residents spread out over an area of more than 8,300 square miles, almost as large as the entire state of New Jersey, making it the quintessential poster child for metropolitan sprawl.

In 1973, the growing electoral power of Black Atlantans led to the city electing its first Black mayor, Maynard Jackson, Jr. Jackson followed mayors Ivan Allen, Jr., and Sam Massell, both of whom continued to facilitate the white-Black regime that Hartsfield had managed over his long tenure. Jackson, who had served as somewhat of an oppositional vice-mayor under Massell, ran on a platform that promised to support the interests of the city's poorer Black residents. As vice-mayor, Jackson had been outspoken on some racial and economic justice issues, especially police brutality against Black residents.[66] Massell ran a racist campaign against Jackson, including using a high-profile slogan proclaiming "Atlanta's Too Young to Die."[67] The corporate leaders of the urban regime worked against Jackson's campaign and, after he was elected, were quick to criticize his administration.[68]

Jackson's first term marked a significant redirection of city policy away from the traditional regime's focus on business-friendly policies that paid little attention to the needs of lower-income residents. Akira Drake Rodriguez has argued that "Jackson's urban governance plan was for reparative growth that specifically sought to empower and grow the most marginalized and distressed communities."[69] The mayor backed a budding neighborhood movement in the city, supporting a new system of neighborhood planning units (NPUs) by providing staff to help each NPU. They would assist the residents of their assigned NPU with constructing and supporting their arguments to the city.[70]

Jackson also developed an affirmative action contracting program, in which city contracts were increasingly awarded to Black-owned firms, strengthening the ties between City Hall and Black enterprise.

Jackson did not break all ties with the corporatist regime, however, and it eventually regained its strength. He retained the city's longtime chief financial officer, Charles Davis, and met regularly with Coca-Cola finance committee chairman Robert Woodruff. By the end of his first term, and especially during his second and third terms, Jackson became a more traditional Atlanta mayor, resuming strong relations with the white corporate power structure and generally moving more slowly in addressing the serious needs of Atlanta's lower-income households. It became less clear how effectively his policies benefitted lower-income Black residents.[71]

In between Jackson's second and third terms, Andrew Young served as Atlanta's fifty-third mayor from 1982 until 1990. Young was, perhaps as much as any of the city's mayors, an enthusiastic champion of the corporate-led urban regime. Young came into office during the Reagan administration, which implemented a new, harsher era of urban austerity, one from which the U.S. has never recovered. Over Young's two-term tenure, federal aid to the city was cut from $49 million to $9 million.[72] Young was perhaps best known for his globe-trotting boosterism of the city, attempting to drum up foreign investment in the city. While some of his efforts likely had the desired effect, as foreign investment in the metropolitan area increased after 1985, it is unclear what portion of this investment flowed into the city versus the suburbs.[73] Moreover, as Maurice Hobson has written, his foreign travels and business attraction focus sometimes made it appear as if he was not terribly concerned with the needs of lower-income Atlantans, including issues of affordable housing, transportation, and public safety. The lack of attention to problems of everyday Atlantans was perhaps best exemplified by the mayor's weakening of the city's NPU system.[74] Perhaps no mayor epitomized or articulated the ethos of the Atlanta urban regime more than Young, who said, "Politics doesn't control the world. Money does. And we ought not to be upset about that." He added that his job was to see that "whites get some of the power and Blacks get some of the money."[75]

A SPRAWLING REGION TURNS AGAINST TRANSIT

As the city of Atlanta and the region grew in the 1960s, the city proposed creating a multicounty regional transportation system. Mayor Ivan Allen, Jr., put forth a referendum to fund the Metropolitan Atlanta Rapid Transit Authority (MARTA) in 1968, but it was soundly defeated, even losing in his own city. In particular, Black voters did not support the proposal in large numbers. Clarence Stone has argued that this was because the organizers did not pay adequate attention to Black concerns, including Black employment and emphasizing service to Black neighborhoods instead of only downtown businesses.[76] After the defeat, the regime leadership formed the Action Forum, a vehicle for discussion and collaboration between the white corporate elite and high-level Black leadership.

A new MARTA referendum was put on the ballot in 1971. MARTA would purchase the privately owned Atlanta Transit Company and expand its services in both the city and the suburbs of Fulton, DeKalb,

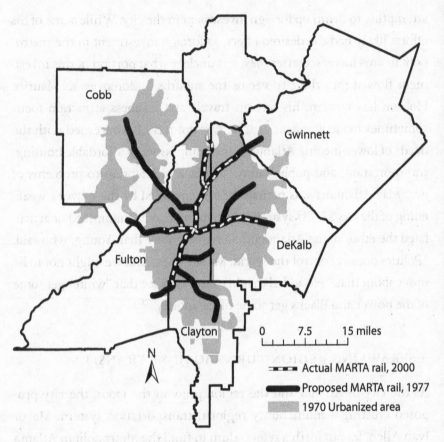

Map 6. MARTA plans and the realities of anti-transit suburbia

Legend:
- ▪▪▪ Actual MARTA rail, 2000
- ▬▬ Proposed MARTA rail, 1977
- ▨ 1970 Urbanized area

Map labels: Cobb, Gwinnett, Fulton, DeKalb, Clayton

Scale: 0 — 7.5 — 15 miles

Gwinnett, and Clayton counties. Cobb County refused to be a part of the planning process. Cobb Commissioner Emmett Burton vowed to "stock the Chattahoochee with piranha" to keep MARTA out of Cobb if needed.[77] But this time, with the help of a more supportive Black electorate, the measure passed in the city of Atlanta as well as in Fulton and DeKalb counties, while still failing in the other core suburban counties.[78] While MARTA served a large portion of the region's population at the time, it was already clear that the area would keep expanding outward, leaving MARTA covering an increasingly smaller part of the region, reaching fewer jobs and residents than a strong transit system should.

The virulent suburban resistance to MARTA in places like Cobb and Gwinnett counties continued well into the twenty-first century. With each proposal to expand the system into more suburban counties, the screeching voices of suburban racial exclusion would resurface. The system never reached even its modest ambitions in the early years (see Map 6). Again and again, MARTA was associated with Black Atlantans, and white suburbanites continued to do what they could to exclude them from their neighborhoods, especially in the more affluent northern parts of Cobb and Gwinnett counties.[79]

MARTA PLANS AND THE REALITIES OF ANTI-TRANSIT SUBURBIA

Arguably, the region, especially as it continued to sprawl over thousands of square miles, should have adopted a more distributed, flexible, and cost-effective metropolitan bus-based system. As early as 1967, a study argued that the region was too low-density to serve well with a fixed-rail system.[80] The region, after all, was one in which growth surged after car ownership had become widespread and after the federal interstate highway system had been developed. While a more robust rail system could have concentrated development along nodes near the rail lines more and slowed sprawl, it seems unlikely that it would have markedly changed the sprawling nature of the region, especially given the lack of political will to adopt other growth-management and land-use planning policies and practices needed to concentrate growth. The approach of local governments and regional planners, however, was to support "unchecked, unregulated atomistic development."[81] Without a willingness to plan for less-diffuse development, creating a reasonably efficient transit system, especially one involving more rail, was increasingly difficult. Moreover, a region built on an ideal of low-density development perpetuated anti-transit attitudes, making the political viability of increased mass transit more challenging. And less mass transit then fed back on the continued reliance on automobility that in turn fed more-diffuse growth, leading to a vicious cycle, one supported by public policy and regional planning.

THE OLYMPICS, PUBLIC HOUSING DEMOLITION, AND SETTING THE STAGE FOR GENTRIFICATION

In 1987, real estate lawyer and former University of Georgia football star, Billy Payne, began to promote the idea that the city of Atlanta should put together a bid to bring the Olympic Games to the city. Payne found a willing partner in Mayor Young because the idea fit so well with his efforts to recreate the image of Atlanta as a world-class, global city.[82] The Atlanta Olympic Committee was formed and began to spend millions on its efforts to win the Olympics for Atlanta. The bid to win the Games was the embodiment of the corporate-led Atlanta urban regime, with Black city government working hand-in-glove with corporate Atlanta, especially Coca-Cola and Delta Airlines. The effort was more than one to win the Olympic Games. It was an effort to reimagine the city and recraft its image into an international city, one extremely hospitable to global capital.[83]

In retrospect, it seems clear that the effort to win the Games was an important event in the city's history, one that likely affected the attention of global capital and real estate markets. While some have debated whether the Olympics provided a net economic or fiscal benefit to the city or the region over the short term, the more important impacts of the Games have been their effects on the long-term trajectory of the city.[84]

Critics have argued that the Olympics hurt the city's poor in various ways. The city accelerated plans to begin shuttering public housing, bused homeless people out of the city, and passed ordinances to remove homeless people from the streets.[85] After the city was awarded the Games, it passed laws banning panhandling, public camping, and the blocking of sidewalks. In the fourteen months before the Games, thousands of homeless were detained in the city.[86] This led to federal courts ordering the city to halt such actions. The state contributed to the anti-homeless efforts and passed a law outlawing removing items from public trash cans. Local governments used public dollars to work with Project Homeward Bound, a nonprofit that gave one-way tickets to homeless people to leave the city.

The city of Atlanta adopted a "twin peaks" effort to prepare for the Olympics but also used the Games as a fulcrum for addressing the disinvestment of poor, predominantly Black neighborhoods. These efforts were combined with efforts like The Atlanta Project and the city's federally funded Empowerment Zone initiative and focused on comprehensive redevelopment planning for a set of "Olympic ring" neighborhoods, Black neighborhoods on the west, south, and east sides of the city. While there were investments in basic infrastructure, parks, and overall quality-of-life planning, these initiatives were also accompanied by various efforts aimed at clearing away problems and less at providing increased and improved housing for low-income and vulnerable families living in these communities. The redevelopment efforts resulted in over 1,300 new and rehabilitated housing units in the targeted neighborhoods by 1996, but it also resulted in the demolition of 3,400 housing units, suggesting a net loss of at least 2,100 units.[87]

In 1996, as the Olympics were ending, Mayor Campbell and the Corporation for Olympic Development in Atlanta (CODA) formed the Atlanta Renaissance Program chaired by Coca-Cola's Robert Goizueta. The large corporate consulting firm McKinsey lent pro bono support and led the drafting of a report for the group. The finding of the report that "seemed most focusing and thus gained the most traction" was to "get more middle-income people to move into the city."[88] The report focused on "shifting the demographic make-up of the city," which "tracked with its analysis of other cities, where a larger middle-class, a smaller low-income component, and a less sharp divide between the rich and poor correlated well with healthier economies and city quality of life."[89] Certainly, the city at this time, especially as of the latest 1990 census figures, had suffered from population loss and seemed in need of a more substantial middle-class. But the Renaissance efforts focused strongly on attracting middle-class in-movers and not on supporting and improving the lives, livelihoods, and economic mobility of existing, lower-income residents, including through providing them with stable, quality, affordable housing. The middle-class attraction route proved to be the preferred strategy. Over the long run, this strategy appears to have succeeded, depending on one's definition of success. However, in recent years, new city residents have increasingly tended to be high- rather than middle-income households, as will be discussed more in Chapter 3.

The Olympics provided renewed motivation to address a problem that corporate leaders had wanted to address for some time—the problem public housing posed to the city's image. The Olympics spurred planning and action to redevelop public housing sites into less-stigmatized properties, thereby recasting the city's image for global capital and dispersing the city's poor. This was particularly true for public housing located in strategic locations such as Techwood Homes, situated between Georgia Tech, north of downtown, just west of Midtown, and immediately east of the Coca-Cola headquarters. In the process, such redevelopment would provide ample opportunities to developers to exploit the rent gap—the difference in land values between what nearby real estate would fetch without the public housing and what it was currently worth.[90]

In the latter decades of the twentieth century, the Atlanta Housing Authority (AHA) faced increasing problems caused by inadequate funding, the exodus of all but their poorest tenants, and, especially beginning in the 1980s with the advent of the crack epidemic, increasing drug and criminal activity. The federal public housing program, which started in earnest with the 1937 Housing Act, was never adequately funded, falling far short of the visions of public housing advocates like Catherine Bauer. The real estate industry lobbied successfully to keep the program small, limit its quality, starve it for operating dollars and reinvestment capital, and allow localities to locate many developments in isolated, disadvantaged locations.[91] At the same time, as Ed Goetz has argued, public housing problems in the U.S. have often been exaggerated and used as a symbol both for the failure of public sector management and the supposed evils of low-income housing. In fact, many public housing authorities and developments successfully managed to provide decent housing despite insufficient federal funding and other obstacles. Moreover, as Akira Drake Rodriguez has chronicled, the history of public housing in Atlanta is one filled with stories of residents, especially Black women, organizing and advocating—often against powerful forces—for "improved infrastructure, economic development, and a built environment that was both safe and welcoming to outsiders."[92]

However, by the 1990s, if not sooner, the AHA had developed a reputation as one of the nation's worst housing authorities. Many developments were continuously being cited with code violations and crime was out of control at some sites.[93] In the late 1980s, Bankhead Courts, which was one of the newer public housing sites in the city, became a particularly egregious example of AHA's problems. Amid the crack cocaine epidemic, several vacant units were used by drug dealers, crime at the complex was a regular issue, and the apartments needed millions of dollars of repairs. Local and federal politicians, including Mayor Young and Congressman John Lewis, routinely toured the complex to see firsthand how troubled it was.[94]

In 1992, the National Commission on Severely Distressed Public Housing released its report. While it found that only six percent of the nation's public housing stock was "severely distressed," it led to creating the federal HOPE VI program.[95] HOPE VI provided federal dollars for the rehabilitation or redevelopment of public housing. In 1993, the AHA secured early HOPE VI funding to rehabilitate most of

Techwood and Clark-Howell's public housing units. However, a new mayor, Bill Campbell, came into office in January of 1994. He was a vocal critic of the AHA and appointed Rene Glover, a corporate attorney who held very dim views of traditional public housing, to lead the agency. Glover shifted the agency's focus to using HOPE VI funding to demolish rather than rehabilitate conventional public housing. When funded by HOPE VI, some sites became new, mixed-income housing developments owned by joint ventures involving the AHA and private developers. Techwood was among the first such redevelopments.[96] Other sites were merely demolished, and tenants were provided with housing vouchers. Techwood was particularly important given its location next to Coca-Cola headquarters, Georgia Tech, and prospective housing for Olympic athletes. Corporate leaders and politicians questioned whether it was appropriate to house Olympic athletes in a high-crime neighborhood. What sort of image would this portray of Atlanta to the world?[97]

After it became clear that Techwood would be redeveloped somehow, the site's vacancy rate began rising. In June 1990, before the city had won the Games, the occupancy rate was over ninety-two percent. By April 1993, after the AHA had stopped admitting new tenants after previous tenants moved, it had dropped to less than fifty percent. By August of that year, it had fallen to thirty-eight percent and then to six percent by the end of 1994.[98] The site was redeveloped into a mixed-income housing development via a partnership with the Integral Group, a developer that became a key partner with Glover's AHA. The joint venture was a key one in the history of public housing and its continuing move to "public-private partnerships." Centennial Place, as the new mixed-income development was called, was the first instance in which HUD had permitted something other than a public housing authority to actually own public housing units. The final HOPE VI plan for the site called for 360 public housing units, with 180 additional units, at somewhat higher income levels, to be financed with Low

Income Housing Tax Credits. This compares to over 1,100 occupied public housing units that were on the site in 1990. Moreover, fifteen years later, only 301 public housing units and 126 tax-credit units were located on the site.[99] Overall, the number of occupied public housing units—those designed for very-low-income households—was only twenty-seven percent of the original number at Techwood in 1990.

The transformation of Atlanta's public housing was spurred and supported by the successful bid for the Olympics. Ed Goetz argues that the AHA's "Olympic Legacy Program" expanded the demolition efforts of the agency far beyond Techwood and Clark-Howell and, together with the new AHA administration, eventually led to the demolition of a dozen public housing sites, seven of which were funded via the HOPE VI program.[100] While there were certainly serious problems at some of AHA developments, the forced uprooting of entire communities was not without significant costs. Residents had developed attachments to their communities, depended on networks within these communities, and many felt a sense of real loss after they were displaced.[101]

Public housing authorities in the 1990s were under pressure, as Akira Drake Rodriguez writes, to "save public housing with no funding, along with that of leaders of depopulated cities with reduced tax bases, and an increasingly low-income and high-need tenant population."[102] As a result of AHA's "neoliberal turn" away from owning and managing public housing, it went from owning more than 14,000 public housing units in 1996 to less than 10,000 units in 2000 and, by 2010, the number had dropped below 5,000 units, including those units in new, mixed-income communities owned by joint-ventures.[103] The agency's remaining traditional public housing was senior housing. During this same period, AHA's tenant-based vouchers increased from just over 5,000 in 1996 to approximately 11,000 by 2000. The AHA effectively became a manager of the housing voucher process and much less a developer and owner of affordable housing. Twenty years later, this left it ill-prepared to develop and create permanently affordable housing stock as the city faced a severe shortage of affordable housing in the 2010s. It was more vulnerable to the whim of private market landlords to accept and manage vouchered housing, which under Georgia law they could, and often did, refuse to do.

Beyond the direct impact that the AHA's demolition endeavors had on the supply of permanently affordable housing in the city, they also have had some effect on setting the stage for the next phase of the city's development beginning after the Olympics and especially in the twenty-first century. By demolishing stigmatized and problematized sites in the city and dispersing the poor residents living there, the AHA provided an important ingredient in the revalorization of the city, including in key locations such as the Old Fourth Ward, Midtown, the East Lake neighborhood, and more recently, even the west side. By dispersing the poor away from these sites, the agency assisted the real estate market in exploiting substantial rent gaps. With public housing removed and the reality or perception of lower crime and fewer Black, low-income neighbors, real estate investors could capture high land values and put the land to its "highest and best use," which often effectively meant more higher-income and fewer Black residents.

AFFIRMATIVELY FURTHERING SPRAWL

If one asked an observer of cities in the year 2000, what word came to mind when they thought of Atlanta, it is likely the answer would be "sprawl." Perhaps no metro in the U.S. represented sprawl more vividly than Atlanta. In this case, such perceptions fit reality quite well. The city of Atlanta accounted for about one-half the metropolitan population in 1960 but, by 2000, its share had fallen to less than ten percent.[104] In the early 1970s, new regional shopping malls and planned unit developments began proliferating "outside the perimeter" (OTP) in places such as Sandy Springs, Dunwoody, and east Cobb County, creating new clusters of jobs and residences that accelerated the growth of the collar counties.

In the late-twentieth century, the sprawling of Atlanta did not mean that wealth spread uniformly in all directions outward from the city. The area north of both I-75 and I-85 became a particular locus of economic and population growth, including a substantial in-movement of higher-income households from other parts of the country. This area has been called, at different times, the "golden crescent," the "northern arc," or the "favored quarter"[105] Whatever the area's moniker, the center of jobs and affluence continued to move northward and farther away from the expanding Black community in the southern part of the metro. This northward shift in wealth was accompanied by exclusionary zoning, gated communities, and new clusters of concentrated affluence. For example, in the northernmost tip of Fulton County, an area later incorporated as the city of Milton, multi-acre single-family lots were common. The city's logo is now a horse due to the number of single-family homeowners who keep horses. Such exclusionary suburbs were able to adopt zoning ordinances that protected affluent homeowners from encroachment by lower-income families. Cobb, Fulton, and Cherokee counties adopted ordinances that included minimum lot sizes for their most exclusionary single-family zoning category.[106]

With their growing affluence and predominant whiteness, the northern suburbs continued to be a locus of conservative politics. But now, instead of working-class native Georgians, the politics of these communities were increasingly driven by more middle- and upper-income corporate transplants into the region. Newt Gingrich, who represented east Cobb County and ascended to being Speaker of the House in 1994, became a perfect statesman for north-suburban Republican power. "These people want safety, and they believe big cities have failed and are controlled by people who are incapable of delivering goods and services," he told the New York Times in 1994.[107]

The State of Georgia created the MPC in 1947. The MPC was not given the powers of a regulatory agency, but rather was designed to be a research and planning operation only. In 1952, the MPC released one of its early major products, a regional development plan for the region, named "Up Ahead." This plan called for limits to the geographic growth of the two-county (Fulton, DeKalb) metropolitan area using a greenbelt, similar to the London Greenbelt.[108] Within two years however, a modified plan, called "Now . . . for Tomorrow," turned away from any notion of regulated growth and a greenbelt. Instead, it called for "unlimited but planned, incremental concentric growth," stating that the 1952 plan was "highly unlikely to be implemented."[109] In 1960, in response to the planning requirements of the 1956 interstate freeway act, the State of Georgia abolished the MPC and replaced it with the larger Atlanta Metropolitan Regional Planning Commission (AMRPC), which covered a broader, federally defined metropolitan area. The AMRPC began to take on more significant planning functions, especially as they related to transportation planning.

Then, in 1971, the state created the Atlanta Regional Commission (ARC). ARC was given more resources and stronger powers to convene local governments around land use and economic development issues. It developed a regulatory context that supported the development of low-density development dominated by large-lot single-family homes, strip malls, and highly segregated land uses that furthered sprawl and allowed for economic and racial exclusion by local governments and individual subdivisions. Carlton Basmajian argues that Atlanta's form of regionalism was "almost completely at odds with that of a place like Portland or Minneapolis, the two American cities most often identified with good regional planning."[110] Basmajian argues that, in fact, given the region's relatively lower level of local government fragmentation, at least before the 2000s, ARC failed to use the advantages and power it had to further goals of environmental sustainability or social and racial equity. In the postwar period, the federal government repeatedly gave regional planning agencies tools to steer growth in ways that could both limit environmental damage and promote more equitable development. But ARC, like many regional planning agencies around the country and especially in the South, chose not to pursue these ends. Given its significant influence over roads and water, especially, ARC could have done more to shape metropolitan growth patterns more equitably and sustainably.[111]

One critical tool within ARC that facilitated the planning of sprawl was adopting and using an opaque urban growth model. Basmajian argues that "the model ended up co-opting the process, helping suppress public discussion and providing justification for a rather narrow analysis and a limited slate of policies . . . The model submerged a set of predetermined outcomes that supported continued, low-density growth . . ."[112] The technical opacity and sophistication of the models helped create a "presumptive veracity" in the agency's regional plans, which was very helpful when dealing with highly political development decisions.[113] Growth projections generated from the models, which were the product of deliberate assumptions and inputs, were then used to justify infrastructure investments in areas identified as prone to growth, creating a self-fulfilling prophecy of continued, sprawling, low-density development.

NO LONGER JUST AN ISSUE OF BLACK AND WHITE

The last two decades of the twentieth century saw the population of the Atlanta metro basically double, from just over 2 million to over 4.1 million.[114] Black, Latinx, Asian and other persons of color constituted over fifty-three percent of this growth so that, by the end of the century, the region was just over forty percent persons of color, up from twenty-six percent in 1980. The white population had grown by 65 percent, but the Black population had increased by 138 percent, the Latinx population by over 1,000 percent, and the Asian/AAPI population by over 900 percent. While the region was still majority-white, it was well on its way towards no longer being so. Although the white and Black population, combined, still accounted for about eighty-nine percent of the metro's population, that was down from ninety-eight percent in

1980, pointing to the region becoming a multiethnic metro in the twenty-first century.

The racial dynamic of the region was no longer one defined by a Black-white dichotomy, but by a multiracial dynamic, one that played out mostly in the context of increasingly diverse, but often not highly desegregated, suburbs. The Latinx population had grown to over six percent of the total metro population by 2000, but the vast majority of census tracts in the region had a Latinx population of less than five percent. Neighborhoods with larger Latinx populations were generally clustered along the Buford Highway corridor, near the towns of Doraville and Chamblee in northern DeKalb County and western Gwinnett County, near Marietta in Cobb County, and northern Clayton County. Similarly, the Asian population in 2000 was also geographically concentrated, especially in northern DeKalb along Buford Highway, and northwest Gwinnett, and the northeastern most tip of Fulton County in the Johns Creek area.

A significant share of the growing Latinx and Asian populations were immigrants, although many were coming from other parts of the country. Atlanta was similar to other "emerging immigrant gateway" metros, in that immigrants were increasingly arriving not in the central city neighborhoods as they did in the older immigrant gateways of Chicago or New York, but instead moved directly to the suburbs.

DREAMS OF BEING A "WORLD-CLASS" CITY

Most cities pay a good deal of attention to their image or, in marketing terms, to their "brand." Perhaps because of its roots in the Confederacy and the Jim Crow South, Atlanta seemed to focus on its image more than most cities during much of the nineteenth and twentieth centuries. From Henry Grady's orations calling for a "New South" to Mayor

Hartsfield and Mayor Allen's peddling of the "city too busy to hate," Atlanta's civic leaders have been masters of public relations. Larry Keating has argued that "being in the South translates into a sort of inferiority complex and city leaders have tried to demonstrate . . . that . . . Atlanta is a progressive, enlightened city."[115]

The city's Olympic bid, together with the global ambitions and background of Mayor Young, accelerated this public relations focus, aggressively peddling the notion of Atlanta being a "world-class" or "global" city. However, the city had been working towards this image well before seeking the Olympics. The push for MARTA heavy rail in the 1960s and early 1970s aimed to internationalize the city's image, a theme that arose again in the twenty-first century in the debate over light rail on the Beltline, as will be discussed in Chapter 2. The city waged a "world's next great international city" campaign in the early 1970s, in which it renamed Cain Street as International Boulevard.[116] The city did become a stronger locus of international investment and national and regional headquarters of multinational firms in the last two decades of the twentieth century.[117] But many cities saw similar trends as the economy became increasingly globalized. In serious analyses of global cities at the end of the century, Atlanta did not tend to make the cut.

By themselves, foreign investment and the branches of multinationals do not seem to be sufficient to increase the sense of whether a city is truly a world-class one. As Rutheiser writes, the notion of a world-class city goes beyond the bean-counting of such activities. It goes to the internationalization of the culture, something in which most southern cities did not have a comparative advantage due to the historic anti-immigrant xenophobia of the larger region.[118] A world-class city is generally viewed by many, especially by outsiders and visitors, as cosmopolitan, and renaming a few streets or creating a streetcar is not enough to develop such perceptions.

CHANGING COALITIONS, CHANGING POLITICS, BUT STILL CATERING TO CAPITAL

The roots of the city of Atlanta's urban regime, one in which a mostly white corporate elite develops a coalition with, and sometimes co-opts, Black middle-class political leadership, goes back to at least the first decade of the twentieth century. Although Mayor Hartsfield is often credited with refining and solidifying the Atlanta regime, the white elite adopted such strategies well before his tenure. In the wake of the 1906 race massacre, for example, white civic leadership, including realtors, bank presidents, and railroad executives, formed a committee and then asked many Black leaders, including leading Black clergy, to join them for discussions of how to avoid further racial violence.[119]

The dominant force in the city's urban regime was the white "community power structure," which consisted largely of men who had, as Ivan Allen, Jr., put it, "gone to the same schools, to the same churches, to the same golf courses, to the same summer camps. We had dated the same girls. We had played within our group, married within our group, partied within our group, and worked within our group."[120]

The Black leadership that formed the junior partners in the Atlanta regime was less comprised of businessmen than it was of ministers and politicians, although Black businessmen were part of the coalition and benefitted from a wide variety of its activities, including the negotiated expansions of Black neighborhoods that involved Black financial institutions and Black developers. Of course, Atlanta was the seat of the civil rights movement, and Black leadership was critical to making gains in voting rights, access to public schools and public facilities, and other areas through strong social and political resistance and protest. At the same time, Black radicals were often unable to gain a significant power base in Atlanta's urban governance itself, especially when it came to issues of housing and other issues that concerned poor, Black

Atlantans the most. This is not to say that there was no progressive or radical resistance to dominant political power by Black organizations in the housing or neighborhood affairs arenas. There certainly was. For example, Akira Drake Rodriguez has detailed the organizing, advocacy, and community-building work of Black-women-led tenant organizations in Atlanta's public housing. And Lee Ann Lands has described the history of Emmaus House, an organization based in the Peoplestown neighborhood that helped form the groups Tenants United for Fairness and the Georgia Poverty Rights Organization.[121] However, the cumulative effect of such organizing and advocacy, while important and impactful, was not able to rise to the level of a strong, lasting base of political power that would shape the longer-term trajectory of the city and effectively contest the dominant urban regime. As historian Alton Hornsby, Jr., wrote, "Black radicals in Atlanta could only whistle Dixie. They could not hope to achieve Black power there."[122] Tomiko Brown-Nagin calls the Atlanta approach one of "pragmatic civil rights," one of politics over litigation and one that sometimes resisted that idea that desegregation was necessary for equality, at least in housing. While mainstream Black leaders enthusiastically supported the NAACP voting rights campaign, in some other areas, they pursued "reform within the confines of Jim Crow."[123]

The rise of Black electoral power and the formal Black governance of the city, derived from Black legal and political activism on voting rights, did not mean an end to the Atlanta regime, especially when it came to issues of urban governance and planning. Despite some short-lived challenges to the corporate regime in the first Jackson term, it returned in fairly short-order. Black electoral power and white economic strength continued to perpetuate a system that favored the interests of capital over the city's less affluent residents. Whether facilitated by white- or Black-led city administrations, the fundamental goal of the regime remained generally consistent, with some temporary diversion along the way during Maynard Jackson's first term. As

Clarence Stone described, "by preserving wide investor prerogative and drawing on a broad array of business-provided benefits, Atlanta enables the downtown business elite to promote civic cooperation on the basis of "go along to get along." Those terms are well understood."[124] Thus, capital, both local and global, was the persistent power-behind-the-throne in city government. It did change some over time, as locally based captains of finance and industry gave way some to national and international real estate investors, developers, and the U.S. or regional headquarters of multinationals, but the focus on catering to capital did not. And the strategies of co-opting potential opposition via a "go-along-to-get-along" ethic remained.

In the later decades of the twentieth-century, corporate headquarters, new operations, and centers of real estate investment increasingly suburbanized, and corporate leadership and real estate investors recognized that they had to spend more time engaging with a different set of political leaders, including suburban governments, state legislators, and the ARC. Corporations and investors pursuing new development wanted new infrastructure, regulatory approvals, business-friendly policies, and explicit subsidies, and so turned their attention more to the political actors who could deliver them.[125] The city proper became relatively less important, less central to the concerns of corporate and financial interests in the region.

As early as 1971, the editor of the *Atlanta Constitution*, Jack Spalding, lamented the demise of the "old Atlanta" regime. Spalding wrote that "the old Atlanta was cohesive. When its captains gave the command, the troops fell in. Simple as that. The new Atlanta? Its old captains and kings barely know the lieutenants. Nor do the troops charge anymore when they hear the bugle from the Chamber of Commerce. In short, the new Atlanta has outgrown the old Atlanta which served so well for so long."[126]

Along with the sprawling of the region's economic base and investments, the economy had become more globalized, and corporate decision-making less under control of Spalding's local "captains and kings." However, what had not changed was a focus on ensuring that the city's and the region's policies and planning were welcoming to the business community and catered to the desires of investors and employers. An "anti-public-planning ideology," as Larry Keating has called it, has always been a principal reason as to why the city and the region are not able to "translate a robustly expanding economy into closing historic gaps."[127]

Efforts to advance stronger and more equitable forms of regional governance, especially around land use and economic development, were ultimately unsuccessful. Under Governor Jimmy Carter, proposals to adopt stronger growth management policies, which could have provided greater environmental sustainability and more social and racial equity, had been pursued, but such plans were effectively derailed under Governor Joe Frank Harris. Harris' chief of community development, Jim Higdon, changed the trajectory of growth management policy and argued that, as opposed to fighting the "evils associated with urban decay and urban sprawl" or considering "radical forms of regulation," the state should focus on making "jobs available for all Georgians."[128] Higdon argued that regional planning should "not be designed to direct growth to certain areas." Higdon also worked to ensure that the Commission on State Growth Policy should be made up of members of the private business community.

Besides the sprawling of corporate investment and the globalization of the economy, another change affected policy and planning in the region, and further supported the long-term trend of governance that catered to capital. In the early 1990s, a new group of conservative Republicans, supported by the influx of affluent, suburban homeowners, increasingly gained power, and any fledgling notion of regionalist planning broke down. As Carlton Basmajian writes, the growing Republican power base was "openly hostile to regulations that supported coordinated planning" and favored "protecting the low-density, single-family subdivisions that many believe gave the region much of its appeal."[129] By the early 2000s, anti-government conservatives had consolidated control of state government, and this solidified an anti-planning and anti-regulatory ideology across a broad swath of state and local government. When Democrat Roy Barnes lost reelection to Republican Sonny Perdue in 2002, and then Republicans gained complete control of the legislature in 2004, it marked a clear turn away from any substantive regional planning, even if such planning had mostly catered to the desires of capital and corporations. Any thoughts of strengthening development regulations or creating a stronger regional planning agency to address, or redress, the decades of sprawl that pro-growth regional planning had wrought, were pretty much off the table.[130] Barnes' initiatives like the Georgia Regional Transportation Authority (GRTA), an attempt to build an actual regional transportation infrastructure, were quickly curbed. The growing racial and ethnic diversity of the region, including in the suburbs, could ultimately create a long-term threat to this new anti-planning ideology, especially if control of the legislature eventually falls out of Republican rule.

Most of the last three decades of the twentieth century in the Atlanta region were ones of massive suburban sprawl, accompanied by central-city population loss, white avoidance of the city proper, and the beginnings of a more multiethnic metropolis. The region had earned the moniker, "Sprawl City."[131] However, the Olympics, the early demolitions of key public housing sites, and the continuing of the urban regime in the city presaged a change in trajectory that had begun in the 1990s. At the same time, there was little indication that the expansion of the suburbs farther outward would slow, though the increasing diversity of the sprawl was perhaps not well-enough acknowledged.

2

THE BELTLINE AS A PUBLIC-PRIVATE GENTRIFICATION PROJECT

NO REDEVELOPMENT PROJECT IN THE ATLANTA REGION, and arguably in the country, has been more transformative than the Atlanta Beltline. Its principal designer envisioned a streetcar line and trail that would wind through more than forty neighborhoods in a ring around the city, connecting rich and poor, Black and white. But the developers, consultants, urban boosters, and many public officials saw something more. They saw the promise of a major city-led public-private partnership, built on the back of expected rising property values, to reshape the city, both physically and demographically. To many, the Beltline has been a key factor in the city's "turnaround," following on the heels of redevelopment efforts initiated before and after the 1996 Olympic Games.[1] There is little doubt that the Beltline has had a profound impact on the city and many neighborhoods. What has often been missing in the enthusiasm for the project, however, is serious, critical analysis about its contribution to gentrification and exclusion—both economic and racial—in the city. Even before the first trails were opened at the tail end of the foreclosure crisis, the signs were there. As early as 2004, well before the Beltline tax allocation district (TAD) was adopted in late 2005, property values near the TAD began rising rapidly, and speculators began scooping up nearby properties. Promoters were writing about the potential for increasing property values early in the project's planning. Yet few expressed concerns about what this would mean to housing affordability, displacement, and the ability of future modest-income families to move into neighborhoods near the project. City officials were still clearly in the mindset of the 1980s and early 1990s, when the focus was on attracting more-affluent residents into the city, not on worrying about excluding or displacing lower-income ones.

This chapter discusses the origins and development of the Beltline, and its effects on surrounding neighborhoods and the city. The project's inception was an opposing bookend of sorts to the period beginning before the 1996 Olympics and its associated redevelopment projects, including the demolition of a great deal of public housing in the city. This period from about 1994 to about 2007, includes the first two key inflection points in the city's post-decline "turnaround" centered around the Olympics and the adoption of the Beltline, respectively. Instead of focusing on responsible reinvestment and community development efforts inclusive of existing and future low-income Atlantans, the corporate-led urban regime focused on a vision of a new, more-affluent, and whiter Atlanta. In some sense, the Beltline represented the long-held dream of the urban regime to identify, promote, and fund the "one big project" that could reverse decades of decline in the city. If this meant that the project would cater to the demands of mobile capital and investors without the bother of having to worry about bringing along less-affluent Black residents, so be it. Instead of focusing on acquiring property for affordable housing while land values were low, and putting in place measures that would protect existing residents from rising property taxes and rents, the focus was on building trails and parks that would enhance land values within the TAD, so that bonds could be supported to build yet more trails and parks. The fact that the beneficiaries of these trails and parks would increasingly become white and affluent seemed to be of little concern.

THE STAGE HAD BEEN SET: EMERGENT GENTRIFICATION IN THE WAKE OF THE OLYMPICS

From 1990 to 2007, a period including the demolition of a large portion of the city's public housing stock and the early 2000s subprime boom, the city of Atlanta underwent a significant shift towards gentrification and the exclusion of low-income families.[2] For the first time in decades, the city of Atlanta saw the reverse of its population loss, with a modest gain of 9.8 percent in its population from 394,000 to over 432,000. The city gained about 22,000 of these 38,000 residents during the 1990s, for a ten-year growth of 5.6 percent, and kept up a similar pace in the first seven years of the 2000s. This was a notable change in trajectory in the city's history and was considered a victory by city leaders. Atlanta was no longer a "shrinking city."

Signs of "revitalization" were evident, including some of the former public housing sites that became nationally prominent examples of mixed-income housing. But underlying this seeming urban success story was the fact that this "turnaround" was coming at a price of less access to the city by those with the least resources. The college-educated population increased by almost 60,000 from 1990 to 2007, while the number of adults without a college degree dropped by over 18,000. The median family income in the city rose from $50,880 in 1990 to $71,794 in 2007 (both shown here in 2021 dollars), a 41.1 percent increase. Perhaps most telling is that the number of families in poverty fell by forty-one percent. This decline wasn't because the city had figured out how to lift families out of poverty or due to some sharp drop in poverty more broadly. Relative to the metro, the city poverty rate had declined about one-third, from being 3.2 times the metro rate to 2.1 times the metro rate. Families in poverty were precisely the sorts of families most affected by public housing demolition and rising housing costs. This was a combination of some lower-income families being forced out of the city and others finding fewer affordable housing options in the city as they moved into or around the region.

The increased exclusion of lower-income families from the city was occurring just when the city proper had begun to see a turnaround in firms moving into the city, creating jobs, but jobs that would be increasingly distant from the regions' poorer residents. Some neighborhoods, including traditionally lower-income and Black ones, had had their share of problems caused by years of wealth extraction and disinvestment. But just when the city's economic prospects and finances were improving, lower-income households found it more difficult to stay in, or move into, the city. Some were skeptical that this had not been the plan of city leadership all along, especially when witnessing the highly visible demolitions of traditional public housing.

The economic shifts in the city were heavily racialized. While the city was seeing some influx of higher-income Black residents, the overall effect of the exclusion of lower-income families was a decline in the Black population of six percent, from 263,000 in 1990 to 247,000 in 2007. This, combined with the fact that the city's white population grew by almost 37,000, meant that the city was becoming significantly less Black, shifting from sixty-seven percent to fifty-seven percent Black over this period.

In many ways, this "turnaround" in the city's trajectory had been a long-sought-after goal of the city's governing regime. From the middle of the twentieth century, the corporate-led white-Black regime had supported efforts, including a massive annexation in 1952, to keep the city from becoming a Black-majority city. And once it did, in 1970, the corporate elite worked hard to oppose forces, including Maynard

Jackson, Jr., during his first term, that might prove too welcoming and supportive of a large, lower-income Black population. Instead, the regime continued to pursue efforts to continue to keep the city, and increasingly the region, as one that supported investors, employers, and more-affluent residents first.

In February 2000, the Atlanta City Council appointed a Gentrification Task Force to consider what appeared to be growing gentrification in the city and to report back with policy recommendations to the City Council. The city had seen gentrification in previous decades in a few neighborhoods, but there was a sense that the issue had been becoming more serious, especially since the Olympics. The Task Force held twenty public meetings over approximately a year, including five public hearings across the city. The Task Force final report, entitled "A City for All," was issued in September 2001, containing forty specific policy recommendations.[3] These recommendations included defining "affordable housing" to mean housing affordable to families with incomes at less than fifty percent of the metropolitan median income, and mixed-income housing as including no less than thirty-three percent affordable housing units. It also called for creating higher homestead exemptions for low-income homeowners, which would effectively reduce their property taxes, and for eliminating the sale of property tax liens, which allow speculators to control and hold vacant properties hoping that at least some of them will increase dramatically in value due to gentrification. The Task Force also recommended that the city adopt a fair-share housing law in which neighborhoods with too little affordable housing would be unable to block proposed affordable housing projects.

The City for All report identified five neighborhoods where home prices had risen considerably faster than the overall city, including Cabbagetown, Ormewood Park, Poncey-Highland, West End, and Grant Park. These neighborhoods represented a mix of Black and white communities as the locus of gentrification. Larry Keating, a member of the Task Force, also noted the stronger role of government in catalyzing gentrification compared to the more "mom and pop" nature of earlier phases.[4] Of the forty recommendations in the Task Force report, only a handful resulted in policy changes. The most important recommendations, such as defining affordable housing at less than fifty percent of metropolitan median income or reducing the property taxes based on homeowner income, were either not enacted or not enforced.

BUILDING THE BELTLINE

Since the mid-2000s, one of the strongest catalysts of urban change in Atlanta has been the Atlanta Beltline. The Beltline is a twenty-two-mile ring of trails, parks, and proposed transit that circles the city's core (see Map 7). It is a still in-process project being built out in stages as funding becomes available. Overall, the costs of the Beltline are now expected to reach at least $4.7 billion over the twenty-five-year development period, up from the $2.8 billion projected in 2005.[5] The path of the Beltline follows those of four historic rail segments developed after the Civil War that were built primarily to support the city's industrial base, including Atlanta & West Point, the Louisville & Nashville, the Seaboard Air Line, and the Southern Railway.

The original concept for the Beltline, somewhat appropriately perhaps, has roots in the 1996 Olympic Games. Randall Roark, who directed planning operations for the CODA, had been approached by a developer about the idea of a "cultural ring" around the city using the Beltline right of way as the path. It would be a corridor for connecting cultural and artistic sites and encouraging tourism in the city.[6] A few years after the Olympics, one of Roark's graduate students in urban design at Georgia Tech, Ryan Gravel, developed his Master's thesis on the Beltline, but this time Gravel proposed that it be used primarily for a circular ring of light rail that would touch on forty-five neighborhoods throughout the city. He saw the Beltline as connecting residents and communities in the city and not as a vehicle to entertain tourists.

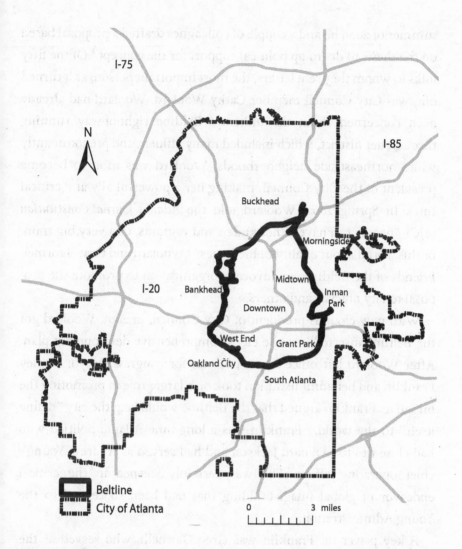

Map 7. The Atlanta Beltline

Gravel's plan called for stops in every neighborhood, and he argued that the project should break ground first in the southern part of the Beltline because it had a "tremendous amount of developable territory,"[7] presaging the ability of the Beltline to catalyze developers' interests and a revalorization of lower-income neighborhoods. After grad school, Gravel went to work with a local architectural firm. In the summer of 2001, he and a couple of colleagues drafted a proposal based on the thesis to drum up political support for the concept.[8] Of the fifty folks to whom they sent letters, the most important person, as it turned out, was City Council member Cathy Woolard. Woolard had already been concerned about the unkempt Beltline right-of-way running through her district, which included many affluent and predominantly white northeast-side neighborhoods. Woolard was soon to become president of the City Council, making her a powerful ally at a critical time. In Spring 2002, Woolard told the *Atlanta Journal-Constitution* (*AJC*), "people can have either kudzu and vagrants, or a very big train, or this. It's all about quality-of-life issues."[9] Woolard and Gravel formed Friends of the Beltline, an advocacy organization to promote the proposal to city officials and others.

With new clout as president of City Council, in 2003, Woolard got the Beltline inserted into the city's comprehensive development plan. After Woolard left office in 2004 to run for congress, Mayor Shirley Franklin and her administration took on a larger role in promoting the initiative. Franklin argued that the Beltline would help the city "define itself" to the world.[10] Franklin was a long-time Atlanta politico who had close ties to Maynard Jackson and had served as Andrew Young's chief operating officer. She was certainly steeped in the critical endeavor of global image-building that had been so central to the Young Administration.

A key player for Franklin was Greg Giornelli, who served as the director of the Atlanta Development Authority (later renamed Invest Atlanta). Giornelli, as it turns out, was the son-in-law of Tom Cousins, the very well-known, well-heeled, and well-connected real estate developer. Cousins' senior vice president for government affairs, Lisa Borders, succeeded Woolard as president of City Council in 2004.[11] And Giornelli and Franklin had both worked with Cousins and his foundation to redevelop the East Lake Meadows public housing site, a redevelopment not without its critics.[12] Franklin continued to collaborate with

Cousins' foundation and the nonprofit Purpose Built Communities that continues to promote the "East Lake Model" of community development. Soon Franklin created the Atlanta Beltline Partnership, an organization designed to raise political and financial support for the Beltline, and appointed Ray Weeks, a developer who had been a joint-venture partner with Cousins, as its chair. In keeping with the "Atlanta Style," or the "Atlanta Way," as it has been increasingly called, she appointed several prominent members of the established Black leadership to its board as well. At the time, some observers raised questions about the close relationships between Cousins, other developers, and public officials involved with the Beltline. State senator Vincent Fort told the AJC, "It just begs the question of whether or not the business community is the power behind the throne for the Beltline . . . More importantly, it begs the question of who City Hall is being run for."[13]

Well before the city formally adopted the legislation key to establishing the Beltline in November 2005, the project received critical support from the real estate community. Developers saw its potential to create a tremendous amount of real estate value, including areas where values had been low for a long time, especially where it ran through the city's south, southwest, and west sides. As Gravel's 2005 addendum to his thesis argued, "Residents love (the Beltline) for all its promised amenities. Developers, transit advocates, and other groups love it for all kinds of other reasons."[14] In fact, developers recognized that the Beltline itself could become "the" amenity in the region, the one that would be capable of moving real estate markets and reshaping the city. In April 2005, developer Beau King proclaimed that the Beltline was the "most exciting real estate project since Sherman burned Atlanta."[15] The statement, if jarring, was revealing, because decades of disinvestment, stemming both from racist housing and urban development policies as well as from discriminatory and predatory lending and investment practices by the private sector, had effectively devastated the neighborhoods surrounding many parts of the Beltline. This disinvestment and wealth extraction led to low land values and hundreds, if not thousands, of vacant and abandoned properties, ready for the taking by speculators hoping that the Beltline would bring back such property to its "highest and best use."

Alexander Garvin's December 2004 *Emerald Necklace* report clearly shifted the Beltline from a project focused on transit to one focused on trails and parks. The report was commissioned by the Trust for Public Land, a national nonprofit focused on securing land for parks and greenspace. Garvin was a nationally recognized urban designer based in New York city and a long-serving adjunct professor at the Yale School of Architecture. Garvin was a fan of Frederick Law Olmsted, the designer of Central Park who also influenced, at least indirectly via his sons' firm, the design of the wealthy and exclusionary Druid Hills neighborhood. Olmsted also designed Atlanta's Olmsted Linear Park, which beautifies Ponce De Leon, the east-west arterial running out of downtown through the east side. Garvin saw the Beltline as an opportunity "to transform what was once an industrial sewer of smoke into Atlanta's emerald necklace, studded with urban nodes and open space jewels."[16] The "emerald necklace" label refers to Boston's chain of parks and waterways, which Olmsted had also designed.

Garvin's report explicitly recognized the real estate value that the Beltline could catalyze. "The Beltline's future users are an attractive market. Early word of the project has already accelerated real estate values and increased property values in northeast Atlanta."[17] But the idea that speculators were already scooping up properties and bidding up land values wasn't a problem for Garvin and many other boosters of the Beltline and certainly not for the development community in the city. As suggested by developer Beau King's allusion to the rebuilding of Atlanta after it was burned to the ground in the Civil War, this was an opportunity to acquire low-priced land in disinvested Black neighborhoods. Then developers would wait for the magic of the Beltline, with its massive public and philanthropic investments, to reshape the city and, in the process, generate huge gains in values for the speculators.

Garvin clearly favored building the trails and parks before taking on transit, arguing that the parks would more quickly generate political support for the project. "If there is no visible progress, support will evaporate."[18] Transit would take years to break ground and perhaps a decade or two to be completed. Garvin recognized that trails and parks could be developed much more quickly and would build and maintain a constituency for the Beltline. He likely also realized that it would generate a large group of property owners and investors that would come to depend on the Beltline, and even the promise of the Beltline's completion near their property, as a way to support much higher property values. The potential displacement and gentrification impacts were not discussed in Garvin's report.

The idea of using a TAD to fund a significant share of the Beltline was proposed by a former city planning department staffer who wrote a white paper in 2003 arguing that land near the Beltline project would generate significantly increased tax value that could be used to fund a TAD.[19] TADs were used to support various targeted redevelopment efforts around the city, including the redevelopment of the Atlantic Steel plant site into the New Urbanist neighborhood of Atlantic Station just north of Georgia Tech. But no previous TAD covered the ground that the Beltline TAD would, which eventually encompassed over 6,500 acres, about eight percent of the city's land area. When the TAD was being championed by City Hall in the summer of 2005, the city and the Atlanta Development Authority cleared the decks of potentially competing TAD proposals to ensure that the Beltline was the focus and that it would not run up against the state's limits on how much of the city's tax base could be put into TADs overall. Council member C. T. Martin told the *AJC* that city staffers would not do feasibility studies for four other special taxing districts despite the City Council requesting that they be done.[20]

TADs are a common redevelopment financing device in Georgia, although the Beltline is far larger than most TADs. In other states,

TADs are called tax-increment financing districts, or TIFs. When a TAD is designated, the assessed value of the property tax base that is available to regular government operations (local government and schools) of a targeted geographic area is frozen. Then, as property values increase, the increase, or "increment," in tax revenue after the designation is diverted away from funding regular government services and schools, and towards the redevelopment expenses of the project or initiative, including repaying bonds that may have been floated backed by TAD revenues. These expenses can include payments to bondholders and private developers and other expenditures in the TAD area. The Beltline TAD spans twenty-five years.

The Beltline TAD, adopted in November of 2005, encircles the central business district and is approximately four miles west to east and six miles north to south. Most neighborhoods that the TAD runs through on the north and northeast sides of the city are high-income, majority-white areas, including parts of Buckhead, Ansley Park, and Morningside. At the other end of the socioeconomic spectrum, the TAD runs through and near lower-income, predominantly Black neighborhoods on the south and west sides of the city, such as Pittsburgh, English Avenue, and Oakland city.

Despite understanding that the Beltline could spur large increases in land values within and near the TAD, few mainstream boosters of the Beltline were speaking publicly about the threat such an effect would pose to housing affordability in nearby communities. The 152-page 2004 Garvin report does not contain a single mention of the terms "affordable," "gentrification," "lower-income," or "low-income." Yet the report authors and Beltline boosters likely knew that these issues would arise. Their preference, it seems, was to minimize attention to such concerns.

As the Beltline TAD was being debated in City Council, affordable housing advocates argued that affordable housing funds should be devoted to those with incomes lower than what the Atlanta Development Authority had proposed.[21] The Atlanta Housing Association of Neighborhood-based Developers (AHAND) argued for a significant commitment of TAD dollars to go to affordable housing. As Andy Schneggenburger of AHAND put it, "OK, revitalization of communities is the mission, but how do we do that without displacing all the folks who've been there, and how do you execute revitalization projects to leave an economically sustainable and diverse community when you're finished."[22] In the end, advocates were able to secure several community benefits provisions into the final TAD ordinance. In addition to the requirement that fifteen percent of TAD bonds go into the Beltline Affordable Housing Trust Fund (BAHTF), they were also able to insert conditions that a small portion of bond proceeds can encourage private development in disinvested neighborhoods and the use of a first-source hiring system.

OVERCOMING BARRIERS TO THE BELTLINE

In the few years following the adoption of the TAD, the Beltline suffered a key setback. In June 2006, John Woodham, a maverick, solo-practicing lawyer from Buckhead, sued the Beltline, claiming that the diversion of property tax revenues from school districts was not permitted under the Georgia constitution. Basically, because the schools' portion of property taxes account for on the order of half of the property taxes, the suit threatened the fundamental viability of the TAD and the financing plan for the Beltline. After losing his claim at the county level, Woodham appealed to the state supreme court, and in February 2008, the court sided with him, dealing an unexpected and serious blow to the project.[23] As a result of the ruling, the first TAD bond issued in 2008 had to be severely cut back because it could only be based on the portion of the tax base devoted to the city and county. The timing was unfortunate because this shrank the overall funding base for the project. The smaller TAD bond also meant less money for affordable housing because the affordable housing funding formula was tied to the size of the TAD bonds, which were now severely constrained by the lawsuit, as well as by the 2008 global financial crisis and its impact on municipal bond markets.

The Beltline's boosters moved quickly into action after losing the state supreme court case. Mayor Franklin, the business community, and localities across the state that were planning to use TADs to finance redevelopment projects joined in a campaign to amend the constitution to permit the diversion of schools' tax base into TADs. By the November 2008 election, a constitutional amendment was on the ballot. The proposal passed, allowing TADs to freeze property taxes once again going to schools as well as to cities and counties, and diverting any increases to fund redevelopment projects. The Beltline's TAD game was, at least theoretically, back on, although the continuing turmoil in financial markets was not a welcoming environment to float municipal bonds.

Another key development in the early history of the Beltline was the difficulty of dealing with land speculators. Once a massive project like the Beltline is announced, it is difficult to prevent speculators from snatching up key properties vital to the project. This was precisely the problem as early as 2004, when the Beltline was a concept on the move. In October, Wayne Mason, a suburban Gwinnett County developer, and his son Keith snatched up a prized and critical piece of the Beltline, a 4.6-mile corridor that included much of the needed property for the northeastern section. The Masons purchased the property from the Norfolk Southern railroad for $25 million. At first, Beltline boosters were quick to praise Mason, seeming to ignore the likelihood that such an action was an attempt to extract value and public subsidy from the project and the city. "Wayne Mason is a successful businessman, so his interest in inner-city development is a positive," Mayor Franklin said shortly after the purchase.[24] It is unclear whether the mayor actually thought this or simply attempted to distract from the fact that a well-heeled speculator had just purchased a large part of the Beltline property before the city could secure it. The Masons appeared to be capitalizing on the likely flow of subsidy to the project and the fact that the city had to have a portion of this property to make the entire project work.

The Masons joined forces with Trammell Crow, a large national builder of apartment buildings, to form a joint venture, the Northeast Atlanta Beltline Group. The partnership submitted rezoning plans to build two large towers, one thirty-eight stories and the other forty stories, in an affluent northeast Atlanta neighborhood dominated by single-family homeowners. The former city planning staffer who proposed the Beltline TAD in 2003 served as a consultant to the project.[25] The plans for the two towers did not go over well with many neighborhood residents. The city distanced itself from the proposed towers and eventually was forced to purchase the property through a joint venture with another developer, Barry Real Estate Company, in November 2007. In the end, by December 2008, the city ended up paying the Masons a total of $71 million, including interest payments, for a tract of land for which they had paid only $25 million a few years earlier.[26] And this was at a time when property values had begun to plummet as the foreclosure crisis had been well underway. Moreover, the city was forced to provide Barry Real Estate with a $3.5 million payout after the firm had only put $1.5 million into the deal only a year before getting bought out, netting a cool 133 percent annual return.[27]

The Beltline and the city had fallen into a classic trap that can accompany large, high-profile redevelopment projects. The enthusiasm, profile, and expectations of such projects can prompt speculation and rising land values. If key parcels are not controlled early on, some speculators often gain control of them well before the redevelopment agency can, and then hold the parcel hostage in an attempt to extract as much as possible from the agency. In the end, much of the Beltline's first TAD bond went to pay the profits made by the Masons and Barry

Real Estate, who in the end were effectively nothing more than land speculators in Beltline property.

A BELTLINE FOR WHOM?

Two issues concerning the Beltline are emblematic of the question of for whom the Beltline was being built. The first concerns transit, and the second concerns housing. Gravel's original thesis was fundamentally a vision of a circle of light-rail transit running along the Beltline. From the earliest days, fundamental questions have continued to resurface about the wisdom and feasibility of this plan. These include whether a circular loop along this route would be effective at connecting working people to jobs, whether it would connect well with or complement the existing MARTA system, and whether light-rail would be the best use of always-scarce mass transit dollars, as opposed to a bus or bus rapid transit alternative. These questions were not just about transit engineering but also ones of transit equity and transit justice. Advocates for Beltline rail were generally passionate advocates of rail over all other transit modes and, sometimes, appeared more concerned with what a large light-rail line might do for the city's image in the eyes of the country and the world, and less about how much it would help reduce commuting burdens or the region's carbon footprint.

In September 2005, a couple of months before the City Council approved the Beltline TAD, the "Beltline Transit Panel," a group of leading transit experts from Georgia Tech and the transportation planning industry issued a brief white paper on transit feasibility on the Beltline.[28] The report was less than supportive. It included the following statements:

> The Panel is surprised at the paucity of credible information relating to the expected ridership of the Beltline alternative . . . .no integrated picture of transit ridership potential for the Central Atlanta area has been developed.

There are very few locations along the Beltline where large and dense concentrations of jobs are expected—these are mostly projected for the Lindbergh area, already served by MARTA bus and rail service.

Operating costs for Beltline transit have not been addressed as far as the Panel has been able to determine . . . Yet operating costs can be a make or break issue for viability of transit projects.

The panel expressed skepticism that Beltline transit could compete for scarce federal transportation dollars, a critical issue, especially for relatively expensive rail transit. Michael Mayer, a transportation engineering professor at Georgia Tech, told a small group at City Hall, "Is transit justified? I have to say—some segments, I'm not so sure. Some people are going to kill me for that, but I have tenure."[29] Despite the panel's conclusions, advocates of Beltline rail were not deterred, nor was the Beltline organization, which continued to include transit in its funding plans.

In 2006, MARTA conducted a study of potential alternatives for building and operating transit along the Beltline. The study found that bus rapid transit offered a far less expensive option than light rail, with estimated costs running about $570 million versus $885 million.[30] It was clear that based on technical feasibility and cost-effectiveness, light rail was not the better alternative, especially because cost-effectiveness is a key criterion in the competition to win federal transit dollars. But public comments were dominated by rail advocates. Some public comments during the assessment of bus versus rail included:[31]

It is fun for a tourist to see a trolley—have you ever heard a tourist say "cool a bus is coming"?

I would like to see light rail. I have traveled to Amsterdam ten times in the last seven years and I am very impressed with the flexibility of the vehicles that they use there.

We are an international city. We need to think on a global scale . . . It's amazing that we have a world class baseball team yet we don't have easy transit to the stadium.

A bunch of buses is the future of Atlanta's great initiative? Show me a poll where people don't say they hate buses.

Buses contribute to the existing urban blight. Give us something to be proud of, like the San Francisco streetcars.

The merits of light rail on the Beltline then, at least for these commenters, seemed to have little to do with how effectively it would perform as transit for working residents of Atlanta and the region. They appeared more concerned with visions of the city's future, what it will look like to a tourist, a visitor, and the world. This is related to the "world-class city" vision discussed in the last chapter, to the quests of people like former Mayor Young and corporate boosters to reimagine the city, to recast its image, and to reposition the city in the eyes of the world. The comments also revealed an anti-bus stigma, one associated here with "urban blight," a term that has a troubling racialized history in the U.S.

Those advocating for light rail over buses in public comments rarely mentioned the transit needs of lower-income, Black residents of the city. How would rail versus bus affect their ability to get to better jobs? How would it allow them to connect to the broader MARTA system that they relied on, especially since the Beltline itself was unlikely to link them directly from their home to their place of work? These questions seemed subordinate to those that spoke to the city's image, to the physical appearance or "shininess" of a new train, and to Atlanta achieving "world-class city" status.

Housing affordability is the second area where the question of who would eventually benefit from the Beltline arose. If the Beltline were to catalyze housing demand and gentrification nearby, it could mean the direct displacement of existing lower-income residents as rents rose. In addition, nearby neighborhoods, and perhaps the city overall, would become less affordable to lower-income families who had traditionally considered living in these communities when moving into or around the region. Without efforts to preserve affordability for both existing and potential new residents, the core city could become a new place of economic and racial exclusion, a role wealthy suburbs had traditionally played. Merely inverting the spatial arrangement of poverty and affluence, so that lower-income families would need to look outside the city to find affordable housing while core neighborhoods become areas of concentrated affluence is not a clear improvement on a situation where the core had been disproportionately Black and poor. Arguably, such a "great inversion" would be worse, as lower-income families would be effectively steered to areas farther from transit and jobs.[32]

There was limited public debate around housing affordability issues on the Beltline, at least before the authorization of the TAD came in front of the City Council in the fall of 2005. Until that time, no local media gave significant attention to the issue, despite increasing press coverage on the project since 2004. Only one article in the *AJC* touched on the topic, and that wasn't until the last day of October when the proposed TAD was being discussed in the City Council.[33] Advocates like the AHAND managed to insert some community-benefits and affordability language in the TAD ordinance in late 2005. When the Council passed the TAD on November 7, 2005, the same month that the Beltline Redevelopment Plan was issued, it included a provision that fifteen percent of the proceeds of TAD bonds be put into an affordable housing trust fund.

There were at least five problems with the fifteen percent affordable housing provision, and all but one of these were highly foreseeable. First, the ordinance did not define "affordable housing." There was no guarantee that Beltline resources would go to truly lower-income families. Second, the TAD was never projected to comprise the bulk of Beltline funding. Over the first five years of the Beltline, it accounted for only thirty-five percent of spending.[34] Third, the fifteen percent set-aside of dollars in the ordinance was only to be applied to TAD bonds, specifically. The problem with this was that dollars generated by the

TAD could go to pay project costs in the TAD area rather than towards repaying bonds issued to fund large, up-front expenses. If the ordinance had required that fifteen percent of *total* annual Beltline spending be devoted to affordable housing, it would correspond to a much larger sum, on the order of $420 to $700 million over twenty-five years, depending on whether one uses the earlier or later total cost estimates for the project. And the amount would not have relied on the precise source of funding but ensured that a significant percentage of overall Beltline spending was devoted to affordable housing. This would have meant heavier investment in affordable housing when property values were dropping in the wake of the foreclosure crisis, and dollars could have been more cost-effectively devoted to acquiring and banking land for affordable housing development. Instead, Beltline spending on affordable housing was pitiful, especially from 2008 to 2012, before values began increasing.

A fourth problem with the TAD-based affordable housing funding was that TAD dollars could only be spent on activities located within the narrow, meandering TAD district, and not in the bulk of the area near the TAD where most of the resulting housing development would eventually occur. Finally, and less foreseeable, was the impediment created by the lawsuit filed by John Woodham seven months after the TAD was adopted.

In September of 2007, Georgia Stand-Up, a community benefits advocacy group, released a study that I conducted for them on the effects that planning and media attention around the Beltline had on home values and home-buying near the Beltline TAD.[35] The study examined home sales from 2000 to 2006 near the Beltline TAD and compared them to home sales farther away from the area. It also looked at changes in homebuyers' incomes in nearby neighborhoods using federal mortgage data from 1999 to 2005. The homes sales analysis revealed that the median sales price of homes within one-eighth of a mile of the Beltline TAD increased by more than 130 percent, or about 15 percent per year, from 2000 to 2006. This rate of increase was much higher than the 9.8 percent annual increase for homes 1 to 1.5 miles from the TAD, and more than three times the rate of growth for homes over two miles from the TAD.

While comparing changes in median sales prices is useful to assessing affordability changes over time, because the composition of the sales may change over time, it does not tell us enough about the appreciation rate of a typical house or its underlying land value. This is because comparing medians does not adjust for changes in the types of or more-precise neighborhood locations of the homes sold and other factors affecting home prices. To detect changes in appreciation due to the Beltline, we need to compare changes in home sales close to the Beltline to those of similar homes farther away. Because we know that real estate market participants more generally were aware of the enthusiasm for the Beltline, and the public and philanthropic dollars that could pour into the project, it is important to look at changes in home values as early as 2002 and 2003.[36]

The media coverage of the Beltline is a good signal of enthusiasm and public attention to the project. The *AJC*'s first mention of the Beltline was in December of 2002, with a few more articles in 2003. In 2004, coverage increased significantly and then continued to grow. From 2002 through 2006, when Beltline organizing and media coverage grew a great deal, homes within a half-mile of the lower-income, southern section of the Beltline TAD appreciated at substantially higher rates than homes more than two miles from the TAD. Appreciation ranged from twelve to twenty-two percent higher over this period, after controlling for other characteristics of the homes and their neighborhoods.[37] Moreover, the greatest period of growth was from 2003 to 2005, when the planning and policy work for the Beltline was most intense.

The same Georgia Stand-Up study also used federal data on mortgage lending to corroborate the notion that the early buzz around the Beltline was inducing gentrification in nearby neighborhoods. The share of owner-occupied homebuyers who were upper-income increased by more than ten percentage points from 1999 to 2005 in most neighborhoods close to the Beltline TAD. In some of these tracts, the increases exceeded twenty-five percentage points. Lower-income neighborhoods within a half-mile of the TAD experienced an average increase in the share of upper-income buyers of 13.4 percentage points.[38] This compares to an average increase of only 3.9 percentage points in similar-income neighborhoods more than two miles from the TAD. The bottom line was that the market enthusiasm for the Beltline, the planning for significant public subsidy, and the speculation that flowed from this excitement generated substantial housing market pressure in the neighborhoods bordering the TAD, especially in the lower-income, predominantly Black ones.

As the evidence of the Beltline's impact on housing costs and gentrification mounted, Georgia Stand-Up organized for stronger accountability of the Beltline to the lower-income communities it was affecting. The organization created a set of community benefit recommendations for the Beltline, including a comprehensive set of policy recommendations around employment issues for community residents. Stand-Up also mobilized residents to engage in Beltline study groups, which was the primary community engagement method that the Beltline employed.[39]

AFTER THE FORECLOSURE CRISIS, BELTLINE GENTRIFICATION IS RESURGENT

The initial phases of detailed planning and physical development of the Beltline began during the foreclosure crisis, especially from 2008 through 2011. The groundbreaking for the Historic Fourth Ward Park was held in October of 2008, and the park and the initial segment of the East Side Trail were opened in 2010 and 2011. By 2012 the housing market had begun its recovery, and the Beltline once again became a locus of gentrification and rising housing costs in the city. Development around the Beltine picked up in 2012 and accelerated in the following years. Home values and rents rose, and speculators increased their acquisition of nearby properties.

Tharunya Balan and I updated my earlier 2007 analysis of pre-crisis Beltline housing prices by examining post-crisis trends (2011 to 2015) around the Beltline compared to other locations in the city.[40] Using hedonic regression to control for differences in housing types, neighborhood conditions, school attendance areas, and other factors, we found that the prices for homes located within a half-mile of the Beltline—effectively the Beltline Planning Area—increased at much faster rates from 2011 to 2015, compared to similar homes farther from the Beltline. The increases were at least eighteen percentage points greater, over this brief period, than for sales in the city farther from the Beltline. Moreover, the increases were greatest near the southwest segment of the Beltline, where many neighborhoods most vulnerable to gentrification were located. Within a half-mile of the Beltline on the southwest side, homes increased in value at a rate that was twenty-seven percentage points faster than parts of the city farther from the Beltline. Given that the rest of the city had increased at a very strong thirty-two-percent rate itself, this meant that home values near this segment of the Beltline had increased by an average of fifty-nine percent since 2011. The bulk of that growth occurred in the three years since 2012. Values have continued to increase at a fast pace in these areas since 2015.

While housing values near the Beltline were beginning to accelerate, Atlanta Beltline, Inc.'s (ABI) affordable housing efforts lagged. Despite efforts by advocates to get the organization to prioritize the issue, ABI's very modest efforts were fundamentally ill-matched for the real estate fervor that the Beltline had generated. The Beltline's reliance on fifteen percent of TAD bond proceeds proved to be far too weak of a vehicle to fund meaningful levels of affordable housing.[41] The TAD funded only about one-third of the expenditures of the Beltline, most of which were put into the developments of the trail and associated parks. While the aggregate assessed property values in the TAD increased from 2006 to 2008, they then stagnated, at least through 2014. This occurred despite a significant increase in actual market values in and near the Beltline after 2012. However, Fulton County's tax appraisal system failed to keep assessed values in line with real market values, stifling the funding capacity of the TAD. On top of this, the two development finance authorities granted property tax breaks to some large properties, weakening TAD revenues further.

Moreover, TAD proceeds, including the set-aside that funded the BAHTF, could only be used in the spidery, narrow TAD district itself, and not in the much broader Beltline Planning Area that covered an area within a half-mile of the TAD, where much of the development occurred. The BAHTF, funded by the bond set-aside, was also aimed at supporting new housing development, but that did little to help renters and homeowners who saw their rents and property taxes accelerate early on. The majority of Beltline expenditures were not funded with TAD dollars, and some of these funds, including the philanthropic dollars, might have been devoted to affordable housing outside the TAD.

Besides the delays caused by the lawsuits against the Beltline discussed earlier, another problem involved a dispute between the Atlanta Public Schools, on the one hand, and ABI and the city of Atlanta, on the other. It centered over a 2005 agreement specifying that the Beltline would make fixed payments to the schools as compensation for lost revenues due to the TAD. ABI had agreed to provide a series of payments in lieu of taxes to the schools amounting to $162 million over the life of the TAD in exchange for the school system forgoing its share of the increment over this period. When the increment failed to materialize as projected, however, ABI reneged on its agreement. After years of back-and-forth, the school system ultimately conceded to accepting only about $88 million plus a small amount of land to settle the disagreement.[42]

In September 2016, two key members resigned from the board of the Beltline Partnership, the booster-fundraising affiliate of ABI, over the issue of affordable housing. One of the resigning board members was Nathaniel Smith, the director of the nonprofit Partnership for Southern Equity, and the other was Ryan Gravel, a key architect of and advocate for the Beltline. Their resigning from the Partnership board because the Beltline had done little in the way of generating affordable housing was a powerful statement. Smith was particularly pointed in his criticism of the Beltline. "What's going to happen to the west and south side if light rail is built and we have no affordable housing provisions," he told Creative Loafing's Thomas Wheatley after resigning. "We're going to see displacement like we haven't seen since urban renewal in the 50s and 60s."[43] Shortly after Smith and Gravel left and the media coverage that followed, ABI announced increased funding goals for affordable housing from a new bond issuance.[44]

The issue of the Beltline's poor performance on affordable housing did not go away. In July 2017, the *AJC* ran a front-page investigative story on the failures of ABI towards making meaningful progress on its affordable housing goals.[45] The article pointed to how, after eleven years, ABI had created under 600 affordable units, had funded affordable homes that could be quickly resold to high-income buyers, and had not pursued funding sources for affordable housing while raising tens of millions of philanthropic dollars for trails, parks, and other activities. The *AJC* also found that as TAD increment dollars began to increase by 2012 because ABI did not float bonds, it was not required to spend fifteen percent of TAD proceeds on affordable housing. Of course, the larger problem was that the TAD generated only about one-third of ABI's revenues. An overall commitment of fifteen percent of ABI spending and investment to affordable housing would have funded much more affordable housing production.

The leadership of ABI did not apologize for its weak progress on affordable housing, with its board chair telling the *AJC*, "All I hear is positive. Everybody has a little different view about priorities."[46] Community members, including housing advocates on the board of the Beltline Partnership, minced few words. Mtamanika Youngblood, a veteran community developer, commented, "I get no sense of a commitment. Now we get lip-service."[47] The article also noted how, in 2016, Invest Atlanta's finance committee had criticized ABI for devoting less than one percent of its 2017 budget for affordable housing and not establishing milestones for reaching its 5,600-unit goal. The *AJC* also reported that ABI leadership made efforts to expand the definition of the housing it could count towards its affordable housing goals.

The *AJC* article, following less than ten months after the well-publicized resignations of Gravel and Smith from the Beltline Partnership board, caused a further uproar over ABI's lack of commitment to affordable housing. Within a month, the ABI CEO was forced to step down. Smith told the *AJC*, "To be honest, it should have happened a long time ago."[48]

The *AJC* had brought to light what many Beltline observers had known for years, that ABI was not making serious headway on its affordable housing pledge, mostly due to a lack of political will. City and ABI leadership saw ABI's mission as building trails and parks, not providing affordable housing. This remained so despite ample evidence that the Beltline was transforming real estate markets in the city, causing rapid increases in home values and rents. The Beltline's original 2005 funding model, at least as portrayed in public documents, had anticipated over $340 million in funding for affordable housing and economic development. But in the ten years following the adoption of the TAD, it had only spent $13 million on affordable housing, only four percent of the projected twenty-five-year amount, despite being forty percent into the project's funded life.[49] Moreover, given that the Beltline had caused property values to increase even before the TAD was adopted, it was critical to front-load affordable housing investments to maximize the amount of property that could be acquired for long-term

Figure 2. The Housing Justice League releases its report on the Beltline, October 12, 2017

Source: Housing Justice League/American Friends Service Committee.

affordability before land values became exceedingly expensive. Unfortunately, this wasn't done.

In October 2017, the Housing Justice League and the Research/Action Cooperative released a study of residents living near the Beltline, focusing on residents of Black neighborhoods on the southwest side of the city.[50] (See Figure 2.) They surveyed 143 residents across sixteen neighborhoods, with an oversampling of three southwest side neighborhoods particularly vulnerable to gentrification: Peoplestown, Pittsburgh, and Adair Park. Ninety percent of the total set of respondents expressed a desire to remain in their communities, with sixty-two percent expressing concern about rising housing costs. Of the sixty-five respondents from the three target neighborhoods, sixty-two percent were concerned about rising housing costs, with ninety-three percent expressing a desire to remain in their community. Thirty-seven percent stated that they would likely move out of the neighborhood if housing costs increased.

ABI was masterful at moving the affordable housing goal posts even after ABI's CEO was forced to leave after the *AJC* expose. And this occurred despite a modest original goal, 5,600 units over twenty-five years for an average of only 224 units per year, in a city of half a million people.[51] ABI moved the goalposts in at least three different ways. First, the original Beltline planning documents called for new or preserved affordable rental units affordable to households earning less than sixty percent of the metropolitan area median income (AMI). Over time, that threshold moved up to eighty percent of AMI.[52] This is a sizable difference, especially because the housing affordability problem is much more severe in Atlanta for families at lower income levels. The second game that ABI played was including housing units subsidized not just by ABI, or even by just ABI and Invest Atlanta (the city's development arm), but by pretty much any subsidy source in the region. This included the Development Authority of Fulton County, the Georgia Department of Community Affairs (which allocates Georgia's Low Income Housing Tax Credits), and the Atlanta Housing Authority. As a result, ABI began counting pretty much every potential source of subsidy towards its own affordable housing goals. These were sources, including Invest Atlanta, that predated ABI and the Beltline TAD. The 5,600-unit goal was clearly intended to cover units generated by the Beltline funding organization, first Invest Atlanta and then ABI. It was disingenuous to count a stream of activity that would have existed with or without the Beltline towards the goal and then imply that this activity was due to the ABI's efforts. Finally, ABI expanded the geographic area for which it counted affordable housing units. Instead of counting just units produced in the TAD itself, which was the constraint of the 5,600-unit goal, it began counting activity in a far larger area, the entire Beltline Planning Area, extending a half-mile on either side of the Beltline.

At the end of 2020, ABI listed a series of claims in its annual report of affordable housing units created and preserved from 2006 through 2020.[53] According to the parameters for the original 5,600-unit goal, which was supposed to only include units in the Beltline TAD and funded by the Beltline, the maximum number of affordable housing units that it should have claimed would be 871 through 2020. This number is generous because it likely includes affordable units at only eighty percent of AMI and not at sixty percent of AMI, as the original Beltline Plan specified. Even setting aside this issue, ABI, over fifteen years had only created or preserved less than sixteen percent of the 5,600-unit goal over sixty percent of the TAD's twenty-five-year life. Even if one counted all the other, preexisting subsidy sources as ABI does, it had only reached thirty-eight percent of the original, modest goal. Over time, ABI expanded its metrics to claim credit for 487 units of affordable housing outside the TAD, presumably funded primarily by Invest Atlanta through its regular development subsidy programs. It also threw in another 555 units subsidized by the housing authority, the county, and the state, outside the TAD, again through programs that preexisted the Beltline.

Finally, in 2020, the Beltline began to devote more significant dollars of its own budget, from TAD dollars, towards affordable housing. The TAD increment had grown substantially, and ABI allocated a larger amount, approximately $11.9 million, in its budget to affordable housing. This was more on the level of the annual dollars needed at the beginning of the Beltline project, a time when dollars would have gone much further due to much lower land values.[54] After several years of pressure to do more about affordable housing, and especially triggered by the *AJC*'s exposé in 2017, ABI appeared to understand that they needed to do more on the issue. With the new revenue from the growing increment in the TAD, it was easier for ABI to do this while still funding trails and other activities. It also began to focus more on acquiring land.[55] Again, of course, if it had made such moves much earlier, before the boom in housing costs and land values, the organization could have created far more units and more units per dollar of subsidy, rather than continually moving the goalposts to make it appear as if it was creating more housing than it actually was.

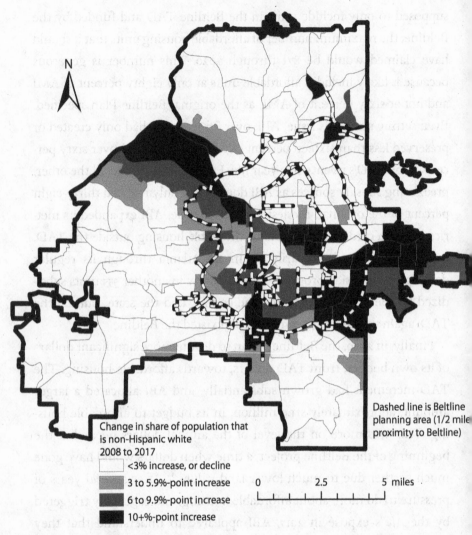

Change in share of population that is non-Hispanic white
2008 to 2017

- ☐ <3% increase, or decline
- ☐ 3 to 5.9%-point increase
- ☐ 6 to 9.9%-point increase
- ■ 10+%-point increase

Dashed line is Beltline planning area (1/2 mile proximity to Beltline)

0   2.5   5 miles

Map 8. Increases in non-Hispanic White population share in the city of Atlanta, 2008 to 2017
Data source: American Community Survey 5 year estimates, 2006–2010, and 2015–2019

One result of the boom in home values and rents near the Beltline, especially in places where rents and values had previously been relatively affordable, was a marked demographic shift in many neighborhoods on and around the Beltline. Map 8 shows the percentage-point increase in the share of the population that was non-Hispanic White from 2008 until 2017. Much of the city's east side experienced increases of at least six percentage points in their white population. Some of these neighborhoods, such as Kirkwood, had already experienced significant gentrification in the late 1990s and early 2000s, and continued those trajectories. In other neighborhoods, the changes were more recent, especially after 2012. Proximity to the Beltline, especially on the east, southeast, southwest, and west sides, was associated with increases in the white population share. (Many of the neighborhoods near the northern and northeastern sections of the Beltline were already predominantly white, so substantial percentage-point increases in the white population would not be expected.) It is important to point out that these increases in white households occurred during a period in which the white share of the metro population was actually declining.

BUFFETED BY THE BELTLINE: THE WHITENING OF THE OLD FOURTH WARD

When people who have lived in Atlanta for a while are asked to name an example of a gentrified or gentrifying neighborhood, they might mention Kirkwood, Reynoldstown, Adair Park, or others. But one neighborhood has, for some time, been perhaps the quintessential example of gentrification in the city, partly due to the historic importance of the area to the Black community. This area is called the Old Fourth Ward, which depending on whom you ask, takes on different boundaries and may or may not include the small historical area known as Sweet Auburn. For the sake of this discussion, the Old Fourth Ward follows the boundaries described by the Old Fourth Ward Economic Security Task Force, and includes the Sweet Auburn area.[56]

The Old Fourth Ward is particularly notable for being the earliest locus of major park and trail development efforts along the Beltline. The east side of the neighborhood borders the Beltline, as shown in Map 9. The neighborhood has a storied history in Atlanta. It is the birthplace of Dr. King and home to Ebenezer Baptist Church as well as many key twentieth-century Black leaders, businesses, and organizations, such as John Wesley Dobbs, Reverend William Borders, Atlanta Life Insurance, and the Southern Christian Leadership Conference. *Fortune Magazine* reportedly dubbed Auburn Avenue the "richest Negro street in the world" in 1956.[57] The area was also home to The *Atlanta Daily World*, the city's historic black-owned daily newspaper.

The Old Fourth Ward area also included Grady Homes, one of the oldest public housing projects in the city, dating back to 1942. Before its demolition and redevelopment beginning in 2005, Grady Homes housed just under 500 families. The 2005 HOPE VI redevelopment plan called for mixed-income housing redevelopment, with just 141 of the 545 units in the new development remaining as public housing.[58]

In the late 1920s, Sears Roebuck built a massive brick building on Ponce de Leon Avenue to serve as their distribution hub in the Southeast.[59] The neighborhood had been one of the denser neighborhoods in the city, with a population of over 20,000 in 1960, but urban renewal—including the clearance of a Black community, Buttermilk Bottom, that was replaced by a now-vacant civic center—and highway construction hit the community hard, led to a steep decline in population over the next twenty years.[60]

In the late 1980s, Sears sold its warehouse and, after a couple of years of vacancy, the city of Atlanta purchased the building, dubbing it "City Hall East." The city never fully occupied the property and put it on the market in the early 2000s, reaching an agreement to sell it to a developer in 2005. But after some delays, the deal fell through. Then, in 2011, near the end of the foreclosure crisis when land values had bottomed out, Jamestown Properties purchased the building for $27 million.[61] The city worked closely with the developer for over a year to package the financing, subsidy, and regulatory approvals used to create the large, mixed-use, high-profile property. This was also around the time of the development of the adjacent Eastside Trail of the Beltline and the Historic Fourth Ward Park,

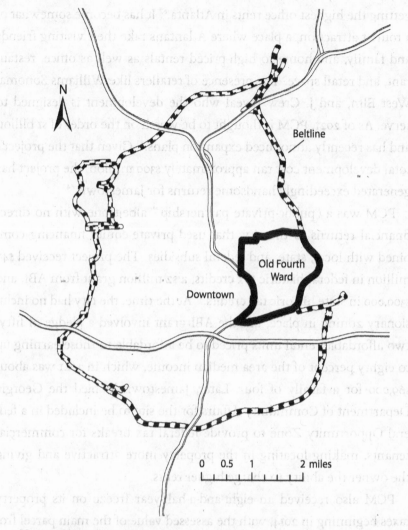

Map 9. Old Fourth Ward/Sweet Auburn

major investments by the city and ABI that would add major value to the new development—Ponce City Market (PCM). Construction of PCM began in 2011 and proceeded in phases with an initial opening in 2014, when the real estate market was in full recovery mode.

After 2011, the site gained enormous value, due primarily to the huge public investment in the immediate area. By 2017, PCM was getting the highest office rents in Atlanta.[62] It has become somewhat of a tourist attraction, a place where Atlantans take their visiting friends and family, and home to high-priced rentals as well as office, restaurant, and retail space. The presence of retailers like Williams Sonoma, West Elm, and J. Crew reveal who the development is designed to serve. As of 2021, PCM is thought to be worth on the order of $1 billion and has recently announced expansion plans.[63] Given that the project's total development cost ran approximately $300 million, the project has generated exceedingly handsome returns for Jamestown.[64]

PCM was a "public-private partnership," albeit one with no direct financial returns to the city, that used private-equity financing combined with local, state, and federal subsidies. The project received $48 million in federal historic tax credits, a $2 million grant from ABI, and $300,000 in state historic tax credits.[65] At the time, the city had no inclusionary zoning in place, but the ABI grant involved a pledge of fifty-two affordable rental units priced to be affordable to those earning up to eighty percent of the area median income, which in 2021 was about $69,000 for a family of four. Later, Jamestown lobbied the Georgia Department of Community Affairs for the site to be included in a federal Opportunity Zone to provide federal tax breaks for commercial tenants, making locating in the property more attractive and giving the owner the ability to charge higher rents.

PCM also received an eight-and-a-half-year freeze on its property taxes beginning in 2014, with the assessed value of the main parcel frozen at less than $5.2 million over this period.[66] Given that assessed values are set at forty percent of the appraised market-value, even if the county valued the property at only $500 million by 2020, over time this effectively amounted to tens of millions in cumulative subsidy and, by 2020, an effective tax rate of well under one-tenth of one percent of market value. Ironically, perhaps, the increase in taxes that the project should have generated would have gone to the Beltline TAD and provided more funding for Beltline activities, including affordable housing.

The statistics on the gentrification of the neighborhood since 2000 are sobering. The area saw its Black population share decline from seventy-six percent to thirty-eight percent in 2017, with a raw decline in the Black population of over 3,400, over one-third of the 2000 level. Over the same period, the non-Hispanic white population increased by over 280 percent, from less than 2,000 to over 7,600. The share of the population with a college degree increased from twenty-six percent to sixty-four percent, and the median household income increased from just over $31,000 in 2000 (in 2021 inflation-adjusted dollars) to just over $64,000 in 2017 (in 2021 dollars).[67] The typical inflation-adjusted income of households in the neighborhood more than doubled over the seventeen years. The number of poor residents in the neighborhood fell by forty-one percent as low-cost housing was replaced by new, higher-end housing. Zillow data shows that the sales price for a typical home increased by 110 percent from January 2013 to January 2021, with fifteen homes listed at more than one million dollars in May of 2021.[68] The neighborhood saw approximately 3,000 new housing units developed in about a decade, the vast majority of those being in apartment buildings, belying the notion that gentrification, at least during this period, was one characterized by individual families moving in and acquiring fixer-upper, single-family homes.

Many other neighborhoods in the city, especially predominantly Black neighborhoods near the Beltline on the south and west sides of the city, are, as of this writing, at earlier stages of gentrification than the Old Fourth Ward. The area was already experiencing early signs of gentrification before the Beltline was adopted, in part because it was sandwiched between whiter, more-affluent neighborhoods to the east and downtown Atlanta to the west. But the Beltline and Historic Fourth Ward Park greatly accelerated this trend.

The initial stages of planning and policymaking for the Beltline, including the adoption of the TAD in late 2005, represent a key missed opportunity. ABI and the city of Atlanta could have redirected the city's trajectory away from one of highly racialized gentrification and exclusion towards one where the project could have produced substantial affordable housing and mitigated the adverse effects of rising rents and property taxes on nearby lower-income households. It was a second major inflection point in the post-decline trajectory of the city, following closely on the heels of a previous one surrounding the 1996 Olympic Games. The Beltline was a public-private partnership billed as benefitting the city as a whole and even as disproportionately helping low-income Black Atlantans, in part by creating a more direct physical connection to whiter, more affluent neighborhoods. But the motivations of the Atlanta regime for backing the Beltline were more complex, and the project relied heavily on the enthusiastic support of real estate developers and investors, public officials, and others traditionally involved in the regime. This "transformative" project effectively reshaped and revalorized the built environment in core city neighborhoods, regardless of who would end up living there. Moreover, this urban "turnaround" project was not simply the result of atomistic, unplanned "market forces," but rather the product of a coalition of institutional actors, including core members of the regime, working towards a vision of a more affluent, and whiter, city population. While the Beltline was not the only cause of gentrification and racial exclusion in the city, as discussed in the next chapter, it was a key contributor and was a highly political project emblematic of a city obsessed with the next big thing.

3

PLANNING, SUBSIDY, AND HOUSING PRECARITY IN THE GENTRIFYING CITY

THE STORY OF THE CITY of Atlanta in the last decade of the twentieth century and the first two decades of the twenty-first century is one centered on heavily racialized gentrification. The city went from being two-thirds Black in 1990 to less than half-Black by 2019. It is a story of enthusiastic civic and government support for reshaping the city into a new, more affluent, and whiter citizenry, centered around the apparent success of its major physical redevelopment project, the Atlanta Beltline. The reasons why Atlanta has become a juggernaut of gentrification lie partly in the last decades of the twentieth century, as described in Chapter 1. Civic leadership, including the corporate-led regime, never relished the notion of being a majority-Black city. Even after Black elected officials gained power, they generally did not embrace the city's lower-income Black population or focus policymaking on improving the conditions of their lives. The clearance of public housing, the reimagining of the city as a global one seemingly hell-bent on supporting investment capital, and the remaking of places to appeal to more affluent in-movers all set the stage for the city's stronger gentrification in the twenty-first century. This chapter details the demographic changes in the city and some of the key policies and practices supported by the Atlanta urban regime, beyond the Beltline, that accelerated gentrification and racialized exclusion during this period.

ATLANTA AS A NEW TECH HUB AND JOB GROWTH MAGNET

During the twenty-first century, and especially following the Great Recession and foreclosure crisis, employers began practically tripping over themselves to locate in the city of Atlanta, partly to be near Georgia Tech, Georgia State, Emory, the Atlanta University Center, and other incubators of talent. Coming out of the foreclosure crisis, the city of Atlanta began adding jobs at a steady pace starting in 2012. According to Census Bureau data, private-sector jobs in the city increased steadily from just over 330,000 at the end of 2011 to over 437,000 by the end of 2019, a thirty-two percent increase.[1] Moreover, the city began to add increasing numbers of high-paid jobs, including in various tech sectors, which often paid starting salaries of over $100,000 per year. The result was that the average salaries of jobs located in the city proper increased, especially starting in 2014, rising from just over $81,000 (in 2021 dollars) to just under $90,000 by 2016 (2021 dollars) and remained roughly at this new higher level through 2019.[2] Some of the new jobs were due to firms relocating operations from other states, while others were relocations from the suburbs. In 2015, NCR announced that it would move approximately 4,000 jobs from Gwinnett County to the eastern part of Georgia Tech's campus in Midtown, only about six years after relocating from Dayton, Ohio.[3] Other large firms that moved into or expanded in the city after 2012 included

Honeywell, Athena Health, Google, Microsoft, Invesco, GE Digital, and Equifax.

Atlanta became a growing tech hub, with a large pool of talent and a growing tech "ecosystem." According to the real estate consultancy CBRE, Atlanta saw a twenty-eight percent increase in its tech talent pool from 2013 to 2018.[4] The region also ranked seventh in the country in the number of completed tech degrees in 2018. In just five years, through early 2021, venture capital investments in the metro reached over $2 billion, with approximately $1 billion invested since 2020, with activity especially focused on financial technology, cloud-based computing, and internet security.[5] The development of new sources of venture capital in the city facilitated the growth of new tech-based firms, although the in-movement and expansions of larger firms drove most of the employment growth.

As high-wage firms moved jobs into Atlanta, this created a strong demand for housing, driving up rents, especially in the city proper, close to many of these new jobs and offering the amenities that younger, higher-income workers wanted. This, in turn, made affordable housing a greater challenge for lower-income residents. As demand for high-end housing grew and real estate capital flowed into the city, the construction of new apartment buildings increased in Midtown and Buckhead, but also in newer areas, including near the Beltline. The ready supply of private equity capital was attracted to the Beltline as a key, high-profile amenity, as ABI, the Beltline Partnership, and the city had laid the groundwork for a new spatial target of development. The Beltline, of course, was not a sole or sufficient cause of the strong housing demand in its path. But it combined with, and supported, the growth of high-wage jobs in the city to push up land values in its wake. The fervor over the project concentrated real estate market demand, resulting in a phenomenon that moved markets. As discussed in Chapter 2, the result was that land values increased sooner and more rapidly in areas near the Beltline, putting severe pressures on many lower-income neighborhoods.

EXCESSIVELY CATERING TO CAPITAL

Some portion of the greater demand for housing and urban space by the new, higher-wage workers in the city could, and should, have been transformed into streams of public revenue that could have been used to subsidize the housing needs of lower-income Atlantans. Instead, the city and local economic development agencies remained stuck in the mindset of a shrinking city, as if it were still 1980, when the city was losing population and focused on retaining middle- and upper-income residents. The two major development finance agencies operating in the city, Invest Atlanta and, especially, the Development Authority of Fulton County (DAFC), continued to grant large property tax breaks to developers of offices and large luxury apartment buildings, as if the signs of rapid gentrification were not staring them in the face each day.

The city had become a smaller share of the region, and Republicans exercised a firm grip over critical state policy, constraining both regional planning and the self-governance of the city. The old "go-along-to-get-along" corporate-government regime still survived, if not precisely in the same form as it took under Mayors Hartsfield, Allen, or even Young. Major civic action was still very pro-business and eschewed most things that smacked of redistributive policies, regulation, or the like. Leaders from the Metro Atlanta Chamber of Commerce, the United Way, the Community Foundation of Greater Atlanta, and the ARC collaborated around major issues facing the region and deliberated together about which civic efforts should get more support, or less.

One critical group that became a key part of the Atlanta corporate-led urban regime was the Atlanta Committee for Progress (ACP), which had been put in place under Mayor Shirley Franklin in 2003. ACP describes itself as allowing the mayor to "gather input and collaborate with c-suite level business, civic, philanthropic, and academic leaders on issues of critical importance to the city;" its membership includes

"40 highly-engaged chief executive officers, university presidents, and civic leaders."[6] The most recent five board chairs of ACP have been white male CEOs of major firms, including Cox Enterprises, Delta Airlines, Georgia Power, and Invesco. The forty members read like a who's who of corporate Atlanta, including Arthur Blank, Dan Cathy (the CEO of Chick-fil-A), an executive vice president of Koch Enterprises, and the CEOs of a good number of developers and firms that have received major tax breaks and subsidies from Invest Atlanta or DAFC, including NCR, Jamestown Properties, Invesco, Georgia Pacific (part of Koch Enterprises), Norfolk Southern, Carter, and UPS. ACP boasts of marshaling $10 million towards completing the Beltline's West Side Trail. Mayor Franklin had relied on ACP heavily in building corporate support for the Beltline.[7] ACP is particularly active in mayoral election seasons, trying to influence the policy agenda at such times. In October of 2017, it issued a five-point platform that focused on fiscal strength, expanded economic opportunity, student achievement, transit connectivity, and crime.[8] Notably, despite affordable housing being a major issue during the fall mayoral debates, the ACP platform made no mention of it as a priority.

As in many southern cities, there has been little philanthropic support in Atlanta for activism or advocacy that confronts the dominant regime or pushes for potentially contentious policies that will bring opposition from any significant corner of the civic infrastructure, including the business or real estate communities. Southern philanthropy tends to be conservative concerning issues of social and economic justice.[9] Until recently, many funders based in the South tended to avoid using social justice language to describe their work, at least compared to national funders. They have not supported policy advocacy and community organizing as much as funders in other parts of the country, especially those based on the coasts. Atlanta funders such as the Woodruff Foundation are known more for supporting cultural endeavors and community service efforts than those aimed at structural economic change, especially if it will entail the enmity of corporate leadership. And the Arthur Blank Foundation, a key local funder, is closely tied to enterprises that themselves have benefitted from the corporate-friendly policies of the city, including direct taxpayer subsidies.

RACIALIZED GENTRIFICATION ACCELERATES

When looked at over the last three decades or so, the data make clear that the city of Atlanta has undergone a fundamental change in trajectory, one that can only be characterized as significant, racialized gentrification. The city has shifted towards a less Black, more affluent, and more college-educated population. If current trends continue, there will be little room for lower-income Black families. The city's Black population will likely shrink to become a substantially smaller share of the overall population. If Atlanta remains a Black Mecca, it already appears that it is the region, more than the city, that plays this role and welcomes most new Black residents. The gentrification of the city, which began at a larger scale in the 1990s (despite some earlier instances in a few select neighborhoods), paused briefly during the foreclosure crisis, but then accelerated rapidly coming out of the crisis during the national housing recovery. Atlanta was not alone in experiencing this quickened pace of gentrification after 2012 but was part of what Derek Hyra and his coauthors call "fifth wave" gentrification, enabled by global capital moving rapidly into urban housing markets in new, heavily financialized ways.[10] The crisis had left millions of vacant properties in its wake, often at very low values, prime material for speculation and revalorization as housing demand reemerged. Global capital surpluses that had pushed into private-label loan securitizations in the 2000s were still chasing yield and favored real estate investments. Private equity markets were flush with "dry powder," and rental housing was a prime target for investment.

Over the longer 1990 to 2019 period, the city's population grew from just under 400,000 to over 506,000, with most of the growth occurring after the end of the foreclosure crisis in 2012. (There was a small annexation in December of 2017 that increased the city's population by about 6,400, but this was primarily college students and accounted for only about ten percent of the city's population growth of over 63,000 from 2012 to 2019, and did not have a material impact on the demographic changes described here or in Figure 3 below.[11]) The median family income in the city grew dramatically, from just over $50,000 in 1990 (in 2021 inflation-adjusted dollars) to over $96,000 in 2019 (also in 2021 inflation-adjusted dollars), for a real, inflation-adjusted increase of over ninety percent during this period. The family poverty rate in the city dropped from 24.7 percent in 1990 to 15.5 percent in 2019.

Three statistics paint a vivid picture of the magnitude of gentrification in the city since 1990 (see Figure 3).[12] First, the Black share of the city's population declined from sixty-seven percent to forty-eight percent over these three decades. So the city went from being two-thirds Black to just under one-half Black. From 2012 to 2019, a period of substantial real estate investment flowing into the city and the height of growth around the Beltline, the city went from majority- to minority-Black. A second graphic statistic is that the share of adults twenty-five and older who had a college degree or higher increased from twenty-seven percent to fifty-six percent from 1990 to 2019, so that the college-educated percentage of the population essentially doubled. Finally, the ratio of the city's median family income to that of the metropolitan area as a whole increased from 0.60 in 1990 to 0.85 by 2007. During the foreclosure crisis, gentrification slowed, and incomes overall in the region fell. But then, from 2012 to 2019, the city-to-metro income ratio increased again from 0.87 to 1.10 so that, over the post-crisis recovery period of only seven years, the city had gone from being significantly lower income than the suburbs to significantly higher-income. Over the broader thirty-year period, the city had truly undergone a major

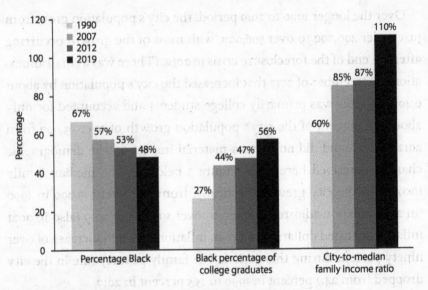

Figure 3. Demographic change in the city of Atlanta, 1990 to 2019
Data sources: 1990 Census; 2007, 2012, and 2019 American Community Survey

shift, what's been called a "great inversion," where the core city is a place of increasing affluence, and where lower-income families are less welcome and pushed to the suburbs.[13]

The city's gentrification was not just the result of higher-income households moving into the city but also a product of a decline in low-income households. The number of families below the poverty line dropped by approximately twenty-nine percent over the thirty years. Some of this was due directly to the demolition of public housing, but much of it was because the city had become increasingly expensive, and low-income families were often forced to look elsewhere for housing.

Gentrification in the city accelerated after the foreclosure crisis ended as the real estate economy regained steam. Demand by investors, renters, and homebuyers in the city surged, and the growth in both rents and home values began a long period of strong appreciation. From early 2013 to early 2021, all zip code areas of the city saw home values increase by over thirty-five percent, with over half the city's geography seeing values more than double (see Map 10). The largest

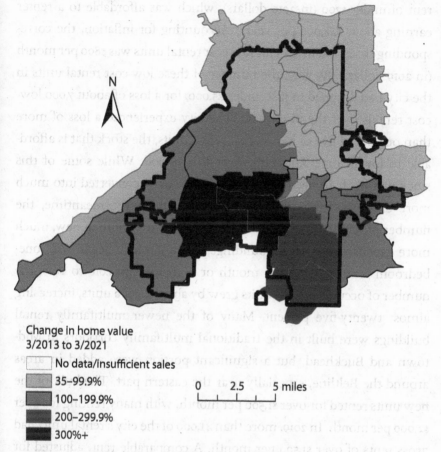

Change in home value
3/2013 to 3/2021

☐ No data/insufficient sales
35–99.9%
100–199.9%
200–299.9%
300%+

0   2.5   5 miles

Map 10. Changes in home values by zip code, city of Atlanta
Data source: Zillow.com

increases, exceeding 200 or even 300 percent over eight years, occurred in neighborhoods on the south, southwest, southeast, and west sides. These were mostly areas that still have significant Black populations, with the more expensive and historically whiter north and northeast sides of the city experiencing slower but still mostly strong gains in value.

Rising home prices were accompanied by rising rents and by the shrinkage of the lower-cost rental stock. In 2010, the city had just over 32,000 low-cost rental units, defined here as those with a gross monthly rent of under $700 (in 2010 dollars), which was affordable to a renter earning about $28,000 per year.[14] Accounting for inflation, the corresponding threshold in 2019 for low-cost rental units was $800 per month (in 2019 dollars). By 2019, the number of these low-cost rental units in the city had dropped to just under 25,000, for a loss of about 7,000 low-cost rentals over the nine years. The city experienced a loss of more than one out of five of its low-cost rental units, the stock that is affordable to low-income Atlantans, over this period. While some of this stock was likely in need of repair, it was usually converted into much more expensive units if it was redeveloped. In the meantime, the number of rental units overall ballooned due to a boom in new, much more expensive apartment buildings, most of which began with one-bedroom rents at $1,500 per month or higher. From 2010 to 2019, the number of occupied rental units grew by about 24,000 units, increasing almost twenty-five percent. Many of the newer multifamily rental buildings were built in the traditional multifamily corridors in Midtown and Buckhead, but a significant portion were added in areas around the Beltline, especially near the eastern part. The bulk of the new units rented for over $1,500 per month, with many renting for over $2,000 per month. In 2019, more than 41,000 of the city's rental units had gross rents of over $1,500 per month. A comparable rent, adjusted for inflation, was about $1,250 in 2010, but in 2010, there were only about 19,000 units priced at that level. The higher-cost rental stock had effectively doubled over the nine years, while the low-cost stock had declined by more than twenty percent.

In a relatively brief seven-year period coming out of the foreclosure crisis, from 2012 to 2019, Atlanta had moved from being a city where most of the population was Black and not college-educated with a median income well below that of the suburbs, to one that was minority-Black, majority college-educated, and with a median income significantly above that of the suburbs. The gentrification trends that had begun during the 1990s had reached a full head of steam, and the city was now on a rapidly gentrifying trajectory. In fact, a study by researchers at the Federal Reserve Bank of Philadelphia identified the city of Atlanta as the fourth-fastest gentrifying city in the U.S. from 1990 to 2014, trailing only Washington, D.C., Portland, and Seattle.[15] Others in the top ten included Sunbelt cities such as Austin, Charleston, Raleigh, and Richmond. The study found that one-third of the city's ninety-seven low-income tracts experienced gentrification over this period, which these authors define as a very large increase in college-educated adults compared to other neighborhoods across the U.S. Moreover, because this study did not capture most neighborhood change after 2012, it missed much of the accelerated changes during the post-crisis period of "fifth-wave" gentrification.

FRITTERING AWAY THE GAINS OF A GENTRIFYING CITY AND DYSFUNCTIONAL PUBLIC FINANCE

In the city of Atlanta, there have been at least three structural problems with the property tax system and development subsidies that have combined to create a public finance system that is fundamentally dysfunctional. These include 1) two competing development authorities operating in the city that have given excessive property tax breaks to large commercial real estate projects, mostly in hot-market neighborhoods where subsidies are not needed; 2) a fundamentally skewed property tax appraisal system that favors large commercial property owners who pay specialists to get their appraised values lowered far below true market value; and 3) property tax limitation policies that disproportionately benefit owners of larger and more valuable single-family homes.

An overarching result of the structural problems with property taxes and subsidy practices has been that, despite the city's land values growing tremendously from the beginning of the 2010s through the end of the decade, the citizens of Atlanta, especially the non-property-owning ones, did not benefit nearly as much from the city's growth and increased land values as they should have. Instead of the public coffers benefitting from the growth in population and land values, the vast majority of the benefits accrued to landowners, speculators, and investors. Rather than having much more revenue to address issues of affordable housing, repairing sidewalks, and other essentials, the finances of the city remained highly constrained. This begs the obvious question as to why a city should bother to promote economic development and growth if a fair portion of that growth is not captured by the tax system so that it can be reinvested in improving the lives of ordinary citizens. The answer, unfortunately, lies in the continued power and persistence of the urban regime that continues to work for the benefit of investors, real estate interests, and affluent homeowners, rather than for the benefit of working-class residents.

The explicit subsidy problem has received the most media attention, in part because it is the least complex and offends many Atlantans' sense of fairness when larger property owners and developers receive subsidies to locate or develop in hot neighborhoods. In November 2019, for example, the Invest Atlanta Board awarded a $700,000 tax break to Blackrock, the world's largest asset management firm to locate right next to the Beltline on the east side, one of the hottest parts of the city. About a year later, the development agency awarded the firm another $500,000, this time in a cash grant.[16] (This $1.2 million is effectively a rounding error to a firm the size of Blackrock, which has over $7 trillion under management.) All of this came just a few years after Invest Atlanta had given a ten-year tax break with a present value of over $7 million to the office building occupied by Blackrock.[17] Another example of excessive tax subsidy occurred around the surging gentrification of the Old Fourth Ward after the development of the East Side Trail of the Beltline. As Chapter 2 details, Ponce City Market, the poster child of mixed-used development on the East Side Trail, saw a remarkable rise in market value after its development, yet its property taxes were frozen at recession-era levels. In this case and others, the share of the value that the Beltline TAD was supposed to recapture for affordable housing and other purposes, was effectively gifted back to the property owners instead.

As of 2021, two competing development authorities provided property tax breaks to developers and large firms in the city. One was Invest Atlanta, the city's development finance arm, and the other was the DAFC. DAFC had an even worse reputation than Invest Atlanta for subsidizing development in hot parts of the city. In 2019, DAFC approved a $3.5 million-dollar subsidy for a hotel to be located in the hot, well-gentrified Old Fourth Ward. The representative from the developer, Portman Holdings, told the DAFC that it aimed to "draw demand out of other districts, out of Downtown we would hope, that we can bring more people to this market."[18] The developer went on record admitting that the DAFC subsidy would help the new hotel compete and draw business away from downtown Atlanta, actually a weaker submarket than the planned location, the Old Fourth Ward.

In just one meeting in January of 2019, the DAFC approved over $100 million in property tax breaks, including a $57-million-dollar, ten-year tax abatement to the insurance company MetLife for a nine-acre development in Midtown, perhaps the hottest submarket in the city.[19] The DAFC board voted 6–2 in favor of the subsidy despite the superintendent of Atlanta Public Schools voting against it and arguing that the project—or a similar one—would have proceeded without the subsidy. Most of the remaining subsidy voted on that day was for projects in other hot neighborhoods such as the Upper West Side and Reynoldstown.

Journalist Maggie Lee analyzed all of the property tax subsidies granted to developers by DAFC and Invest Atlanta over sixteen months, from July 29, 2019, to December 8, 2020.[20] During this period, the two agencies granted over $239 million in tax abatements, with the ten largest abatements accounting for over $156 million of that amount. Most of the $239 million went to large real estate projects—typically dominated by offices and commercial space—in hot submarket areas, including Midtown, the Upper West Side, and the east side of the city. This was despite the fact that employers were clamoring to locate in these areas. The presence of two development authorities giving incentives in the same city had resulted in a race-to-the-bottom with both agencies excessively catering to capital, especially the DAFC, which accounts for a large majority of the tax breaks. They both generated fees for their operations from granting subsidies, which increased as the size of the deals did, giving them strong incentives to woo developers to their agency and for developers to shop between the two agencies, seeking the best deal. After being heavily criticized earlier in the 2010s, Invest Atlanta focused more on requiring modest levels of affordability in residential and mixed-use projects, but both agencies continued to finance large commercial developments in hot neighborhoods through the end of the 2010s and into the 2020s. In 2021, critics of the DAFC revealed that the agency's board members received very generous per-diem fees from the agency, enabled largely from revenues derived from the tax break transactions. This revelation received a good deal of media attention and led to some turnover on the agency's board.[21]

Another structural problem that has kept the public from benefitting from the city's economic growth has been the practice, implemented primarily by Fulton County but effectively sanctioned by the State of Georgia, of under-taxing large commercial properties. In late 2018, the *AJC* examined 264 sizeable commercial property sales that occurred since 2015 in Fulton County. The paper compared the sale prices to the tax-appraised values that Fulton County had set for the properties.[22] It found that 119 properties, forty-five percent, sold for more than twice their appraised values. Despite the city's hot real estate market and public investments in projects like the Beltline generating rising property values for owners of commercial real estate, many, if not most, were not paying close to their fair share of regular property taxes, never mind any notion that the city deserves to capture a larger share of the land value gains created through public investments. In Fulton County's own review of 175 appraisals of commercial properties, it found that the properties appraised for only $2.8 billion despite selling for about $4.2 billion, for an aggregate appraisal-to-sales ratio of only sixty-seven percent.[23] It also found that sixty-one percent of the 175 properties had their tax levels appealed, leading to billions in decreased appraised values from 2016 to 2018. More than half of the properties had had their appraised values frozen for three years—during a period of quickly rising land values in the city—after the owners had appealed their values in earlier years. Most appeals by these larger property owners involve firms that specialize in appealing property taxes, and these firms tend to be very successful in getting their clients' appraisals substantially reduced.

Later in 2019, the city of Atlanta hired a firm to conduct its own study of county tax appraisals and found that appraisal levels were much lower for high-valued properties than for low-valued ones. In a sample of 176 properties, the firm found that properties valued at $20 million or more were appraised by the county at only about sixty-eight percent of market value compared to about ninety-eight percent for properties worth less than $250,000.[24] A large portion of this difference was due to frequent, successful appeals of tax-appraised values by the large property owners and taking advantage of legal loopholes that reduce the tax-appraised value of the properties. Of course, the owners of high-value properties can easily afford to spend the money on a tax appeal expert if it will save them millions over the long run.

In November 2019, Julian Bene, a retired management consultant who had served on the board of Invest Atlanta for eight years, estimated that the county's underappraisals of commercial property in the city cost the city, county, and public schools over $300 million per year in the city of Atlanta alone.[25] That is the equivalent of over $1,300 per household per year. Even a moderate slice of that could provide a great deal of funding for affordable housing, with the rest providing much-needed resources for schools and other critical local services.

Some efforts were made to remedy the underappraisal problem. A few county commissioners and state legislators proposed that commercial property tax appeals be less of a cakewalk for owners of large properties. They called for the county to require detailed, audited financials from the property owners when they file appeals and that owners pay taxes on the full appraised value, instead of a discounted rate, during the appeals process.[26] To do this, however, they needed state legislation, and a bill proposed by Representative David Dreyer of Atlanta died in the Republican-controlled legislature in 2020.

A third fundamental problem with the city's public finances is one that was partly a response to the rapid decline and then subsequent rise in home values in the city during and after the 2007–2011 foreclosure crisis and the political challenges that they caused. Homeowners enjoy periods when their taxes decline as property values fall but tend to resist mightily when values recover. As home values began to rise around 2012, the Fulton County Assessor failed to keep appraised values current. Therefore, many homeowners did not see assessments rise for several years. Then, in 2017, when the Assessor's office finally did reset values to reflect the considerable growth in values across the city from 2012 to about 2016, many of the notices sent out to homeowners showed large increases, often well over thirty percent, in appraised values.[27] Homeowners received these notices during 2017, a mayoral election year. As it turned out that year, the chairman of the Fulton County Board of Commissioners at the time was a candidate for mayor of Atlanta. In response to the political heat generated by the rising assessed values, the county placed a freeze on property tax assessments at the older, much lower 2016 values. It kicked the can down the road until after the 2017 election. In 2018, the new values shot up again so, after pressure from some homeowners, state legislators in Atlanta, led by a Republican from Buckhead, the wealthiest part of the city, supported a policy change doing two main things. First, it allowed home-owners to roll back their appraised value to as far back as 2016 when the assessor had not updated appraised values from recession-era levels. Second, it limited subsequent growth in the city's portion of property taxes to less than three percent per year as long as the homeowner stays in the home. This was a significant windfall for owners of expensive homes that had appreciated a good deal during the post-crisis period, especially in affluent neighborhoods in Buckhead and northeast- and east-side neighborhoods. Besides the windfall disproportionately ben-efitting more-affluent homeowners, the policy change shifted the city portion of the tax burden going forward to rental properties. This shift will be mostly passed on to renters, who tend to be less affluent. More-over, this structure will create significant horizontal inequities between newer and longer-term homeowners and discourage wealthy owners from selling their homes as they age. Although some argued for more progressive approaches to cushion the blow to low-income homeown-ers from the rapid rise in home values, the rollback-plus-limitation pro-posal was approved by voters in 2018.

HIGH PROFILE PROJECTS AND PUSHING
THROUGH COMMUNITY RESISTANCE

The post-crisis period included a series of controversial, large real estate development projects in the city. These included the construc-tion of a new stadium for billionaire Arthur Blank's football and soccer teams, the sale of the shuttered Fort McPherson to movie mogul Tyler Perry's production studio, the redevelopment of Turner Field (the base-ball stadium abandoned by the Atlanta Braves who left for suburban Cobb County), and the proposed redevelopment of the "Gulch" a forty-acre site in the southern part of downtown Atlanta.

In 2013, the city of Atlanta agreed to a massive subsidy of a new stadium proposed by local billionaire and philanthropist Arthur Blank, owner of the Atlanta Falcons football team, to replace the twenty-five-year-old Georgia Dome. While Invest Atlanta portrayed the subsidy as amounting to $200 million out of a total $1.6 billion price tag, the details of the deal revealed that the subsidy would amount to a much larger cash flow stream to the project, one that Arthur Blank himself estimated as having a present value of $700 million. More recent estimates have pegged the value at as much as $900 million.[28] While the city subsidy, funded by bonds backed by the city's hotel-motel tax, ostensibly covered $200 million in bonds to pay upfront development costs, hundreds of millions more in subsidy will go to pay the stadium's ongoing operating and financing costs over time. Blank told the *AJC*, "We've got close to $700 million in public money, if you look at the net present value of the stream over a long period of time."[29] Blank pegged the private dollars in the project at $850 million, meaning that the city subsidized well over forty percent of the full cost of the project. The good news for the city, though, was that Blank's stadium only charged $2 for hot dogs when it opened.[30]

The sale of the bulk of Fort McPherson to Mr. Perry for his movie studio was heavily criticized as a sweetheart deal to a high-profile celebrity close to then-mayor Kasim Reed.[31] Perry purchased 330 of the former army base's 448 acres for a price of only $30 million in 2016. At under $91,000 per acre, this was an extremely low price for a site only five miles from downtown Atlanta and seven miles from one of the world's largest airports. The deal was announced abruptly in 2014. It ignored years of planning involving numerous community meetings and charrettes. Many in the neighborhood felt blindsided. "When I saw the mayor's announcement, that's when I knew we had gotten the banana in the tailpipe," one resident told *USA Today*. "It felt like a trick. A dirty, dirty trick."[32] Earlier plans that the base redevelopment authority had developed with a great deal of local community input had called for a more diversified and publicly accessible multi-tenant, mixed-use development, including open space. The sale of most of the site to Perry made those plans moot.[33]

The Turner Field controversy focused largely on the likelihood that the redevelopment of the nearly seventy-acre stadium area into a large-scale mixed-use development by a partnership involving Georgia State University (GSU) and Carter, a real estate development firm, would accelerate gentrification and displacement in a south side Black neighborhood already under gentrification pressure from the Beltline. Carter's CEO was a strong supporter of Mayor Kasim Reed and was involved in several important projects involving the city.[34] The firm received an Invest Atlanta tax break for an early phase of the project. The controversy was exacerbated by the refusal of GSU to engage in negotiations with community groups to develop a community benefits agreement (CBA) involving Carter, GSU, and the community organizations. Neighborhood groups near the stadium had formed the Turner Field Community Benefits Coalition (TFCBC), which approached GSU president Mark Becker about entering into a CBA that would help ensure that neighborhood residents would benefit from the redevelopment, including initiatives to reduce displacement.

President Becker refused to engage in any meaningful discussions with the TFCBC. In March 2017, Becker told GSU's student newspaper, "Don't believe for a second that the TFCBC speaks for those neighborhoods. It is a self-interested group of people that have their own agendas that have historically been able to line, in some cases, their own pockets through money that looks like it's going to an organization you can never track. There's a long history of that."[35] This was quite the statement coming from the president of a public university based in downtown Atlanta and generally perceived as the flagship urban university for the city. While GSU, as a public university, was limited in providing funding to a CBA, it certainly could have encouraged Carter as the for-profit partner to provide affordable housing and community development resources as part of a CBA. Instead of engaging in a CBA, Carter and GSU wrote letters to some select organizations in the area that were not part of TFCBC saying that they would do some local hiring and offer after-school programs. Carter wrote that ten percent of housing units would be affordable to those earning less than eighty percent of the metropolitan median income, an income level considerably higher than the median income of most of the surrounding communities.[36]

The largest redevelopment deal in the city in the twenty-first century, and the one involving by far the largest amount of public subsidy, was a project called the "Gulch." The Gulch is a forty-acre site that appears sunken relative to most of downtown Atlanta. This is because the streets surrounding the area were elevated in the early-twentieth century to allow automobile traffic to run above railroad lines passing through the city. The site is adjacent to downtown's Centennial Olympic Park and near the CNN Center.[37] Mayor Reed, followed by Mayor Bottoms, proposed massive public subsidy for a redevelopment proposal led by the developer the CIM Group, a firm headed by the brother of the owner of the Atlanta Hawks. The plan is to build a mini-city of over nine million square feet of office space, 1,000 housing units, 1,500 hotel rooms, and a million square feet of retail space. According to estimates by the *AJC*, the public subsidy would reach as high as $1.9 billion, both through a tax allocation district, in which any increase in property taxes is diverted to the development and the diversion of state and local sales tax revenues to the developer.[38] This would represent approximately thirty-eight percent of the $5 billion cost of the project. The developer agreed to contribute $28 million to a housing trust fund, which would likely generate on the order of about 500 units of affordable housing, in addition to the ones that existing ordinances would require for subsidized projects. Part of the development budget was to buy the land for $100 million from Norfolk Southern, which likely extracted some of the subsidy by charging a higher price for the land than it would have otherwise received. This was despite the fact that Norfolk Southern would receive a $24 million property tax break from Invest Atlanta for its new headquarters in December of 2018, thus benefitting from two large-scale subsidy deals within a period of a few weeks.

Some of the Gulch subsidy comes from tax increment financing that will draw millions in revenue from other local government uses, including schools. The superintendent of the Atlanta Public Schools, Meria Carstarphen, objected to the continued use of tax-increment financing (called tax allocation districts in Georgia) in the city, which was effectively shrinking the footprint of land that the schools could rely on for tax growth, even as the city's population grew. Carstarphen went public with her concerns, and the pushback from the mayor's office in 2018 was swift and strong. Tharon Johnson, a Democratic Party operative, had strong words for Carstarphen on a local public radio politics show in October of 2018, the month before the Gulch deal was approved by City Council: " . . . if you don't bring anything to the table, if you don't have any skin in the game, then keep your mouth shut . . . don't interfere with this deal and go out and trash publicly or privately a mayor who has worked with you."[39] It is unclear how Johnson could reasonably argue that Carstarphen had no skin in the game of a deal that would wind up diverting hundreds of millions of dollars away from the school system for which she was responsible. Carstarphen's outspokenness against this deal and the increasing share of the tax base covered by tax allocation districts made her few friends in the governing regime. Within a year, the school board, some members of which had strong ties to the Mayor, voted not to renew Carstarphen's contract despite the superintendent being generally popular in the community. Carstarphen had made the fatal "mistake" of refusing to quietly "go along to get along" with the Atlanta regime.

In addition to opposition from Superintendent Carstarphen, the Gulch deal was opposed by a coalition of community organizations called "Red Light the Gulch." Their membership included Georgia Stand-Up, the Housing Justice League, and subsidy critic and former Invest Atlanta board member Julian Bene. In October 2018, the coalition released a compilation of expert opinions on the Gulch subsidy proposal, including comments on the likely benefits, costs, affordable housing provisions, and overall economic impact on the city.[40] The authors argued that any purported benefits of the Gulch would mostly occur at the expense of shifts in economic activity from elsewhere in the city, resulting in little net benefit to the city. Economist J. C. Bradbury argued in the memo that the city's economic impact analysis was "non-rigorous fluff, full of flawed assumptions that should not be taken seriously as objective or realistic estimates of economic impact." Bradbury wrote that the city's consultant gave no "consideration as to how a future Gulch development would compete with other parts of the local economy."[41] Resistance to the Gulch subsidies by both the Red Light the Gulch Coalition and by Superintendent Carstarphen did reduce the period of the property tax subsidy. However, the size of the overall subsidy is still likely to exceed $1.9 billion, a very large share of total project costs. Ultimately, even after persistent legal challenges by the coalition after the City Council's narrow 8–6 approval, the project and subsidy package seem likely to move forward.

RHETORIC AND REALITY ON AFFORDABLE HOUSING POLICY

As will be discussed more in Chapter 4, during and after the 2007 to 2011 foreclosure crisis, the city of Atlanta did little to prepare for the coming rise in rents and home values. It was pockmarked with thousands of vacant homes, particularly in lower-income Black neighborhoods, that investors had snatched up for bargain-basement prices. As the national housing recovery began in 2012 and global capital began flowing rapidly into the housing market, land values and then rents began to increase. This was precisely when the city should have been racing to acquire land and homes, especially around the Beltline, before prices rose more rapidly. However, despite some outrage expressed by

Mayor Reed over the vacant homes, the city took little action. The civic community seemed unable to appreciate the real estate frenzy that had begun.

Civic and media coverage of affordable housing in the city increased in the second half of the 2010s. One indicator of public attention to affordable housing is the media attention it receives over time. The number of articles in the *AJC* including both the terms "affordable housing" and "city of Atlanta," went from an average of just under two per year from 2010 through 2012 to an average of five from 2013 to 2015, and then shot up to eighteen in 2016, and twenty-eight in 2017, the year of the Mayoral election and the *AJC* exposé of the Beltline's poor performance on its affordable housing targets. The number of articles increased even more in 2018 to thirty-seven, but then dropped to twenty-three in 2019, and even further, to fifteen in 2020.[42]

In May 2015, the *Wall Street Journal* ran a story about how, during the first three years of the post-crisis multifamily housing construction boom, from 2012 to 2014, eighty-two percent of apartments built in large U.S. cities were considered luxury units, those commanding rents in the top twenty percent of the market.[43] Atlanta fared particularly poorly in the analysis, which was conducted by the CoStar Group, a leading authority on multifamily real estate; ninety-five percent of all new construction in the city during this period was comprised of luxury units. This was not a surprise to many Atlantans but mostly confirmation of the new, pricey apartments springing up in Midtown, Buckhead, and around the Beltline. The next month, the city's deputy planning commissioner wrote an op-ed in the *AJC* calling affordable housing a "key goal" for the city.[44] The op-ed also stated that the city hoped to have inclusionary zoning legislation adopted by the end of 2015. (Inclusionary zoning legislation was not adopted until late 2017, and even then, it covered only a small portion of the city.)

At the beginning of 2016, in the middle of Mayor Reed's second term, he met with the editorial board of the *Atlanta Business Chronicle*. He focused much of his remarks on his desire to improve social equity in the city, including working to ensure that more low-income folks could remain in the city.[45] The city had been ranked among the three large cities in the country with the worst income inequality by the Brookings Institution. However, the Mayor was short on specifics in terms of new policies to generate more affordable housing.

In May 2016, the Federal Reserve Bank of Atlanta released a study showing that the share of renter households earning under $35,000 a year who were cost-burdened had risen to 83.5 percent, up from 79.9 percent just four years earlier.[46] The study found that the number of units renting for less than $750 per month in the city had declined by more than 5,300 over this brief period, despite very little overall inflation. Over the same period, the city gained over 4,800 units renting for over $1,500 per month. The report was widely cited by housing advocates pointing to the need to do much more about affordable housing in the city.

In the same month, the City Council finally passed an ordinance requiring Invest Atlanta and other subsidy providers to require new apartment buildings receiving a subsidy to set aside ten to fifteen percent of their units at affordable levels. However, the measure gave developers the option of setting aside fifteen percent of units for tenants with incomes under eighty percent of the area median income or ten percent for tenants at under sixty percent area median income. Most developers chose the former. John O'Callaghan of the Atlanta Neighborhood Development Partnership told WABE radio, "I am concerned that even though they have the option of serving 60 percent or below of area median income families, they are not required to."[47]

In late 2017, a couple of weeks after the mayoral election, the Atlanta City Council finally passed mandatory inclusionary zoning (IZ) for two parts of the city: a half-mile buffer around the Beltline TAD and a set of neighborhoods near the new Mercedes-Benz Stadium. The argument for limiting the policy to just these areas is that they had been the result of major city subsidies and development interventions. So those developing multifamily rental properties in such areas should have some obligation to provide affordable housing in return for the benefits of such interventions. The city had been working at least a couple of years considering various aspects of inclusionary housing policy and had adopted a weak affordability requirement for developers receiving public subsidy in May 2016. This legislation was, to some degree, an extension of that policy. It required new multifamily rental developments over ten units to set aside at least fifteen percent of their units at lower rents for households earning less than eighty percent of the metropolitan median income. If the developers set rents to be affordable for those at sixty percent of area median income, they only had to set aside ten percent of their units. The developers were compensated by a mix of density bonuses, parking minimum waivers, and expedited reviews of building permits. Atlanta's IZ was criticized as too marginal, both in terms of not serving folks at lower-incomes (especially because most developers chose to serve renters up to eighty percent of area median income) and not covering a large portion of the city.[48]

The city appeared concerned that the ordinance not be perceived as too taxing to developers. State law preempted local governments in Georgia from passing rent control, and city officials feared that strong regulation might trigger a developer lawsuit on that or other grounds, which, if victorious, could nullify the IZ. In the bargaining to get the ordinance to be more palatable to local developers, the definition of affordable rents allowed for higher rents than most affordable housing programs would permit for a given income level. Typically, "affordable" rents are set so that the nominal net rent, plus an allowance for utilities, would be no more than thirty percent of the tenant's income. The utility allowance can be a sizeable amount, often running $150 or more per month depending on the size of the apartment. But the city agreed to redefine "affordability" so that "rent (not including utilities and mandatory fees)" would not exceed thirty percent of the tenant's monthly income.[49] Therefore, while normally HUD or similar agencies would consider a net rent of say $850 plus a $150 utility allowance to be the maximum rent affordable to a household with an income of $40,000 per year, the IZ ordinance would allow the net rent to be $1,000, not including any allowance for utilities. So, in reality, a tenant's full housing cost burden in the IZ program might be well above thirty percent of the tenant's income.

While the IZ ordinance was working its way through the City Council, the fall of 2017 was mayoral election season, and Georgia Advancing Communities Together (Georgia ACT), a statewide affordable housing advocacy organization, led a coalition of housing groups called "City for All." A key goal of City for All was to elevate affordable housing as an issue in the November mayoral election in Atlanta. Despite limited resources, City for All's advocacy managed to raise the profile of the issue during the election season, with several of the candidates ranking it as one of the top one or two issues facing the city, including future Mayor Keisha Lance Bottoms. City for All also released a ten-point policy platform that it advocated for during the election and surveyed all the candidates on their housing policy positions.[50] The most critical item in that platform was a call for $250 million in new city funding to create a housing trust fund. The platform called for the fund to be capitalized through annual budget appropriations and potentially new dedicated sources of revenue. It also specified focusing on low-income households, those with incomes below fifty percent of the metropolitan median, and called for a citywide inclusionary zoning ordinance.

One result of the increased profile of affordable housing in the campaign was that it became a frequent topic in several mayoral debates in the fall of 2017. Most importantly, the eventual victor, Keisha Lance Bottoms, made a public pledge to *raise* $1 billion in funds for affordable housing, with half coming from the government. This pledge clearly implied that, if elected, she would work to create new city funding for affordable housing. As the *AJC* reported later, "as a candidate for mayor, Bottoms also left many housing advocates with the strong impression she would seek mostly new local revenues to build the $500 million in public dollars for her $1 billion housing pledge."[51] While the number was perhaps aspirational and perhaps unrealistic politically, it signaled a serious commitment to affordable housing should she be elected. Even if she raised $250 million in new city dollars for affordable housing, that would be a sea change in city policy and meet the City for All's key recommendation.

As the City for All coalition was pushing mayoral candidates to speak to the affordable housing crisis, a group of civic heavyweight organizations discussed plans to further affordable housing programming and policy after the election. Once Mayor Bottoms won the election, given her $1 billion pledge, there was a key opportunity to work towards holding her accountable to that pledge. This new coalition, called House ATL, was in a very good position to develop some program designs and policy proposals, but it was unlikely to be a group that would hold the mayor publicly accountable to her pledge, especially because it adopted a "big tent" approach that included the city itself as a key partner.

The Blank Foundation initially funded the House ATL effort. It was staffed primarily by the Atlanta chapter of the Urban Land Institute, an association of real estate developers and owners. House ATL invited membership from for-profit developers, lobbyists for landlords (the Atlanta Apartment Association), utilities, banks, and nonprofit affordable housing advocates and practitioners. It listed as its "vision partners" the Metro Atlanta Chamber of Commerce, the city of Atlanta, Central Atlanta Progress (the downtown business improvement association), the Center for Civic Innovation, the Urban Land Institute-Atlanta, and the Blank Foundation.[52] "Support partners" included over seventy organizations from the real estate industry, utilities, nonprofits, and government. House ATL was a public-private-philanthropic partnership, not a hard-edged, independent affordable housing advocacy coalition. That was clear from the get-go.

Over a few months spanning the mayoral election, the momentum shifted from the more grassroots, pre-election City for All advocacy coalition to the better-funded, more corporate House ATL organization, a coalition involving members of the traditional urban regime such as the Chamber of Commerce and Central Atlanta Progress as well as the apartment association and many developers. The City for All coalition faded quickly, with most of its members joining the House ATL effort. This quick capturing of the issue by a more corporate-led group was a reminder that the traditional corporate-government regime, and the Atlanta Way, was alive and well in the city. The new House ATL coalition included firms and organizations with something to lose if housing advocates were to make a meaningful push for shifting subsidies away from large commercial developments towards benefitting low-income families or enacting stronger tenant protections in the state legislature.

House ATL set up working groups and held numerous meetings over the next eight months. In September, they presented a set of recommendations, many of which were detailed and substantive.[53] Echoing the mayor's campaign pledge, they called for raising $1 billion of "local, flexible resources that enable 20,000+ new and preserved homes over the next 8–10 years." In particular, the recommendations called for $500 million in new public resources, including a $250 million bond for affordable housing and new dedicated city funding sources yielding $5 to $15 million annually. They stipulated that public funds should prioritize serving households with incomes below fifty percent of area median income. House ATL also called for private-sector initiatives, including funding through social impact funds and philanthropy, and for reforming zoning regulations and other initiatives. While public dollars were to be targeted towards low-income households, private funds and regulatory reform could be targeted towards housing needs for those in the 50 to 120 percent of area median income. Missing from House ATL's recommendations, however, were any substantive proposals to strengthen tenant protections in state law. Also, while the coalition called for new funding streams and bond financing, it did not suggest fundamental reforms of property tax and incentive systems that under-taxed large commercial property owners and gave property tax breaks to firms, both of which reduced the ability to capture even a modest share of rising property values as a means of funding affordable housing programs.

Despite its central involvement in House ATL, the city was not quick to respond to the recommendations. It wasn't until nine months later, in June 2019, that the city released its "One Atlanta Affordable Housing Action Plan."[54] This was also eighteen months into the Mayor's term, despite repeatedly claiming that affordable housing was one of her top priorities and receiving national media attention for her rhetoric on the issue. The One Atlanta "Plan" was more of a statement of principles and ideas than a concrete plan, with some of the ideas being ones that had been around for years and others that were more defined in previous documents, such as the House ATL recommendations. The One Atlanta document was often quite vague with language such as "leverage vacant public land for housing," "create and expand housing affordability tools," "revise the zoning code," and "develop new funding resources."[55] Despite the campaign pledge of $500 million in new city funding and Mayor Bottoms' own campaign website's language of "raising" $1 billion, the One Atlanta document stated that the city would "invest" $1 billion from "public, private, and philanthropic sources." It indicated that existing federal and state sources would be counted towards the public sector portion of the goal. The mayor's office had now clearly shifted away from a notion of raising $500 million in new, city funding towards a revised goal of simply spending $500 million in mostly pre-existing federal, state, and local dollars, much of which came from higher levels of government.

In 2020, the administration proposed $100 million in bond financing for affordable housing after continued scrutiny revealed that the city's progress towards its $500 million pledge contained few new city dollars. The number was increased to $200 million after advocacy from the chair of the City Council's Community Development Committee, who had proposed the higher figure. After COVID-19 hit, bond markets were unsettled, and the proposal was revised downward. Finally, in 2021, the city of Atlanta issued $50 million in bonds for funding affordable housing, with a proposal to issue another $50 million later.[56] It remains unclear how effective this program will be in providing funding for projects that serve the needs of low-income renters. Still, after three years into the administration, it finally represented some new city dollars allocated to affordable housing, although it was only one-tenth of what the mayor had pledged during her campaign.

A PUBLIC-PRIVATE PARTNERSHIP BREAKS DOWN

As described in Chapter 1, the AHA in the 1990s, under CEO Rene Glover, had developed the nationally recognized "Atlanta Model" of public housing redevelopment. It demolished essentially all of its traditional family public housing. It vouchered out most of the displaced tenants. It then entered into joint ventures with private developers who took control and ownership of redeveloped, mixed-income housing developments, typically resulting in far fewer low-income units at the redeveloped sites. Some demolished buildings were not redeveloped at all, so AHA was left with hundreds of vacant parcels across the city.

AHA CEO Glover had remained popular under multiple mayoral administrations. However, in June 2010, just six months into Mayor Kasim Reed's administration, after the AHA board approved Rene Glover's fifth consecutive contract, the mayor publicly stated that a "lame duck board" had extended her a new five-year contract and that he had wanted to "pick [his] own team."[57] After three more years of a contentious relationship between Glover and the mayor, Glover announced her departure in the fall of 2013, before her contract expired. After this, Reed was able to put in his pick for AHA CEO.

In March 2017, the *AJC* ran a front-page story on a major conflict between the AHA, led by Mayor Reed's ally, and the Integral Group, the firm that had been Glover's first developer partner and co-creator of the "Atlanta Model," beginning with Techwood Homes in the 1990s. Integral had developed a strong relationship with the AHA under Glover. AHA had signed contracts with Integral in 2011, giving Integral options lasting seven years to purchase about 100 parcels of vacant land, amounting to almost eighty acres, for potential redevelopment in collaboration with the AHA. These contracts did not require that the land be developed for affordable housing.[58] Integral had notified AHA of intent to exercise these options in 2016. The options allowed Integral to purchase the land at prices using formulas developed in 2011, at the bottom of the housing market. It was difficult to foresee how valuable many of these parcels would become during the option period. Some of these parcels were in desirable, gentrifying locations, including the old Grady Homes in the Old Fourth Ward, Capitol Homes in southeast downtown, and other places that had experienced significant increases in land values since the early part of the decade. Affordable housing advocates, including the Housing Justice League, were critical of the loss of so much land that could be used for affordable housing to the control of a private developer. The Housing Justice League organized a petition against Integral's proposed exercising of the options, gathering 1,200 signatures, and picketed outside of a talk that the Integral CEO gave in downtown Atlanta.[59]

Mayor Reed and the CEO of Integral were apparently already not on good terms. Both the city and the housing authority ended up filing suit against the developer to nullify the contracts. Integral and former AHA chief Rene Glover later filed countersuits. Prominent journalist Maria Saporta, who had praised Glover's and Integral's "Atlanta Model" over the years and who had squabbled with Mayor Reed over the questionable sale of Fort McPherson to Tyler Perry, used her column in the *Atlanta Business Chronicle* to relay the Integral CEO's side of the story.[60] In the end, the courts sided more with Integral and Glover, pushing the AHA to settle the suit.

The primary matter appeared to be settled in December of 2019. The authority agreed to a total sale price of just under $22 million, almost certainly well under the market value of the land, and to a partnership between Integral and the AHA to develop over 2,000 units of housing, in which the housing authority would receive a fifty percent, non-controlling interest in the venture.[61] This fifty percent stake for AHA would hopefully make the deal a fairer one for the AHA.[62] More worrisome, however, was that the settlement called for only a minimum of fifteen percent of the 1,600 or so rental units to be affordable, with ten of that fifteen being affordable at under eighty percent of metro median income and five percent affordable at under 100 percent of metro median income. These are incomes far above the typical housing authority resident, where incomes tend to be well below fifty percent of metro median income. The settlement also called for almost 400 homeownership units, with two-thirds of those set at prices affordable to those with incomes below eighty percent of metro median income and one-third affordable up to 120 percent of metro median income.

The almost exclusive reliance of the AHA on public-private partnerships that ceded ownership or control to private-sector partners, and the close relationship it had with a small group of developers, raises the larger question of whether this approach has yielded good or equitable results for the city in the long run. Integral clearly felt that the firm created the increased values of the affected parcels. As the CEO told WABE radio when asked if he contributed to the hot housing market of early 2018, he replied, "I don't just feel that. I know that."[63] He had told the *AJC* almost a year earlier that the projects had been "occupied by some of the most pathologically deficient people in society."[64] The firm's claim to being responsible for the much higher land values of these parcels has at least some kernel of truth to be sure, as its involvement in the demolition and redevelopment of AHA projects had helped "clear the way" for the gentrification of the city. At the same time, a great deal of land value in many of these locations were arguably as much the product of other, often publicly funded, initiatives, such as the Beltline, as well as the overall housing market pressures occurring across much of the city. Whatever the earlier merits or flaws of the joint ventures, this Integral-AHA partnership did not last for more than about fifteen years before descending into acrimony and lawsuits. As the partnership fell apart, the lawsuits and discord appeared to distract the AHA from its core mission. The agency was very slow to produce new affordable housing during this period despite some high-profile plans initiated earlier.[65]

A FRAGILE HOUSING SYSTEM, EVICTIONS, AND NEIGHBORHOOD RACIAL CHANGE

The demolition of most traditional public housing in the 1990s and 2000s left the city relying increasingly on tenant-based vouchers and buildings financed by the federal Low-Income Housing Tax Credit (LIHTC) program and owned by for-profit firms and nonprofits. In Atlanta, the subsidized housing industry has been driven heavily by for-profit, specialized firms, such as Columbia Residential, the Integral Group, and others. As of May 2021, data from the National Housing Preservation Database indicated that for-profit firms, including their joint-ventures with nonprofits, together controlled more than seventy-two percent of the rental units in subsidized buildings in the city of Atlanta. This does not count units with tenant-based vouchers.[66] Nonprofit owners accounted for only just over eleven percent of the units in subsidized properties, with the housing authority accounting for less than ten percent. The dominance of for-profit ownership of subsidized housing in Atlanta should be of significant concern. In a gentrifying city, when the subsidy compliance period ends, owners can sell off their properties to owners who may be likely to convert them to market-rate apartments, causing significant losses in affordable housing. Therefore, the subsidized stock in Atlanta is expected to be more vulnerable than in cities where a larger portion of such supply is either public housing or owned by mission-driven nonprofits.

It is also important to note that the LIHTC program, by itself, does not provide the depth of subsidy that traditional public housing or vouchers provide. LIHTC affordable units generally have rents set, so that they are affordable to households earning sixty percent of the metropolitan median income (equivalent to about $52,000 for a family of four in 2021) even if tenants' incomes are significantly below this level. Public housing units and vouchers generally limit a tenant's rent to no more than thirty percent of their income, and if their income goes down, their rent is adjusted down accordingly. While LIHTC units can be accompanied by additional subsidies, including vouchers, many LIHTC tenants do not receive such additional subsidies. One result of the more limited LIHTC subsidy, and the fixed nature of the rents, is that, in the Atlanta metro, many LIHTC properties have eviction rates close to those of similarly situated market-rate units.[67] Research has shown that public housing and other types of project-based subsidies tend to have lower eviction rates.[68]

Housing stability has been a major problem in Atlanta for a long time, but worsened during the post-crisis era. Of the fifty-seven U.S. cities with populations of over 300,000 for which Princeton's EvictionLab had collected data, the city of Atlanta ranked third, with 17.6 percent of rental units receiving an eviction filing in 2016, compared to a median rate of just over six percent.[69] Evictions in Atlanta are highly racialized, with rates in majority-Black neighborhoods much higher than in majority-white neighborhoods. Even when adjusting for a wide variety of neighborhood characteristics, including income, poverty rate, home values, and rent levels, Black neighborhoods have much higher eviction rates than white neighborhoods. For every ten-percentage-point increase in the share of Black residents, the 2016 eviction rate was expected to be 0.9 percentage points larger, even after controlling for these other neighborhood factors.[70]

Georgia is a landlord-friendly state, where evictions are cheap, fast, and easy to file and where, unlike most states, tenants have no "right-to-cure" notice period before the formal eviction filing. Megan Hatch categorized the landlord-tenant legal regimes of the fifty states into three categories, ranging from protectionist, where tenants are provided with significant legal protections, to pro-business, in which tenants receive few protections under the law.[71] Georgia falls firmly into the third category. Industry observers tend to agree, with one website classifying Georgia as one of eleven "landlord-friendly" states.[72]

Gentrification pressures and landlord-friendly housing laws are a toxic mix for vulnerable tenants, especially in low-income Black neighborhoods with many single-earner families. Institutional investors seek out multifamily properties in communities susceptible to gentrification, especially in places with few tenant protections. Unregulated rental markets provide a lubricated path for investors wishing to make "added-value" moves to "reposition" properties to produce stronger cash flows. Atlanta has been a prime market for such investors, especially as private equity firms moved more aggressively into the multifamily rental market after the foreclosure crisis.

Elora Raymond and her colleagues found that from 2006 to 2016, evictions in Fulton County, which contains the bulk of the city of Atlanta, rose from 4,406 to 10,753, more than a 140 percent increase.[73] This increase was much greater than for the larger five core county region, where evictions increased at only a moderate seven percent rate over the same period, from 30,922 to 33,172.[74] Raymond and her coauthors also found that apartment sale prices in Fulton County increased markedly from 2005 to 2018, with average sale prices for the same property increasing by approximately $5.5 million. Apartments were a hot commodity in a gentrifying city. This hot market brought with it the displacement of Black renters. When larger institutional investors purchased an apartment building, the odds of a subsequent spike in evictions increased by one-third, with even greater odds of a spike when garden-style properties were purchased. Critically, the researchers found that purchases of apartment buildings by institutional investors in a neighborhood led to an expected decline of 166 Black residents and an expected increase of 109 white residents in the neighborhood, compared to adjacent neighborhoods with no institutional investor purchases of apartment buildings. The magnitude of these effects were significant given that the average neighborhood (census block group) in the county had a population of fewer than 1,700 residents. Thus, larger investors moving into Atlanta were associated with racialized displacement and exclusion. The investor- and landlord-friendly climate provided by lax state tenant protections provided a welcome mat for the snatching up of older, lower-cost rental properties, displacing disproportionately Black tenants, speeding a transition to a whiter and more affluent Atlanta.

OF ZONING REFORM: LIMITED PROGRESS, BUT PREDOMINANTLY WHITE, AFFLUENT NEIGHBORHOODS RESIST

As described in Chapter 1, the history of zoning in Atlanta, as in many cities, is a racist one. In the 1920s the city repeatedly attempted to maintain an explicitly racial zoning code. After the courts struck down such efforts, the city extracted the explicitly racial language from its zoning maps, but the effects of a racialized system persisted. The city's zoning code continues to exhibit exclusionary effects across the city, especially in the most affluent neighborhoods in the north- and northeast-side neighborhoods.

In 2015, as the city recognized that development pressures were rising, the planning department hired consultants to assess the city's zoning ordinance, which had not received a comprehensive update since 1982. However, the city had made incremental zoning and development practice changes, especially after the 1996 Olympics.[75] In September of 2017, the city released "Atlanta City Design," an overall vision of a denser city that still sought to preserve the city's celebrated tree-canopy. In 2019, the city also passed an ordinance to allow detached accessory dwelling units (ADUs), small units on the same lot as a single-family home, in a larger part of the city, including "R4" or "R4A" districts, where ADUs had been prohibited.[76] This left R1, R2, and R3 single-family districts as places where detached ADUs were not allowed. While previously ADUs were not allowed in sixty percent of the city's land area, these zoning changes had reduced the area where detached ADUs were still not allowed to about twenty-two percent of the city.[77]

While zoning reform can help accommodate the growing demand for housing in a city like Atlanta, it is not a panacea for generating more housing, and certainly by itself is unlikely to generate housing affordable to low-income families. ADUs are small units intended generally for single-person households. Moreover, there are many barriers other than zoning to the development of ADUs, including physical design requirements, setback requirements, and other issues. One example is financing.[78] Without the ability to subdivide a lot to make the ADU lot into a distinct fee-simple lot that can be easily mortgaged, financing the construction of an ADU can be difficult.

In late 2020, the city introduced another proposal to allow ADUs throughout the entire city, including in the R1 through R3 neighborhoods omitted in the previous round of zoning reform. It released "Atlanta City Design Housing," which called for ending at least "pure" single-family zoning throughout the entire city.[79] The proposal also called for allowing small apartment buildings to be built on single-family lots that were within walking distance of mass transit stops. Both proposals generated significant opposition, especially from single-family homeowners in more-affluent parts of the city.

A large share of the remaining no-ADU neighborhoods were in the most affluent and exclusionary parts of Buckhead, where large-lot, million-dollar (and up) homes are common. The response from some voices in the Buckhead community was swift and hostile. One Buckhead blogger wrote that "the premise of 'ending single-family zoning' is shocking and incendiary," adding that retaining single-family-only neighborhoods "does mean that some neighborhoods are 'exclusive.' Is that a bad thing, something that should be changed?"[80] Later in 2021, as the city began public meetings to discuss the rezoning proposals, yard signs sprung up opposing the rezoning plan, especially in affluent, predominantly white neighborhoods.

The resistance to relaxing single-family zoning was effective, as Mayor Bottoms, who had supported the zoning changes, switched gears abruptly in April 2021, saying "it's going to be something that's much more scaled-down, and it may not even look like what was put on the table initially." She added that it would not be a "one-size-fits-all for the entire city. It will very likely be tailored to specific communities."[81] Later in 2021, as the mayoral election got underway, most candidates for mayor opposed the zoning reform plan, although some City Council candidates, usually those not running in the whiter, more-affluent districts, backed zoning reform.

Given the significant resistance that simply trying to allow homeowners to construct small ADUs on their own lots encountered and that it took several years to phase in even very incremental changes, notions that the city will dramatically relax most zoning restrictions to allow multifamily apartment construction in many predominantly single-family neighborhoods seem politically naive. Moreover, more than 37,000 multifamily units were permitted from 2011 to 2020 in the city, compared to the city having about 100,000 occupied rental units at the beginning of the decade, indicating a substantial increase in the supply of market-rate rental housing.[82] While accommodating more density is certainly important in Atlanta, up until this point the city has not been as severely constrained in its housing construction as many large coastal cities. Of course, as the city continues to grow, more severe constraints are likely to develop, so it is important to act sooner than later to put in place zoning reforms and other measures to accommodate population growth.

While the city of Atlanta has made some limited progress on reducing restrictive zoning in recent years by allowing accessory dwelling units in more neighborhoods, few majority-white, exclusionary suburbs in the region have taken any significant steps in this direction. It is in these suburbs where exclusionary zoning practices are the most widespread and, together, account for the largest numbers of developable parcels. If anything, as will be discussed in Chapter 5, moves towards greater incorporation and secession among affluent suburbs have increased their power to enact and implement exclusionary and displacement-inducing policies and redevelopment projects.

Together with Chapter 2, this chapter shows that the gentrification and whitening of Atlanta was not simply the result of unplanned, atomistic "market forces." The city of Atlanta has been on a planned and subsidized trajectory supporting gentrification starting before the 1996 Olympic Games. After clearing out most of its public housing, the city was primed for rapid change, especially after the foreclosure crisis, as the real estate economy heated up. Over three decades, the city went from being majority-Black with a median income far below that of the suburbs, to one that is minority-Black and has a higher median income than its suburbs. The trends are all pushing towards continued gentrification—and in some places super-gentrification—of the city, with growing diversity and higher poverty rates in the suburbs. Employers began flocking to the city after the Great Recession to be close to Georgia Tech, Emory University, Georgia State, and the historically Black colleges in the Atlanta University Center. High-wage job growth created an increased demand for housing, pushing up rents. Real estate capital flowed into the city, fueling the construction of apartment buildings, and financing the acquisition and redevelopment of older, lower-cost apartments into more expensive, Class A buildings. The ready supply of private equity capital was attracted especially to Midtown and areas around the Beltline.

Despite the city's transformation, local government continues to act as if it is still the 1980s, and Atlanta is still a "shrinking city," losing population and unable to attract middle- and higher-income jobs and residents. The city continues to cater to capital and excessively subsidize and under-tax commercial property. As a result, as land values boomed after 2012, too little of the value was captured by local government, and tax revenues grew more slowly than they should have. Therefore, the benefits of the city's economic growth were not adequately shared with the public sector. The bulk of the benefits went to landowners—homeowners and commercial property owners—with little going to the city's lower-income residents, including many families of color.

As affordable housing began being recognized as a critical problem in the city, especially in the latter half of the 2010s, politicians made bold, glittery campaign pledges, but after they were elected and it came time to deliver, they claimed that the financial resources were just not there. Again, this was an inflection point, especially after the 2017 mayoral election, when public support for affordable housing had risen. Policymakers chose to let their corporate partners in the urban regime continue to extract the bulk of the benefits of the city's growth, with little remaining to tend to the physical and social infrastructure needs of less-fortunate city residents, especially affordable housing.

4

SUBPRIMED ATLANTA

Boom, Bust, and Uneven Recovery

THE SUBPRIME CRISIS THAT BEGAN in 2007 hit Atlanta hard, and it hit Black families and neighborhoods the hardest. The crisis and its aftermath were the products of a perfect storm of federal deregulation and yield-hungry capital markets, a state government that turned its back on any meaningful effort to reign in subprime lenders, and then a timid federal response to surging foreclosures combined with weak state and local implementation. Subprime lenders targeted Black neighborhoods in the region with high-cost, often predatory mortgage loans, a type of process that Keeanga-Yamahtta Taylor has called "predatory inclusion."[1] Subprime loans were made recklessly, and with far higher rates and fees, than traditional mortgage loans. The result was predictable: much higher foreclosure rates and declining property values in affected communities. Property value declines were larger in Black neighborhoods, especially through about 2013. This left many Black homeowners underwater on their mortgages so that their home values were below the balance due on their loans. Many Black neighborhoods suffered from larger numbers of vacant properties stemming from foreclosures, which further impeded the recovery of home values. In the meantime, federal policymakers encouraged large-scale, Wall Street-backed private equity firms to enter the single-family rental market. Starting in 2012, they began buying up tens of thousands of foreclosed homes in the region and other, mostly Sunbelt metros. Atlanta was an ideal "strike zone" for these private equity giants, given its large number of foreclosures flowing through the system, weak tenant protections, and strong demand for housing, with many households shut out of the mortgage market. The overall result of all these forces was a major transfer of tens of thousands of single-family homes from homeowners, including many families of color, to investors, including a new institutional breed of investors backed by Wall Street capital. With tight mortgage markets and little enforcement by regulators of fair lending rules, Black households found it difficult to purchase homes at the now rock-bottom prices. As a result, Black families, as a group, were excessively harmed during the market's fall and then largely shut out of the recovery and opportunities to benefit from rising home values. Those Black households who could buy homes when values were low tended to see significant gains in home value and equity. But far too many were excluded from a rising market.

RACIALIZED SUBPRIME LENDING AND FORECLOSURES

Many consumer advocates, including some in Atlanta, had argued well before the subprime crisis of the 2000s that subprime lending had the potential to cause a serious crisis of rising foreclosures.[2] They recalled the smaller, earlier boom in subprime lending in the late 1990s that resulted in concentrated foreclosures in Black neighborhoods targeted by subprime lenders in Atlanta, Chicago, and other cities. This first subprime boom was smaller than the second one and, critically, had little impact on broader investment or real estate markets. The bulk of the damage of the first subprime boom occurred among Black homeowners and neighborhoods, limiting the attention it received from both the media and policymakers. Federal regulators did conduct hearings around the country but failed to adopt meaningful new regulations. As a result, the subprime industry came roaring back in the early 2000s, precipitating the foreclosure and global financial crisis beginning in 2007.[3]

The subprime crisis resulted from a policy regime that, rather than providing homeowners and neighborhoods with access to credit, was focused on providing global capital with access to neighborhoods and homeowners, as Kathe Newman has put it so well.[4] The crisis uprooted families from communities and schools, damaged households' credit history and economic opportunities, and left many neighborhoods, often Black ones, pockmarked with vacant homes and many homeowners with mortgages far larger than their homes were worth.[5]

In response to the earlier subprime boom and resulting foreclosure crisis of the 1990s, consumer advocates had argued for more robust regulation at the federal and state level around the turn of the twenty-first century. North Carolina passed the first serious set of subprime lending regulations in the country in 1999. Aided by experts like those at Atlanta Legal Aid and the Center for Responsible Lending, in 2001, State Senator Vincent Fort introduced a strong subprime lending bill in the Georgia legislature. In 2002, Governor Roy Barnes signed the Georgia Fair Lending Act (GFLA). Built off of North Carolina's statute, the Georgia law was even stronger.[6]

As soon as the law went into effect, the lending industry began a concerted campaign to overturn it, especially after Barnes lost his reelection bid in 2002 to conservative Republican Sonny Perdue. Opponents of the law gained a critical ally in early 2003, when the credit rating agency Standard & Poor's loudly proclaimed that it would not

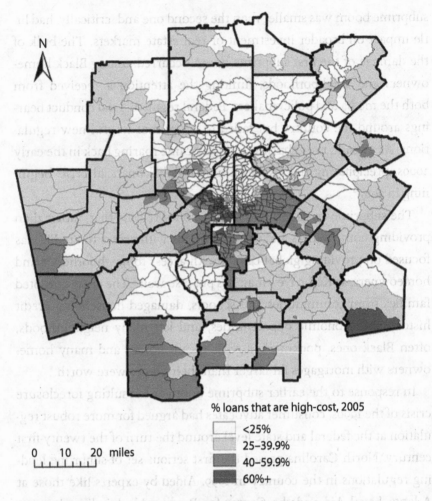

Map 11. The racialized nature of subprime home lending during the 2000s

Data sources: High-cost home loan data for 2005 is from Home Mortgage Disclosure Act data via PolicyMap.com; percent Black is from the 2005–2009 American Community Survey (centered on 2007).

rate securities backed by Georgia mortgages due to GFLA. Soon, lending industry advocates managed to replace GFLA with a much weaker law.

Nationally, subprime lending began increasing in 2002. Subprime mortgage-backed securities increased from $87 billion in 2001 to almost $200 billion in 2003 and over $350 million in 2004. By 2005, subprime

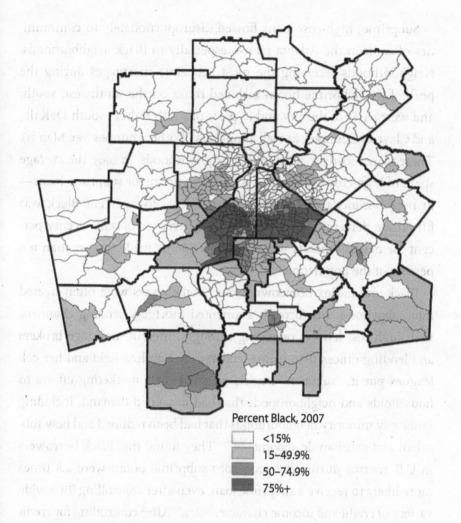

Percent Black, 2007

- ☐ <15%
- ☐ 15–49.9%
- ☐ 50–74.9%
- ■ 75%+

securities peaked at $465 billion, dropping slightly in 2006 before plummeting to $200 billion in 2007 and then to an insignificant trickle by 2008.[7] Over this same period, private-label securities funding Alt-A loans, which mostly went to investors in single-family rental properties, increased from $11 billion in 2001 to $332 billion by 2005, dropping to near zero in 2008.

Subprime, high-cost loans flowed disproportionately to communities of color in the Atlanta metro, especially to Black neighborhoods. Neighborhoods receiving the most subprime mortgages during the peak of the subprime boom included those on the southwest, south, and west parts of the city and in parts of south Fulton, south DeKalb, and Clayton Counties, as well as pockets of other counties (see Map 11). These were mostly majority-Black neighborhoods. In 2005, the average share of high-cost mortgages—a common proxy for subprime loans—in neighborhoods that were at least seventy-five percent Black was fifty-three percent. This compared to an average of only twenty percent for neighborhoods where Black residents made up less than ten percent of the population.[8]

Black and Latinx homeowners and homebuyers were often steered into subprime loans through segmented mortgage lending channels, with high-cost lenders operating through different mortgage brokers and lending offices than prime lenders.[9] As Carolina Reid and her colleagues put it, "subprime lenders targeted their marketing efforts to households and neighborhoods that had untapped demand, including inner-city minority neighborhoods that had been redlined and new suburban and exurban developments."[10] They found that Black borrowers in U.S. metros during the 2004–2007 subprime boom were 2.8 times more likely to receive a subprime loan, even after controlling for a wide variety of credit and income characteristics.[11] After controlling for credit and other factors, Latinx borrowers were still 2.4 times more likely to receive a subprime loan than similarly situated white borrowers.

Foreclosure notices in the thirteen-county Atlanta metro grew modestly in 2003 and 2004, from just over 35,300 in 2003 to about 37,600 in 2005.[12] But in 2006, after the first two-to-three years of the subprime lending boom, foreclosures began increasing much more rapidly, by almost twenty percent in 2006 to just under 45,000, then another twenty-nine percent in 2007, and thirty-seven percent in 2008. By 2008, the thirteen-county region had reached almost 80,000 foreclosure notices annually, well over double the level in 2005. And, as the economy fell into a tailspin and property values dropped in many communities, including increasingly in the suburbs, the crisis moved beyond just subprime loans to imperil prime loans, as many homeowners losing their jobs were unable to sell their homes. By 2010, foreclosure notices peaked at about 135,000, almost four times the pre-crisis 2003 level. In 2011 and 2012, foreclosure notices remained high but began falling significantly, so that they were down to about 100,000 in 2012.

Because subprime loans were disproportionately targeted at Black, Latinx, and lower-wealth homeowners and homebuyers, the initial stage of the crisis was more concentrated in predominantly Black neighborhoods in the city of Atlanta, south DeKalb County, and other closer-in neighborhoods. In addition, investors owning single-family rental homes with high-cost subprime and Alt-A loans were quicker to let their properties fall into foreclosure because they had less of a commitment to hold onto their properties when values began to fall. Investor-owned rental homes are far more common in lower-wealth, Black neighborhoods. However, by 2010, the foreclosure crisis expanded, affecting a larger swath of homeowners and neighborhoods.[13] Unemployment had reached very high levels, and property values had declined markedly in many communities, especially as vacant properties began to accumulate.

The foreclosure crisis began in predominantly Black neighborhoods on the south, southwest, and west sides of Atlanta and in many neighborhoods in south Fulton, south DeKalb, and Clayton counties, where subprime lending levels were generally very high. The subprime crisis then metastasized into a broader foreclosure crisis that spilled over into more and more neighborhoods. By the 2010 to 2012 period, the neighborhoods with the highest levels of foreclosures were no longer in the city of Atlanta. They had spread out to more neighborhoods in south Fulton, the edges of south DeKalb, parts of Clayton County, and new concentrations in central Gwinnett County.

One thing remained throughout the crisis, however. The more affluent and whiter, northern suburbs of north Fulton, north DeKalb, northeastern Cobb, and northern Gwinnett counties were mostly spared the worst of the foreclosures. These communities received few subprime loans and generally had low foreclosure rates, even in the more diffuse later stage of the crisis. Moreover, they benefitted heavily from refinancing their home loans into lower interest rates, due both to the actions of the Federal Reserve's quantitative easing programs and to the Obama Administration's Home Affordable Refinance Program. This helped borrowers who were current on their mortgages refinance into lower-cost loans. At the same time, the federal Home Affordable Modification Program (HAMP), which was designed to help struggling homeowners avoid foreclosure and effectively targeted more at borrowers of color, was slow to roll out.

The story of the policy response to the foreclosure crisis in Atlanta, and in many other cities, is one where the communities hit hardest and earliest by the crisis, due in large part due to regulatory failure by federal and state government, were often ones with large Black and Latinx populations and where the efforts to reduce foreclosures were the least effective. By the time the federal foreclosure prevention response had become somewhat more effective, the locus of foreclosures had shifted farther out into the suburbs.

FALLING VALUES, UNDERWATER HOMEOWNERS, AND VACANT PROPERTIES

From 2006 to 2011, from the peak of the housing boom to the trough of the crash, home values declined much further on average in Black neighborhoods, especially those targeted with predatory subprime lending, than in other parts of the region (see Map 12). At the same time, values dropped the least in the affluent, mostly non-Black neighborhoods in the favored northern arc east of I-75 and west of I-85 in

North Fulton County, East Cobb, North Gwinnett, and up into eastern Cherokee and Forsyth Counties. Across the entire region, tracts that were less than ten percent Black in 2010 saw a median decline in home values of just over eighteen percent, while tracts that were fifty percent or more Black saw a typical decrease of almost twice that, at over thirty-two percent.[14] This left many homeowners "underwater," with home values significantly less than their outstanding mortgage debt, which makes it hard to sell a home, refinance a home, or take out a home improvement loan, all of which are options that can benefit both homeowners and their neighborhoods.

Atlanta was an epicenter of underwater mortgages. Moreover, underwater mortgages were heavily racialized. At the end of 2013, among metropolitan areas with populations of at least one million, the Atlanta metro had the second-largest percentage of underwater homes, only slightly behind the Las Vegas metro. Thirty-five percent of home-owners in the region were underwater.[15] Of the twenty zip codes in the country with the highest percentages of homeowners underwater, sixteen were in metropolitan Atlanta, with at least sixty-five percent of homeowners underwater. These sixteen zip codes were all majority-Black, suburban zip codes, with most being over eighty percent Black. These were mostly moderate- or middle-income suburban, Black neighborhoods.

The racialized nature of the subprime crisis and the uneven recovery was closely tied to the nature of subprime lending. Black homebuyers had been targeted by mortgage brokers with subprime, often predatory, home loans at far greater numbers than white homeowners had been, and the resulting foreclosures created sudden surges of vacant homes that depressed property values, both by rapidly flooding the market with supply and by leaving some neighborhoods pock-marked with empty homes. Many of the neighborhoods that saw val-ues drop by at least twenty-five percent, and especially the ones where declines were thirty-three percent or higher, had been the targets of

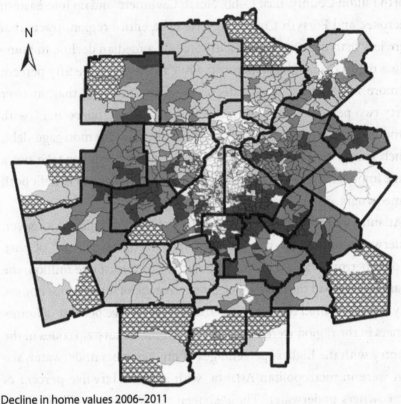

Decline in home values 2006–2011

- ■ >33% decline
- ■ 25–32.9% decline
- ▢ 15–24.9% decline
- ▢ <15% decline, or gain

Cross-hatched tracts =
too few sales to calculate value change

Map 12. The racialized fall of home values during the crash

Data sources: Federal Housing Finance Agency Home Price Index; 2010 Decennial Census

subprime lenders in the early to mid-2000s and experienced a high level of foreclosures following the advent of the crisis.[16] This is consistent with work coauthored with Elora Raymond and Kyungsoon Wang, where we found that many Black neighborhoods—even many with lower levels of poverty—saw rapid price declines with only modest or essentially no recovery by 2014.[17] Meanwhile, many predominantly

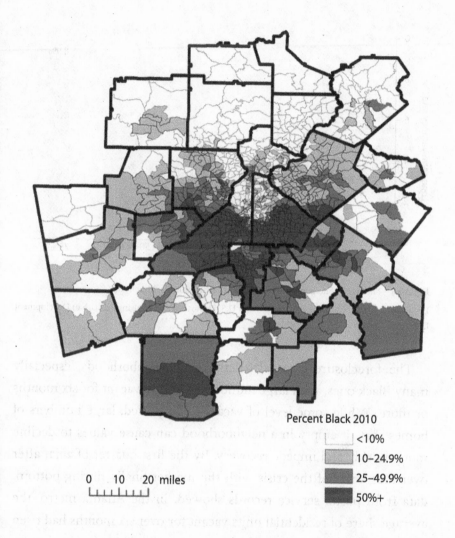

Percent Black 2010

	<10%
	10–24.9%
	25–49.9%
	50%+

0   10   20 miles

white, middle- and upper-income neighborhoods experienced less vola-
tility during the boom and bust. By 2014, they had more than recovered
from the modest housing price declines they had faced. Eventually, the
values of many Black neighborhoods did reach their pre-crisis levels,
but not until the latter part of the 2010s, as overall housing markets
grew increasingly tight.

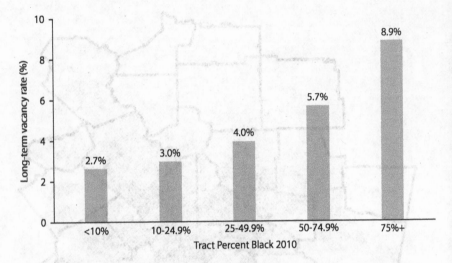

Figure 4. The share of housing units vacant for over six months, March 2012

Data sources: USPS vacancy data compiled by U.S. Department of Housing and Urban Development; Decennial Census 2010.

The foreclosure crisis also left many neighborhoods, especially many Black ones, with large numbers of homes vacant for six months or more. While some level of vacancy is expected, large numbers of homes that sit empty in a neighborhood can cause values to decline more quickly and impede recovery. By the first quarter of 2012, after over four years of the crisis with the market finally hitting bottom, data from postal service records showed, in the Atlanta metro, the average share of residential units vacant for over six months had risen to nine percent in census tracts that were seventy-five percent or more Black. This compared to less than three percent for neighborhoods that were less than 10 percent Black.[18] (See Figure 4.) The vacancy rate of predominantly Black neighborhoods was more than three times that in non-Black neighborhoods. On some blocks within these neighbor-hoods, the long-term vacancy share was considerably higher than the rate for the entire tract, as vacancies tend to be geographically clus-tered on specific blocks. Subprime and predatory lending left scars in Black neighborhoods felt for years after the crisis began.

RESPONDING TO FORECLOSURE CRISIS:
TOO LITTLE, TOO LATE

Public attention to the foreclosure crisis in the Atlanta region began in late 2006 and early 2007 as foreclosure levels, and national attention to the crisis both grew. The region certainly had earlier episodes of increased foreclosures, especially in the 1990s, and corresponding periods of increased local media coverage, but not to the extent it experienced in 2007 and 2008.[19] Beginning in 2007, foreclosure prevention activities in the region included those of both community-based operations, including HUD-certified housing counselors, affiliates of the NeighborWorks network, and a large consumer credit counseling organization, Consumer Credit Counseling Services (CCCS), an Atlanta-based nonprofit. CCCS was also a partner of the HOPE NOW Alliance, a George W. Bush administration initiative.

Atlanta Legal Aid's Home Defense Project (HDP) played a significant role in responding to the crisis. While the organization had dealt with foreclosure issues for many years, in 2007, it began to see dramatic increases in the numbers of foreclosures in which the homeowner received loans they couldn't afford. HDP worked to save clients' homes by negotiating cancellations of mortgage loans or restructuring loans into ones with smaller balances and payments. One approach it utilized was enlisting the aid of state legislators who would make phone calls to banks to access "executive" resolution departments to speed and improve lenders' responses.[20]

The local response to the crisis was severely constrained by slow and timid national and state responses. In September 2007, U.S. Senator Dick Durbin introduced legislation to allow bankruptcy judges to reduce the balance due on home loans on owner-occupied properties, which are explicitly excluded from bankruptcy protection in the U.S. Investors in rental properties or owners of vacation homes can get their loans reduced in bankruptcy court, but not borrowers financing their own homes. Durbin's bill would have provided a key tool to reduce foreclosures and encourage lenders to reduce the balances on loans, especially when the home was worth less than the mortgage. But Durbin's bill went nowhere due to severe opposition from investment and banking industry lobbies and no support from the Bush White House.

Instead of more serious interventions, the Bush Administration offered a voluntary loan-modification initiative, the HOPE NOW Alliance, designed by the American Securitization Forum (ASF), the trade group representing investors in private-label securitizations, the financial product primarily responsible for the subprime debacle.[21] In the first six months of 2008, the ASF-HOPE NOW modification initiative was responsible for only nine percent of loan modifications in the country, dropping to two percent by the end of the year. Most of these modifications provided very short-term forbearance, after which loan payments either increased or did not decline significantly. As a result, many borrowers were quickly forced back into default.

With the election of Barack Obama, many hoped for a more effective response to the crisis. In late 2008, before the President took office, the incoming director of the National Economic Council wrote a letter to Congress that the new administration would direct $50 to $100 billion in existing funding to reducing foreclosures. In March 2009, the Obama Administration announced HAMP to incentivize loan servicers to modify loans more aggressively to reduce mortgage payments and keep people in their homes. Rather than taking a strong, government-led approach to the loan modification issue, HAMP was based on the fundamental proposition that small incentive payments to loan servicers would result in large numbers of affordable, restructured loans. But the program was overly complex and confusing to borrowers, and servicers retained control of most parts of the process. Over the first three years of HAMP, under one million homeowners received loan modifications, far below the goal of several million. And because many of the earlier modifications did not involve reductions in the principal amount of the loan, a practice which became more common in later restructurings, many of the earlier loans ended up re-defaulting.[22]

As weak as the federal policy response to the foreclosure crisis was, the State of Georgia's was even worse. At the start of the subprime boom in 2003, the state had repealed the GFLA, which had essentially shut down the subprime lending market in the state for a few months. With the Governor's office and both chambers of the legislature under full Republican control by 2004, there were few prospects for the state to step in rapidly with any attempts to reduce foreclosures or slow the process. Because Georgia is a nonjudicial foreclosure state with a very fast foreclosure timeline, homeowners could see their homes auctioned at the courthouse steps within a few weeks after receiving their initial foreclosure notice. This gave them little time to access financial or legal assistance to attempt to save their home.

Although several bills were proposed to slow foreclosures in the state during the first two years of the crisis, only one was enacted. It made only very minor changes to the notification process involved in foreclosures. This bill only succeeded because it was so weak that it garnered the support of the Georgia Bankers Association. All the bills proposing more substantive changes, including those calling for bringing back stronger lending regulation or shifting the state to a judicial foreclosure process, went nowhere.

Passing pro-consumer legislation in Georgia is difficult, but passing such laws in the area of banking or real estate is even more challenging. According to the *AJC*, in 2008, thirty-four legislators sat on the boards of directors of banks around the state; twenty-nine more owned bank stock according to their financial disclosure statements.[23] Other legislators worked for banks, were married to bank executives, or represented banks as lawyers. In total, more than thirty percent of the legislature had close ties to the banking industry. Some legislators were not shy about the fact that the general assembly favored mortgage lenders. Representative Calvin Hill (R-Canton), who was vice-chairman of the House banking committee and on the board of a bank in his district, told the *AJC*, "The House and the Senate and all of Georgia want to keep away from————quote, unquote————'predatory lending' and 'bad lending practices' . . . if there's a good, clean agreement between two parties and both parties understand it, then both parties should be held accountable."[24] Other states did far more during the crisis to try to slow foreclosures. By 2008, at least nine states had created funds to assist homeowners to make their mortgage payments or modify their loans. The *AJC* counted thirty-four other states that had adopted policies to reduce foreclosures and help homeowners keep their homes. The lender-friendly nature of Georgia's lending laws remained mostly intact despite the crisis. Later in 2013, the Georgia Supreme Court sided with the banking industry in a lawsuit challenging foreclosure practices in the state. The ruling stated that the "continued ease with which foreclosures may proceed in this state gives us pause in light of the grave consequences foreclosures pose for individuals, families, neighborhoods, and society in general."[25] They urged the legislature to belatedly address Georgia's weak consumer protections, adding, "we leave to the members of our legislature, if they are so inclined, the task of undertaking additional reform." Suffice it to say, the legislature did not act on this admonishment.

Even when the federal government gave the State of Georgia funds to assist homeowners during the crisis, state efforts were ineffective. In 2010, the U.S. Treasury Department awarded Georgia's Department of Community Affairs (DCA) $340 million in federal Hardest Hit Fund (HHF) dollars to assist homeowners at risk of foreclosure. The state began its "HomeSafe Georgia" program in the spring of 2011. By early April of 2012, DCA had provided only $23 million to fewer than 1,000 homeowners across the state via HomeSafe Georgia, its primary HHF program, while the monthly tally of foreclosure notices topped 10,000. Karen Brown of Atlanta Legal Aid told the *AJC*, "This is extremely disturbing . . . the criteria are really strict."[26] The state had not marketed its program effectively and received too few applications, but it also approved only about twenty percent of the applications it did receive. Like some of the federal efforts, the state was too focused on determining who was "deserving" of foreclosure aid and avoiding those perceived as undeserving, rather than focusing on getting the aid out rapidly, which was critical to slowing the crisis.

In 2017, SIGTARP, the special inspector general for the Troubled Asset Relief Program (the bank relief program started during the financial crisis), released a scathing audit of Georgia DCA's HHF program. The SIGTARP press release on its audit stated that "DCA has consistently ranked among the least effective state agencies in the nation in disbursing HHF dollars."[27] Less than half the available $370.1 million had been disbursed to just over 9,000 homeowners. DCA had rejected two-thirds of those seeking assistance, which was one of the highest rejection rates across HHF programs nationally.

DCA argued that it needed to "guard" HHF funds for taxpayers. Yet, SIGTARP countered that DCA was "guarding HHF funds from Georgians who, within 30 days, could not get the IRS to issue and stamp a tax transcript, or their mortgage servicer to provide two years of payment history, or their employer to issue a letter saying the unemployment was not the homeowner's fault . . . They even 'guarded' the funds from one woman who could not continue in her job while undergoing chemotherapy for breast cancer. However, DCA's 'guarding' of funds stopped at its doorstep: it paid itself more than $30 million in administrative fees."[28] SIGTARP found that despite advocacy from nonprofits, the U.S. Treasury Department, and others, DCA remained determined to retain its stringent criteria. These criteria were stricter than required by the Treasury Department or by most other states with HHF programs. DCA had set a goal of helping 18,500 homeowners in its first two years but fell ninety percent short of this goal. This was despite DCA spending over $30 million in administrative costs to distribute only $174 million.

MISSED OPPORTUNITIES: FORECLOSED
PROPERTIES AND LOW PROPERTY VALUES

As foreclosures grew and mortgage markets tightened, the number of vacant, foreclosed properties surged. This occurred first, and rapidly, in Black neighborhoods in the city and many southern suburbs in DeKalb, Clayton, and Fulton counties. The large numbers of single-family homes owned by investors accelerated the problem in many of these neighborhoods. Investors were much more likely than homeowners to walk away from their properties when values fell below the outstanding mortgage balance. For homeowners, foreclosures tended to occur only when the homeowner could no longer afford the monthly payment and could not sell the house for enough to pay off the mortgage.

As the number of vacant, foreclosed homes in a neighborhood grew, the values of nearby properties declined, worsening the downward spiral of the local market. Community development advocates in Atlanta and around the country called on the federal government to step in to provide resources to acquire foreclosed homes to arrest this cycle of decline and to repurpose the homes for affordable housing or other community development uses. In the summer of 2008, the Housing and Economic Recovery Act created the first phase of the Neighborhood Stabilization Program (NSP), funded at $3.9 billion.[29] The Bush Administration had resisted supporting such an effort, but was forced to compromise to pass the broader bill as the November election approached. Over time, from 2008 through 2010, three phases of the NSP program were adopted and funded with $7 billion. Given the more than seven million properties that flowed through the foreclosure process during the crisis, this amount would be far too little to acquire even a modest portion of foreclosed homes.

NSP, especially the first and most significant phase of the program, was cumbersome and burdened by HUD regulations designed to fund traditional local government community development activities.

These programs' bureaucracy and slow pace were not well suited to allow public- and nonprofit-sector actors who were in a race against cash-paying investors clamoring to scoop up foreclosed homes at low prices. Some loan servicers charged with selling foreclosed properties preferred to sell to investors, including those buying in bulk, over dealing with the rules and regulations of NSP-funded cities.[30]

In Atlanta, the surge in foreclosures and the drop in home values meant that loan servicers began selling off foreclosed homes quickly in 2007 and 2008, wanting to unload large numbers of properties for fear of values falling even further.[31] Servicers began selling off lower-valued properties, often concentrated in Black neighborhoods, much more quickly, almost entirely to private investors. Many would end up sitting on empty homes for long periods, or quickly sell to other investors, who would then tend to sit on them or rent them out. In higher-income neighborhoods, foreclosures were much more likely to be resold to homeowners. The speed of the sell-off made it difficult for NSP recipients to compete with cash-wielding investors. Over half of the lower-value homes acquired by lenders in Fulton County in 2008 were sold off by May 2009, when the first phase of NSP money was just beginning to be deployed. These were precisely the sort of homes that could have been most cost-effectively acquired and used for long-term affordable housing. Many were in neighborhoods that, within a few years, would be subject to very strong gentrification pressures, including many within a half mile of the Beltline on the city's south, southwest, and west sides. Had a large number of these properties been secured by government and nonprofits, they could have been used to provide a substantial amount and variety of affordable housing instead of losing those homes to speculators and investors.

Despite the slow and inadequate response of poorly designed federal programs, the loss of so many foreclosed, vacant homes to private speculators was not just a failure of federal policy. It was also a huge, missed opportunity by state and local government. Part of this problem was a slow and ineffective deployment, and lack of leveraging of NSP funding. More broadly, however, little attention was given to the opportunity to acquire large amounts of housing and land during the crisis, when values reached very low levels—often on the order of $10,000 to $20,000 for a single-family parcel. Lots in many of these neighborhoods, especially in the core city, would by the late 2010s reach values more than five to seven times this amount. While public dollars were somewhat scarce during the crisis era, significant dollars were going to other efforts, including paying a speculator $71 million for a relatively small segment of land along the Beltline. And civic fundraising efforts were focused on Beltline-related and other activities, with little attention paid to this key opportunity to bank land for affordable housing in anticipation of the inevitable rebound in land values. Instead, speculators were scooping up properties near the Beltline's path.[32]

In January 2010, HUD admonished the city of Atlanta for its slow deployment of NSP funding. The city had to request an extension of the regular deadline to expend its NSP allocation. The city's slow progress on the first phase of NSP likely contributed to the fact that it was not awarded second-round NSP funds in what was a competitive, rather than formula-driven, process. The city planning commissioner blamed the slow deployment of first-stage funds partly on the time it took to apply for second-round funding, perhaps not a good indicator of the city's capacity to act quickly and effectively during the crisis.[33] Critics of the city's handling of NSP dollars recalled its earlier challenges with effectively deploying federal Empowerment Zone dollars in the 1990s.

In November of 2012, the *AJC* reported that $68 million in first-round NSP funds had been used to purchase, rehabilitate and sell or rent out 445 single-family homes and 366 units of multifamily housing in the city of Atlanta and the four biggest counties in the region, including Fulton, DeKalb, Gwinnett, and Cobb.[34] Looking at a broader set of eight counties in the region, the Atlanta Regional Commission reported that the eight counties had received $93 million in NSP 1 funds and, as of January

2012, acquired over 1,200 housing units.[35] These efforts helped stabilize home values in nearby local communities and provided homeownership opportunities to lower-wealth households, including many Black families.[36] However, the number of properties acquired paled in comparison to the hundreds of thousands of properties that had flowed through the foreclosure process during the crisis and the tens of thousands of vacant homes located throughout the region. DeKalb County alone had compiled a list of 7,000 vacant properties in 2012.[37]

Another issue with the NSP response in the region was that the bulk of the effort was geared towards rehabbing and then selling off the formerly foreclosed homes to individual homeowners. Local governments were under some pressure to demonstrate various forms of "success," and selling homes to homeowners was a simple way to achieve such metrics. Still, they focused much less on creating longer-term affordable housing that would remain under public or nonprofit ownership or permanently preserved as affordable homeownership through shared-equity structures such as community land trusts (CLTs).[38] Although providing lower-wealth families, especially homeowners of color, with opportunities for homeownership while prices were low was certainly a justifiable approach, especially for asset-building purposes, preserving some substantial share of foreclosed homes as long-term affordable housing was an advisable complement, but was not one in which suburban governments appeared interested.

There was simply not enough federal funding available via NSP 1 and NSP 3 (the region failed to compete successfully for NSP 2 dollars) to capture a sizable share of the foreclosed properties in the region. The great bulk of them, especially in lower- to middle-income neighborhoods, were snatched up by investors. What could have made a bigger difference was if the complementary state, local, and philanthropic resources had been devoted to acquiring foreclosed properties and if some of those dollars would have been used to create long-term affordable rental or shared-equity housing.

There was little capacity in the city or region for shared-equity housing, however. No effective community land trust existed in the area during the crisis. Before the crisis took hold and in the wake of increasing evidence that the Beltline was causing home values to spike, there was discussion of forming a citywide community land trust in Atlanta, but it did not really materialize until about ten years later. In the same month (September 2007) that Georgia Stand Up released its report, *The Beltline and Rising Home Prices*,[39] which showed that property values had surged near the Beltline, the Beltline Partnership convened a meeting with housing and community leaders to consider the possible establishment of one or more CLTs in Atlanta. About two years later, in December 2009, the Atlanta Land Trust Collaborative (ALTC) was incorporated.[40] The ALTC was not a traditional land trust, but rather a "central server" that would provide financial and technical support to neighborhood-based land trusts throughout the city. With some exceptions, the ALTC would not be a developer of land trust housing itself, but seek to support the work of other, more locally based CLTs. A fundamental problem with this design was that there were essentially no active land trusts in the city at the time, and the prospects for establishing a substantial number of new ones that could create a substantial flow of new CLT housing were unclear.

In 2015, the ALTC retained the services of CLT expert John Davis to prepare a strategic business plan for the organization, given its lack of success. Eventually, a renamed and reorganized nonprofit, the Atlanta Land Trust (ALT), was the result. ALT would no longer operate as a "central server" but be a fully operational, citywide land trust focusing on neighborhoods near the Beltline. Finally, after hiring a full-time executive director, it began acquiring properties in significant numbers in 2019. By this time, unfortunately, the low land values of the post-crisis period were a distant memory. Land values in many lower-income neighborhoods, especially those by the Beltline, had skyrocketed. While this does not negate the importance of eventually creating the ALT, the more than ten-year road to its full formation was certainly less than ideal. It also, arguably, reflects the priorities of civic leadership in the city over this period, as substantial portions of the Beltline itself had been built out, but far less had been done to secure land for affordable housing.

FEDERAL FAILURE COMPOUNDS A WEAK LOCAL RESPONSE

The combination of weak local responses and poor federal policy around securing vacant, foreclosed homes for affordable housing was perhaps epitomized in the story of the federal takeover of Omni National Bank. This small bank had a large portfolio of mortgages backed by investor-owned properties in Black neighborhoods in the Atlanta metro. Omni was heavily engaged in financing property flippers, some of whom were involved in fraudulent schemes. Eventually, at least four people, including one of the bank's co-founders, went to prison after a federal probe of the bank. Its 2009 failure cost the Federal Deposit Insurance Corporation's (FDIC) insurance fund over $280 million. The FDIC was responsible for handling the bank's assets, including hundreds of vacant, foreclosed homes. Instead of these homes being acquired by the city of Atlanta, perhaps partly with NSP funds, and banked for eventual redevelopment into long-term affordable housing, the FDIC sold off the properties in bulk sales to private investors for pennies on the dollar. The *AJC* found that, on four days in 2009, the FDIC sold 400 homes, many of them located in Black neighborhoods, to investment firms located in Atlanta and Denver. On one of these days, the agency sold 176 properties for only $3 million, an average of less than $18,000 per home, with some selling for a few thousand dollars. Community advocates argued that they were never even aware that the houses were for sale by the FDIC. Meanwhile, these same community organizations had been working with the NSP programs attempting to purchase foreclosed homes to repurpose them to benefit the community. As Brent Brewer, a resident of the West End neighborhood, put it to the *AJC*, "It seems odd that [FDIC] would bulk-sell these properties at very reduced amounts when they had this federal program over here ... The city of Atlanta could have bought all of those properties."[41]

One of the major buyers of Omni National Bank's portfolio was the Carter real estate firm, an established, well-connected real estate developer not generally known for engaging in buying bank foreclosures. (Carter was the firm that later partnered with Georgia State in the redevelopment of the old Turner Field ballpark, as discussed in Chapter 3.) But the company bought 272 of Omni's 450 foreclosed homes, most of them located on the south, southwest, and west sides of the city, but also in the suburbs. The other major buyer was a Colorado private equity firm with the Randian name of John Galt Enterprises. Carter had planned to sell off the least attractive properties, a process often referred to as "dumping," and then rent out the rest for a few years until the real estate market recovered. It had also planned a "rent-to-own" program generally a scheme with a sordid history of exploiting Black families in Atlanta and three other cities, but that plan had few takers.[42] Almost thirty of Carter's homes had received multiple complaints about building code or zoning violations. By October 2012, about three years after purchasing its Omni Bank portfolio, Carter had sold off half of the properties, not to homeowners but to other investors.

RESURGENT RACIALIZED PREDATION IN THE WAKE OF THE SUBPRIME CRISIS

The foreclosure crisis in the Atlanta region, and the sell-off of bulk foreclosures by subprime lenders as well as the government-sponsored enterprises Fannie Mae and Freddie Mac, precipitated a new round of predatory housing market activity, some of which represented a resurgence of pre-Fair Housing Act racialized predation. One such practice that surged in Atlanta and elsewhere after 2008 was contract-for-deed (CFD) home sales. CFDs, sometimes called installment land contracts, have a notorious history of racial exploitation in the U.S. The history of the practice was exposed to a broader public by Ta-Nehisi Coates' 2014 *Atlantic* essay, "The Case for Reparations," and earlier by Beryl Satter's book, *Family Properties*.[43] CFDs were also the focus of a significant racial justice organizing effort that began on Chicago's west side that became known as the Contract Buyers' League. A CFD is neither a conventional homebuying transaction nor a regular rental agreement, but is, instead, a hybrid that Coates has called a predatory agreement that combines "all the responsibilities of homeownership with all the disadvantages of renting, while offering the benefits of neither." With a CFD, the "buyer" pays a large deposit and then makes payments over a long period, and is usually responsible for property taxes, insurance, and, critically, maintenance and repair of the home. So, in this way, the CFD resembles a regular, fee-simple home purchase. One hitch, and it is a big one, is that, unlike in a regular purchase transaction, the new "buyer" is actually just a tenant, and not a homeowner under the law. The family does not gain title to the home at purchase, nor do they build up equity in the home even after years of making payments. If they miss even a single payment, they often lose any claim to the home and can be evicted. Some CFD agreements stipulate that the borrower must bring the property up to code in a certain period.

In the wake of the crisis, as loan servicers and Fannie and Freddie began to unload some of their delinquent loans and foreclosed properties in bulk sales, they sold them to many different sorts of entities, including some private equity firms that specialized in then reselling the homes through CFDs, often to unsophisticated buyer-tenants. In the first half of the 2010s, legal aid and consumer protection lawyers from around the country began reporting that they saw higher incidences of CFDs.[44] This surge was precipitated both by the flood of foreclosures and by the fact that values for some homes, especially in many Black neighborhoods, had dropped below $50,000, a level at which it is difficult to obtain a mortgage. Moreover, mortgage markets overall had tightened drastically during the crisis and did not loosen again for several years.

One CFD seller that had drawn the attention of Atlanta Legal Aid and *The New York Times* was the private equity firm Harbour Portfolio, which had purchased properties from Fannie Mae.[45] From 2011 to 2015 in Fulton County, Harbour was able to buy homes from Fannie Mae in bulk sales at very low values, averaging under $11,000, generally well below the tax-appraised values of the properties. The median ratio of Harbor's price compared to its tax appraised value was less than thirty-six percent. The firm could turn around and sell these houses typically for $40,000 to $50,000 without doing significant renovations or repairs. On top of this, they charged an interest rate in the CFD agreements of 9.9 percent, roughly double the going interest rate at the time. The average racial composition of the neighborhoods where Harbour's CFD sales occurred was eighty-seven percent Black. Even after controlling for median income, owner-occupancy rate, and the age of the housing stock, neighborhoods with larger Black populations were more likely to have been the location of a CFD sale.

There is, at least, one bright spot here. Due to the press Harbour Portfolio received in the *New York Times*, a successful fair housing lawsuit initiated by Atlanta Legal Aid, and investigations undertaken by the Consumer Financial Protection Bureau (which were subsequently suspended during the Trump Administration), Harbour Portfolio was effectively shut down. Moreover, in 2018, Atlanta Legal Aid obtained a settlement from Harbour and firms that had purchased some of the CFDs, obtaining damages for their clients together with actual mortgages, providing them with some much-deserved home equity.[46]

ATLANTA AS A PRIVATE EQUITY "STRIKE ZONE" IN WALL STREET'S SINGLE-FAMILY RENTAL BOOM

In the wake of the foreclosure crisis, millions of single-family homes across the U.S. flowed into the hands of investors. While some of these were then resold to homeowners, many were converted into single-family rental (SFR) housing. In the Atlanta region, most SFR investors were small, "mom and pop" landlords who own anywhere from one to about twenty rental properties in the region. This had been, and in many communities still is, the predominant nature of investment in single-family rental homes, especially in lower-income neighborhoods throughout the country. In fact, in the Atlanta metro, SFR homes had been, before the foreclosure crisis, predominantly located in low and moderate-income neighborhoods. In many middle- and upper-income neighborhoods, rental housing was often scarce, and where it did occur was usually concentrated in large-scale multifamily apartment buildings, often located outside of single-family residential subdivisions, close to expressways and larger arterial roads.

The foreclosure crisis changed this dynamic. Because foreclosures primarily affected the single-family stock in the region, because so many properties flowed to investors after foreclosure, and because of extremely tight mortgage markets that followed the crisis, many single-family homes were converted to rentals. Similar patterns occurred in many Sunbelt metros, but Atlanta was among the leading sites of this restructuring.

In 2012, this trend was effectively "juiced" by a combination of public policy and Wall Street financialization that drove a great deal of globalized capital into this new, burgeoning SFR market. Several large, institutional private-equity firms entered the SFR market, and the Atlanta region was a key early target. The region promised continued population growth, lots of foreclosures, and little regulation of landlord-tenant issues or the prospects of something like rent control. These firms began sending multiple representatives to the foreclosure auctions that occurred each month in the front of county courthouses. They also began buying foreclosed properties off the books of banks and subprime lenders. And because by this time, foreclosures had spread much more into the prime market, some also sought to purchase foreclosed properties or distressed loans from Fannie Mae and Freddie Mac.

Beginning in 2007, millions of families were rapidly pushed into the rental market and then precluded from reentering homeownership for years due to their damaged credit histories. On top of this, mortgage markets tightened drastically, and many would-be homebuyers were burdened with student debt. Finally, capital flooded into the SFR industry, allowing investors the ability to scoop up millions of homes, often paying cash, making it more difficult for owner-occupiers to compete in the market, especially in the lower- and middle-cost tiers. From 2006 to 2015, the number of SFRs in the fifty largest U.S. metros increased by approximately two million, from 3.8 million to 5.8 million. The share of single-family homes that were rentals increased in all fifty of these metros, with the aggregate share increasing from 11.3 percent to 16 percent, a forty-two percent increase in SFR share. Moreover, the nine metropolitan areas with the greatest increases in SFR share were all located in the Sunbelt. The Atlanta metro had the fourth-greatest increase in SFRs, increasing from 11.5 percent to 19.2 percent of the single-family stock, a sixty-seven percent increase in SFR share. Other metros with large increases in SFRs included Las Vegas, Phoenix, and Tampa, all metros that had experienced large numbers of foreclosures.[47]

The growth in SFRs occurred in many parts of the Atlanta region. Most neighborhoods experienced at least a three percentage-point increase in single-family rentership over the 2010 to 2015 period, and many experienced increases of over fifteen percentage points.[48] Surges in SFRs were greater in more diverse suburban neighborhoods, those with larger Black, Asian, and Latinx populations. Many neighborhoods that had experienced higher levels of foreclosures during the crisis experienced larger increases in SFRs, because many new SFRs had been foreclosed homes. There was one notable exception here, however. Foreclosures in neighborhoods with high property values did not result in increased SFRs. SFR investors were not looking to pay the higher home prices commanded in these areas, and wealthier homeowners had strong access to mortgage credit despite the tighter mortgage markets that disproportionately affected lower-wealth households.

In 2016, Amherst Capital Management reported that the Atlanta metropolitan area was the largest for institutional SFR investors, followed by Phoenix, Miami, Tampa, Dallas, Charlotte, and Houston, all Sunbelt cities. It accounted for over fifteen percent of all institutional SFR homes, totaling over 30,000 SFRs in the region.[49] Moreover, the Atlanta metro was the largest SFR market for the largest institutional investor, Invitation Homes, accounting for at least 7,500 of its 48,000 homes by 2016.[50] As the CEO of Colony Starwood, a major SFR investor, proclaimed, Atlanta was one of private equity's "strike zones."[51]

Suzanne Lanyi Charles examined the ownership patterns of four of the largest institutional SFR investors and how their properties were distributed throughout the Atlanta region as of 2018.[52] These included Invitation Homes, American Homes 4 Rent, Front Yard Residential, and Tricon American Homes. Charles' analysis confirmed that Gwinnett County was ground zero for institutional SFR investors, with the four firms owning just over 6,200 SFRs in Gwinnett, almost twice the number of the next highest county, Cobb, at just over 3,200. Gwinnett has approximately the same number of SFR homes as Fulton County, but Fulton only accounted for just under 2,000 of the SFRs owned by these four firms in 2018. Charles also identified the proportion of single-family homes owned by the four large investors in each census tract and found that their combined market share reached as high as eight percent in some neighborhoods. It is important to point out that this is the share of all single-family homes, including owner-occupied ones. Because most single-family homes remain owner-occupied, the four-firm market share of just SFRs certainly runs substantially higher than this in many neighborhoods. This suggests that these firms likely have significant market power in some neighborhoods and therefore have some ability to extract higher rents or provide lower quality housing.

Charles showed that the four firms' SFRs were spread across a broad donut that encircles the city of Atlanta, including running through much of Gwinnett, south DeKalb, south Fulton, Henry County, Clayton County, Douglas, Cobb, and Paulding counties.[53] However, the firms were conspicuously quite thin on the ground both in affluent, high-cost North Fulton and in the city of Atlanta. They were also less present in the farther-flung, more exurban counties of the region. The four firms tend to focus on different parts of the more established suburban areas. Invitation Homes, for example, tends to be heavily invested in Gwinnett County, south Cobb, Paulding, and Douglas counties, while Front Yard Residential focused much more on the predominantly Black areas of south Fulton, Clayton, and south DeKalb counties. This suggests that, by targeting different parts of the region, the firms reduced competition and maximized their market power.

The story of how private equity entered the SFR business in a big way is, like many developments in housing finance, one that involves both private- and public-sector actors, including relationships and policies that accelerated the flow of Wall Street dollars into neighborhoods hit hard by the foreclosure crisis. For starters, the surging rentership and depressed home values that caught the eye of large investment firms, and eventually led to them investing on the order of $60 billion into SFRs, was the result of policymakers failing to regulate the subprime mortgage market and, after the crisis began, to markedly reduce the number of homeowners losing their homes to foreclosure. But policymakers also played a continuing role in supporting this rapid transition by not acting more forcefully to provide a broader spectrum of households with access to mortgage credit after the crisis and by actively courting Wall Street's entrance into large-scale SFR ownership.

In August 2011, the Federal Housing Finance Agency (FHFA) issued a public "request for information" to gather views from industry actors on how Fannie Mae and Freddie Mac could more quickly sell off their large and growing portfolio of foreclosed properties.[54] The response was, to say the least, enthusiastic, with the agency receiving more than 4,000 comments. Several federal agencies met during the year to discuss possible ways to support more "REO-to-rental" conversions. (REO stands for "real estate owned" and essentially means foreclosed properties on the books of a lender or government agency that has ended up owning such properties.) Then, in January 2012, the Federal Reserve released a high-profile white paper in which it laid out the accumulation of REO properties but also discussed approaches for how policymakers, agencies, and the private sector could facilitate, perhaps even subsidize, the flow of properties into investors' hands to rent them out. As the paper put it:

> . . . the challenge for policymakers is to find ways to help reconcile the existing size and mix of the housing stock and the current environment for housing finance. Fundamentally, such measures involve adapting the existing housing stock to the prevailing tight mortgage lending conditions—for example, devising policies that could help facilitate the conversion of foreclosed properties to rental properties— or supporting a housing finance regime that is less restrictive than today's, while steering clear of the lax standards that emerged during the last decade.[55]

The authors of this paper argued that policymakers had a choice between allowing families to purchase more homes at a time when values were relatively low or spurring a speedier flow of these homes to investors and, in particular, to larger-scale institutional investors backed by Wall Street and private equity dollars. It is clear that federal policymakers, in the aggregate at least, chose more the latter route than the former. As a result, policymakers facilitated the transfer of tens of billions in housing value to larger-scale, deep-pocketed investors during a time of low but soon-to-be rising prices. This was on top of the even larger number of homes captured during this period by more traditional, smaller-scale buy-to-rent investors.

The January 2012 Fed "REO-to-rental" white paper was a pivotal document. It gave Wall Street firms the credibility they needed to gather support from broader capital markets and their institutional clientele. The paper was cited repeatedly in investor prospectuses and private-equity pitches at invitation-only country club lunches.[56] As Bret Christophers has written, the Fed had performed the "crucial discursive work in making *conceivable* and *creditable* large investor portfolios such as Blackstone would subsequently build."[57] Within a few weeks, Warren Buffet appeared on CNBC, in a widely cited interview, where the "Oracle of Omaha" proclaimed that he would purchase "a couple hundred thousand" single-family homes if he could.[58] This was somewhat prescient because it was about the number Wall Street firms had purchased by 2016.

In the meantime, a firm named the Treehouse Group had begun buying foreclosed homes in Phoenix in 2010 and 2011.[59] It partnered with another firm, Riverside Residential, to gain more capital to scale up its operations. Soon Blackstone, the international private equity firm, took notice of the Treehouse-Riverside venture just when federal policymakers had begun to discuss the continuing build-up of foreclosed homes and the potential for increasing REO-to-rental pipelines. By early 2012, Blackstone had effectively taken over the firm. In April 2012, about three months after the Fed published its REO-to-rental white paper and about seven months after the FHFA had issued its request for information, the new firm, Invitation Homes, purchased its first home. By the end of 2012, Invitation Homes had moved into the Atlanta region. By March 2013, it had purchased thousands of homes in the region, a substantial portion of the 17,000 homes it had already acquired around the country in less than a year.[60] Other major private-equity firms also pushed early into the region, including Colony Capital, Waypoint Homes, and others.

The Federal Reserve, in its 2012 white paper, had suggested that institutional investors might be given incentives to "provide appropriate property management by deferring some of their compensation" until several years of renting properties in a manner consistent with 'good landlord' practices . . ."[61] The compensation of the corporate leadership of firms like Blackstone and Colony Capital doesn't appear to have been significantly limited during this period. For example, Steven Schwarzman, the CEO of Blackstone, saw his total compensation increase from $223 million in 2011 to $810 million in 2015.[62] Even if Fannie Mae and Freddie Mac did take some measures to incentivize private equity buyers of bulk-sold homes to practice "good landlording," it is unclear what portion of the institutional SFR market this would have affected. Many of the homes that ended up in the hands of these firms were acquired through individual purchases of foreclosed properties via county foreclosure auctions or mortgage servicers and not from Fannie Mae and Freddie Mac.

A variety of investigative journalism, advocacy research, and scholarly literature suggests that there have been some significant problems in how the new Wall Street landlords have treated their tenants. In 2014, the activist groups Occupy Our Homes Atlanta and The Right to the City Alliance issued a report on Invitation Homes.[63] They interviewed a sample of twenty-five tenants in Invitation Homes properties. Eighteen of these respondents reported that they had experienced maintenance problems with their homes. Over two-thirds indicated that they had had no contact with any individual at the landlord. Alana Semuels, a reporter with *The Atlantic*, spoke to two dozen tenants and reviewed twenty-one lawsuits against SFR firms in Gwinnett County, one of the prime submarkets in the region for institutional SFR investors.[64] The tenants reported numerous instances of poor maintenance and problems with their homes.

Elora Raymond and her colleagues examined the eviction behavior of large institutional SFR investors in Fulton County, comparing their eviction activity to that of smaller firms and "mom and pop" investors, which they defined as owning fewer than fifteen properties in the county.[65] They found that, in 2015, nine institutional investors, as a group, had a twenty percent eviction filing rate, more than three times the six percent rate of "mom and pop" landlords. Even after controlling for a wide variety of property characteristics and the neighborhood in which the property is located, they found that, of the nine institutional

investors, all had a filing rate that was higher than other owners and, for seven out of the nine, the difference was statistically significant. The differences tended to be quite large. Colony Capital, for example, was 205 percent more likely to file an eviction in 2015 than a "mom and pop" landlord on an otherwise similar property. American Homes 4 Rent was 181 percent more likely. The increased likelihood of eviction for the nine institutional landlords compared to a mom-and-pop landlord averaged 100 percent higher.

Complaints about institutional SFR homes have not been limited to Atlanta. A 2018 *Washington Post* investigation into First Key Homes, an SFR company owned by the private equity firm Cerberus Capital Management, found that the firm was a leading code-enforcement violator in Memphis and filed evictions at high rates.[66] Its eviction filing rate was consistently higher than the eviction rates of the remaining rental properties in the zip codes in which it operated. In 2021, the *Tampa Bay Times* investigated a private equity firm with ties to the Hermes leather goods dynasty in France, which owned more than a thousand homes in Florida through Lafayette Real Estate.[67] Lafayette began investing in SFRs after the crisis. Lafayette's homes required tenants to be responsible for all maintenance costing $100 or less, regardless of whether the tenant was to blame for the problem. Renters were also responsible for maintaining appliances, gutters, and other parts of the home, and were required to carry liability insurance to cover damage to the property of up to $100,000.

Some of the problems reported with SFR investors are likely driven by their business models, including their focus on cutting operating costs. In 2016, the chief operating officer of American Homes 4 Rent, a major SFR investor, stated that it had reduced its spending on maintenance, repair, and "turn" costs from $2,500 to $1,600 per home.[68] Colony Starwood reported that it had cut its property management costs by twenty-five percent in 2016, including employing video and chat software to show tenants how to repair things like garbage disposals or clogged toilets. Some leases of the large firms required tenants to be responsible for landscaping, insect control, and even repairing sinks and sewer backups. Invitation Homes reported to the U.S. Securities and Exchange Commission in 2016 that it was spending only an average of $1,142 per home annually on repairs, maintenance, and turnover costs (costs entailed in preparing a property to lease a vacated unit to a new tenant). This is well under the average $3,100 per year that homeowners of similarly aged properties pay for repairs and maintenance.[69]

One way to increase a landlord's net operating income is to cut back on maintenance or service. Another way is to create new sources of revenue via new fees and charges. American Homes 4 Rent reported that tenant charge-backs, the monies charged to tenants after they vacate a property, soared by over 1,000 percent from 2014 to 2018, even though the number of homes the firm owned had only increased by seventy percent.[70] In 2016, the CEO of Colony-Starwood lamented the "revenue leakage" allowed by "not getting every charge that you are legitimately due under leases."[71] By shifting maintenance costs onto tenants, reducing their service costs, and charging tenants as much as possible for as many things as possible, the SFR firms could report higher net operating incomes to their investors each quarter, with higher earnings stoking the firms' values.

The rapid emergence of the institutional SFR industry was not just a product of unbridled capital. However, lightly regulated capital markets certainly facilitate the rapid flow of investment into new asset classes. It was also a product of public sector support and facilitation, including the influence that the 2012 Fed white paper had in supporting the industry. At the state and local level, the large SFR firms focused more on markets in Sunbelt states, most of which were landlord-friendly ones, with few tenant protections and little prospects for rent control.[72] Except for deploying limited federal NSP funds, state and local governments in Georgia were mostly nowhere to be seen in terms of helping families access mortgage credit to purchase homes when home values had dropped to bargain-basement prices. The policies of Fannie Mae, Freddie Mac, their regulator, the FHFA, and the FHA, kept mortgage credit extraordinarily tight in the wake of the crisis, which meant that the institutional SFR players would have less competition from families looking to buy their own homes when prices were low.

Sometimes federal policy even provided low-cost financing to institutional investors. In 2017, Fannie Mae and Freddie Mac both began providing financing for large, institutional SFR firms, a practice that consumer advocates argued made little sense from a policy perspective. In January, Invitation Homes revealed that it received $1 billion in financing from Fannie Mae, financing approved by the FHFA. Because Fannie Mae and Freddie Mac can offer lower-cost financing than other institutions, this effectively meant that the institutional SFR firms would be receiving a subsidy to grow their SFR business.[73] Rob Grossinger, president of the National Community Stabilization Trust, argued "These investors so far have had no trouble financing the purchase of tens of thousands of homes without government support."[74] In July, Freddie Mac announced that it would begin financing institutional SFR firms as well. Freddie suggested that it would focus on smaller firms but moved into financing larger SFR firms, including Front Yard Residential's acquisition of HavenBrook partners and a portfolio of 3,200 SFRs in 2018. Shortly after that transaction, in August, however, after continuing criticism about Fannie and Freddie supporting large SFR firms, the FHFA directed them to stop this line of business.[75]

THE FALL IN BLACK HOMEBUYING AND
THE WORSENING RACIAL WEALTH GAP

Federal mortgage data show that home purchase loans to Black households fell precipitously during the 2007 to 2011 foreclosure crisis. This occurred across the country, but the magnitude of the impact in the Atlanta region was stronger due to the large Black population and the size of the Black middle class. Tight mortgage markets and reduced attention to fair lending and community reinvestment policies reduced Black homebuying following the crisis. The Urban Institute compared home purchase lending in 2012 to lending in 2001, a relatively healthy year for home mortgages that predated the subprime boom, and found that home purchase lending to Black families as a group in 2012 was fifty-five percent below 2001 levels.[76] Black families were disproportionately pushed out of the homeownership market via foreclosures, and disproportionately kept out as home values recovered.[77] They were dealt heavy losses during a period of foreclosure and value decline and then were given too few opportunities to participate in the subsequent wealth building by being able to purchase homes when values were low. This process exacerbated the racial wealth gap. Too-few Black families were able to buy homes in the years following the crisis, but those who did tended to gain significant wealth during the recovery. The median estimated appreciation experience of homes purchased by Black homebuyers in the Atlanta metro in 2012 was 49.9 percent over the following five years.[78]

The dramatic drop in Black homebuyers in the region meant that Black households did not experience the same sort of recovery in their aggregate wealth that white families did after 2012. In the five core metro Atlanta counties, the number of home purchase loans to Black homebuyers fell sixty-five percent, from over 21,000 in 2004 to under 7,300 by 2009 (see Figure 6). Even by 2014, the number of home purchase loans to Black homebuyers had risen to only 7,512. But because other

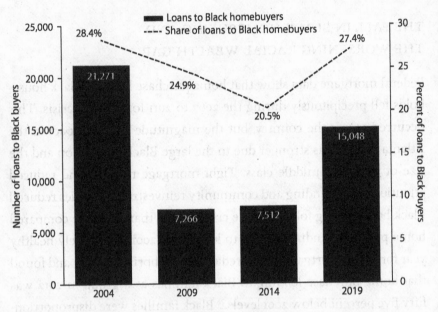

Figure 6. Black homebuying in the five-county Atlanta metro

Data source: Home Mortgage Disclosure Act data via PolicyMap.com

homebuyers were increasing their buying during the early part of the recovery and were able to purchase homes at low values, the share of home purchase loans to Black homebuyers continued to fall, down to 20.5 percent. Finally, by 2019, as access to mortgage credit improved some, Black homebuying began to recover significantly in the region, effectively doubling to over 15,000 buyers from 2014 to 2019 in the five core counties. As a result, the Black share of all homebuyers finally began to increase, from 20.5 percent in 2014 to 27.4 percent in 2019.

The contraction of Black homebuying occurred at the same time that homebuying by investors surged, including that of the large institutional SFR firms. Policymakers opted to facilitate the scooping up of low-valued foreclosed properties by large investors rather than to support the ability of Black and less-affluent families to purchase homes. In doing so, they steered land wealth towards an increasingly concentrated ownership structure and away from the groups who had been hit so hard by the crisis. Even after a few years of gains in Black homebuying, as of 2019, the Atlanta region's Black homeownership of 48.2 percent remains far below the white homeownership rate of 77.3 percent, a gap of twenty-nine points. Moreover, it remains below the 2005 rate of 50.6 percent.

One initiative in the region that pushed against the dominant tide of low-priced properties flowing to SFR investors was an Atlanta Neighborhood Development Partnership (ANDP) program. ANDP demonstrated, through a program funded by the federal NSP and other sources, that supporting Black homebuyers in the wake of the crisis provided a large benefit to those homebuyers, allowing them to build significant wealth during the broader recovery.[79] In 2009, ANDP began acquiring foreclosed homes throughout the Atlanta metro using federal NSP funds through partnering with local governments in the region. The organization rehabbed and sold 284 foreclosed homes to low- and moderate-income families. With NSP funding running out, ANDP turned to accepting foreclosed homes as donations and using other federal affordable housing funds in partnership with local governments. It also obtained federal funding from the Capital Magnet Fund and the New Markets Tax Credit programs. From 2009 through 2018, ANDP was able to purchase, rehab, and sell 482 homes. Of these buyers, as of mid-2019, 447 (92.7 percent) still owned their homes, thirty-two (6.6 percent) had sold their homes, and three (0.6 percent) had lost their homes to foreclosure. Almost ninety percent of ANDP's buyers were first-time homebuyers, about seventy-three percent were Black, and more than half were female-headed households. Sixty-five percent had incomes below eighty percent of the metropolitan median, and the remaining had incomes under 120 percent of the metro median. Over ninety percent received financial assistance in making their down payment or paying their closing costs. The average purchase price of the homes was about $117,000. The buyers bought homes in twenty-two counties across the region, but eighty percent were located in four counties: Fulton, DeKalb, Gwinnett, and Douglas.

To assess its impact, ANDP looked closely at the 215 buyers who had owned their homes for at least five years and used Zillow value estimates to calculate the expected gain in equity each buyer had achieved.[80] These buyers experienced an average appreciation of seventy-seven percent based on the Zillow estimates. The appreciation combined with the down-payment assistance yielded an average gain in home equity—effectively wealth creation—of almost $89,000 per homeowner for an aggregated benefit of $19 million over this group of participants. While the ANDP program was clearly a success, it could reach the scale it did only by cobbling together various federal housing and community development programs. A more muscular response during this period by federal, but also state and local actors, could have generated a much larger program and captured a much greater number of properties. Instead, tens of thousands of single-family homes flowed to investors each year in the region, with a substantial portion flowing to Wall Street firms.

The Atlanta region was hit extremely hard by the foreclosure crisis, and Black neighborhoods were hit the hardest. Georgia's bank-friendly legislature, a lack of regulation, and the region's sizeable Black homeowner population made it a prime target for predatory subprime lenders in the 2000s. Property values in many Black neighborhoods fell sharply after 2007 and sometimes took a decade to recover. Many Black neighborhoods in the region led the nation in terms of the share of underwater homeowners, at least as late as 2013. The federal and state responses to the crisis were weak and slow, and by the time they began to have more significant results, the crisis had moved into more diverse suburban communities. Despite all the damage that reckless lending did to the region, the state legislature resisted strengthening lending regulations or tilting a very uneven foreclosure playing field even moderately towards borrowers. Even when the federal government provided resources to state government to assist homeowners at risk of foreclosure, the state was slow to deploy those resources, worrying far too much about helping "undeserving" homeowners rather than slowing the crisis and saving homes.

In addressing the surge of vacant, foreclosed homes in the region, which were disproportionately concentrated in Black neighborhoods, the federal NSP program was a key intervention. In some cases, these funds were well-deployed in Atlanta, particularly when they were successfully used to help Black homebuyers purchase homes at low prices after 2008. But the magnitude of NSP, by itself, was far too small to make a serious dent in acquiring foreclosed homes for affordable housing or Black homeownership. Moreover, relatively few properties were captured and preserved as long-term affordable housing via nonprofit-owned rental housing or community land trust homes. The entire region missed a key opportunity, a possible positive inflection point towards reduced racial inequality in the housing market. If more Black families could have acquired homes at low values after the crisis, the years of growth in home values would have significantly reduced the racial wealth gap in the region. And if many more of the foreclosed homes that ended up in the hands of for-profit investors had been captured as long-term affordable housing, lower-income renters, many of them people of color, would be in a much stronger position as opposed to facing high and rising rents over the subsequent decade.

Instead, the bulk of foreclosed properties flowed to private investors. A significant chunk of those, especially in moderate- and middle-income suburbs, flowed to private-equity firms who, flush with capital and federal policy support, identified the Atlanta region as a key "strike zone" because of the region's weak tenant protections, growing renter population, and ample availability of relatively newer single-family homes. These trends contributed to continuing gentrification in the city and especially racial exclusion and growing housing instability in the suburbs.

5

DIVERSITY AND EXCLUSION IN THE SUBURBS

AFTER 2000, THE ATLANTA REGION, and especially its suburbs, became much more diverse both racially and economically. The number of Latinx and Asian households and the number of immigrants in the region continued to grow. The metro also experienced an increase of almost 900,000 in its Black population from 2000 to 2019, including many families moving from northern and coastal metros. But the growing racial and ethnic diversity of the suburbs was not spatially uniform or uncontested, especially in many majority-white suburbs. Local officials, homeowner associations, and real estate interests used their redevelopment and exclusionary powers, sometimes newly strengthened after incorporating as municipalities, to reduce the number of lower-income renters—usually renters of color—in their cities and schools. In addition to the well-known tool of exclusionary zoning, these efforts also involved the demolition of low-cost rental housing. By portraying the demolition and redevelopment efforts as "revitalizing" or "retrofitting" their communities, as converting "tired," car-centric development patterns into modern, "live-work-play" environments, local public-private partnerships, with the help of state and federally enabled development finance tools, were able to create new, shinier places accompanied by a replacement of lower-income residents with higher-income households and commercial amenities. The overall result of these changes is that many lower-income households and households of color have been excluded from both the city of Atlanta and many of the most affluent communities in the region, especially in its northern "favored quarter." It was as if the more affluent localities in the region—and the city of Atlanta is on a clear trajectory to joining this group—were competing in a race of exclusion in the face of a more diverse metropolitan region. This race involved using public redevelopment finance tools and exclusionary housing practices to push the poor and people of color over to some other part of the region. They effectively competed for affluence, for the whiter middle- and upper-middle class, at the expense of low-income families and people of color. So, while the suburbs continued to diversify by race and income, majority-white, middle- and upper-income suburbs continued to try to preserve their status, and their schools, as places that would not be too welcoming for families of color and, especially, lower-income households. As the region continues to suffer from very high levels of heavily racialized income and wealth inequality, only aggressive organizing at the metropolitan and statewide levels on affordable and fair housing issues are likely to counter these practices and policies.

TAKING STOCK OF A CHANGING METRO

The population of the Atlanta metropolitan area grew from 4.1 million to just over 6 million from 2000 to 2019, a gain of over forty-six percent.[1] Like many growing metros in the U.S., Atlanta underwent substantial racial and ethnic change from 2000 to 2019. The metro went from being a majority-white region to a minority-white one. The share of the population that was non-Hispanic white in the Atlanta metropolitan statistical area declined from sixty percent to forty-six percent, while the Black population increased from twenty-nine to thirty-four percent. The fastest rates of increase were in the Latinx and Asian populations, which rose at rates of 146 percent and 170 percent, respectively, over the nineteen years. The Latinx population increased from 6.5 to 11 percent of the region's population, while the Asian population increased from 3.3 to 6 percent.

The Black population of the region also grew rapidly, by seventy-five percent over the period. While the Latinx and Asian populations grew at the fastest rates, Black residents comprised over forty-six percent of the overall population growth in the region, accounting for almost 890,000 of the total 1.9 million gain in population. Latinx households accounted for about twenty-one percent of population growth, and Asians accounted for about twelve percent. The numbers show that the region has become a multiethnic one, especially since 2000, with Latinx, Asian, and multiracial residents making up about twenty 20 percent of the population. However, many seem to continue viewing the region as a traditional Black-white binary.

The Black population continued to become more suburban during the first two decades of the twenty-first century. Like most major metros, Black suburbanization in Atlanta was certainly not a new phenomenon in the twenty-first century. As discussed in Chapter 1, Black suburbs had been developed in Atlanta during the twentieth century, starting well before the city's major 1952 annexation of many adjacent suburban neighborhoods. Black real estate developers and Black-owned financial institutions enabled Black suburbanization to get an early start in Atlanta. Later, after many of these early Black suburbs were annexed into the city, Black suburbanization continued, especially after 1970. The share of Blacks living in Atlanta's suburbs increased from about twenty percent in 1970 to over sixty percent in 1990.[2] Then, it increased further to seventy-eight percent in 2000. By 2019, the share of Blacks living in the suburbs had reached eighty-eight percent. The increase in the suburban Black population from 2000 to 2019 actually exceeded the total metropolitan increase slightly because the city saw a decline in its Black population over this period.

Katherine Hankins and Steve Holloway have pointed to several changes in Black suburbanization patterns after 2000, including an increase in the geographic scope and scale of Black suburbs.[3] Black suburbs expanded north of I-20, a traditional boundary between Black and white suburbia, especially to the east of the city, and spread into farther-out areas, especially along major highways. This phenomenon is likely at least partly related to lower housing costs in far-out suburbs, following the well-trod "drive-till-you-qualify" mantra of real estate agents and mortgage lenders. Some of the post-2000 Black suburbs were effectively newly developed suburbs, rather than places that transitioned from white to Black due to white flight.

Map 13 illustrates the spatial concentrations of Black households across the metropolitan area using the 2015–2019 American Community Survey. As of 2017, the midpoint of the survey, there were still many parts of the region where Black residents comprised less than ten percent of residents, despite comprising about one-third of the metro population. These neighborhoods were widespread in the northern suburbs of North Fulton, east Cobb, Cherokee, and Forsyth Counties, as well as in the northern exurban fringe and large parts of Fayette and Coweta counties to the south.

At the same time, substantial parts of the metropolitan area have Black populations above twenty-five and even fifty percent, and these areas have grown substantially since 2000. Majority-Black neighborhoods are in more established Black areas such as the south and southwest sides of the city, south Fulton, south DeKalb, but also in areas that became majority-Black in recent decades, including much of Clayton County, and parts of Douglas, Cobb, and Gwinnett counties. Rockdale and Henry counties also have substantial Black populations, as do

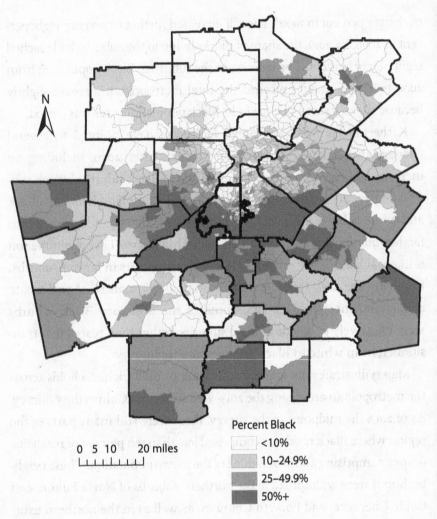

Map 13. Black population, 2017

Data source: American Community Survey 2015–2019 5 year estimates (centered on 2017)

several exurban counties. There are many neighborhoods in the five core counties, including in the large and politically important counties of Cobb and Gwinnett that have seen significant increases in their Black populations. Other research has shown that in the latter 2010s, Black homebuyers were increasingly buying homes in these more diverse, minority-Black neighborhoods.[4]

Comparing tract-level data on Black population share in 2000 and 2017 indicates that the number of majority-Black neighborhoods increased significantly over this period. In 2000, twenty-one percent of the tracts in Map 13 were at least fifty percent Black. This share rose to twenty-seven percent by 2017, due in part to the growing overall metro Black population.[5] Conversely, the number of neighborhoods with less than a ten percent Black population declined by thirty-six percent, from thirty-nine percent to about twenty-five percent. The large growth in the metro Black population led to fewer neighborhoods with very small Black populations. However, many such neighborhoods persist, especially in the northern suburbs. Even in 2017, one out of four neighborhoods in the region remained places where Blacks comprised less than ten percent of the population. And many of these were in the most affluent parts of the region.

The suburbs, as a group, grew more ethnically and racially diverse, especially after 2000, continuing a trend that began in earnest during the last two decades of the twentieth century. By 2019, non-Hispanic whites were a minority of the suburban population, accounting for just over forty-six percent of the population, with Blacks constituting thirty-three percent, Latinx over eleven percent, and Asians over six percent. As shown in Map 14, by 2017, the majority-Latinx neighborhoods were concentrated in central Cobb, northern DeKalb, and eastern Gwinnett along the Buford Highway and northwest I-85 corridors. However, many neighborhoods in different parts of the region had smaller but significant Latinx populations. The share of neighborhoods with a Latinx population of at least twenty-five percent more than doubled over the 2000 to 2017 period, increasing from 4.7 to 10 percent of census tracts. The share of majority-Latinx tracts, while still not large by 2017, almost tripled, from less than 1 percent to 2.5 percent. However, many more neighborhoods had appreciable Latinx populations by 2017. Almost one-third of tracts had a Latinx population of at least ten percent, with ten percent having a Latinx population of at least twenty-five percent.

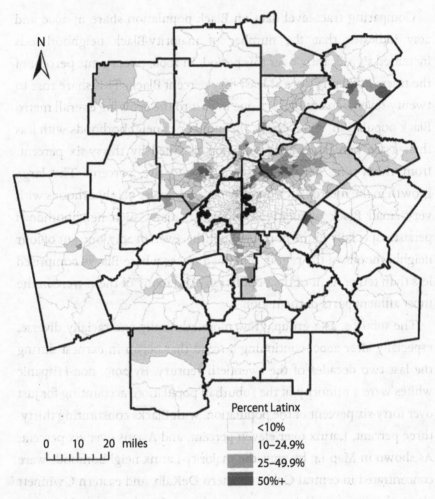

N

Percent Latinx
<10%
10–24.9%
25–49.9%
50%+

0   10   20 miles

Map 14. Latinx and Asian populations in 2017

Data source: American Community Survey 2015–2019 5 year estimates (centered on 2017)

The Asian population was quite spatially concentrated as of 2017. Combined with the growing overall numbers of Asian households, this meant that, by 2017, there were a significant number of neighborhoods where Asians constituted at least twenty-five percent of the population. Map 14 shows that Asian households were especially clustered in northeast Fulton (especially in Johns Creek and Alpharetta), the northern tip of DeKalb, south Forsyth, and in Gwinnett County, especially near and

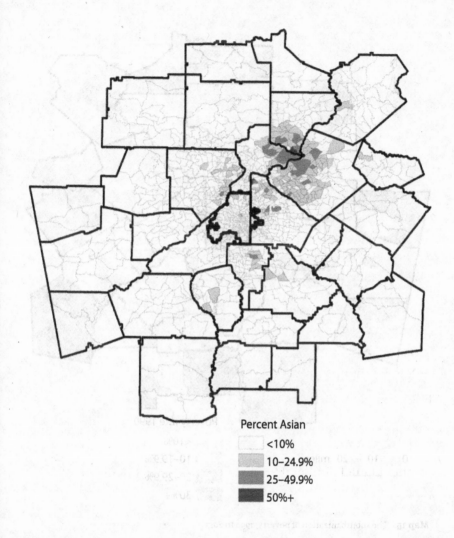

Percent Asian

<10%

10–24.9%

25–49.9%

50%+

north of I-85. In 2000, there were no neighborhoods in the region where Asians comprised more than twenty-five percent of the population. By 2017, thirty-five neighborhoods reached this threshold, with two tracts becoming majority Asian.

As is the case with many metros, the story of the last three decades for poverty in Atlanta has been one largely of increased suburbanization. Atlanta's suburban poverty rate grew from 7.8 percent to 9.7 percent over

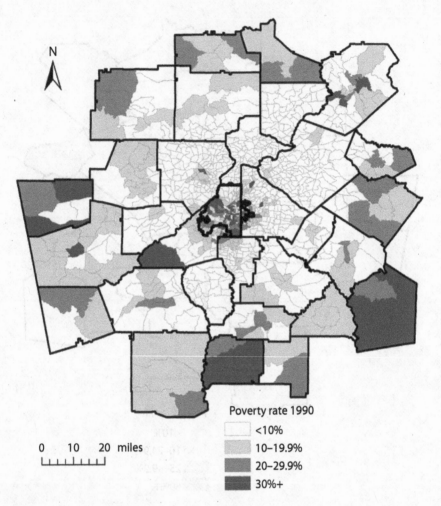

N

Poverty rate 1990

<10%
10–19.9%
20–29.9%
30%+

0   10   20 miles

Map 15. The suburbanization of poverty, 1990 to 2017

Data source: 1990 Decennial Census in 2010 tracts via SocialExplorer.com; American Community Survey, 2015–2019 5-year (centered on 2017)

the 2000 to 2019 period. Moreover, eighty-five percent of poor individuals lived in the suburbs by 2019, up from seventy-five percent in 2000.

Map 15 shows that, while poverty in 1990 was primarily an urban and exurban phenomenon, by 2017, it had also become an entrenched suburban phenomenon. Suburban poverty in 2017 was clustered in certain areas, and many parts of the suburbs continue to have very low poverty rates. In

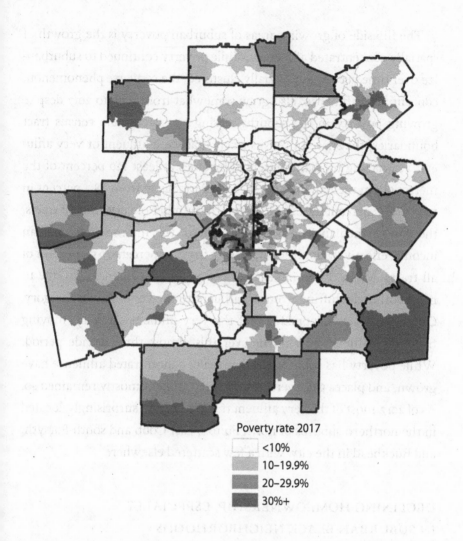

Poverty rate 2017
- <10%
- 10–19.9%
- 20–29.9%
- 30%+

the five core counties, poverty rates are relatively high in a good deal of south-central DeKalb County, Clayton County, Douglas County, central Cobb, and central Gwinnett Counties. As in 1990, 2017 poverty rates were high in many parts of the fringe, exurban counties, some of which remain predominantly rural. Comparing Maps 13, 14, and 15 shows that localized poverty rates in the region have remained highly racialized.

The flip side of growing areas of suburban poverty is the growth of spatially concentrated affluence. While poverty continued to suburbanize over time yet remain spatially clustered, the converse phenomenon, concentrated affluence, also grew somewhat from 1990 to 2017 despite growing poverty in the suburbs.[6] Using consistent 2010 census tract boundaries, the share of census tracts that were affluent or very affluent, i.e., having median household incomes at least 120 percent of the metropolitan median income, increased modestly from 28.2 percent in 1990 to 29.7 percent in 2017. However, the number of very affluent tracts, those with median incomes twice that of the metropolitan median income, effectively doubled, increasing from 2.7 percent to 5.7 percent of all tracts. Much of the increase in concentrated affluence was due to neighborhoods shifting from the affluent to the very affluent category. Only nine tracts dropped out of the very affluent category, moving from very affluent to affluent over this almost three-decade period. While poverty has suburbanized, areas of concentrated affluence have grown, and places that were already very affluent mostly remained so. As of 2017, most of the very affluent tracts were, not surprisingly, located in the northern suburbs of north Fulton, east Cobb and south Forsyth, and Buckhead in the city, with a few scattered elsewhere.

DECLINING HOMEOWNERSHIP, ESPECIALLY IN SUBURBAN BLACK NEIGHBORHOODS

As discussed in Chapter 4, subprime lenders targeted Black neighborhoods in the region during the 2000s, so these communities were hit hardest by the 2007 to 2011 foreclosure crisis. Moreover, Black homebuyers were disproportionately shut out of the mortgage market in the wake of the crisis so that few Black buyers were able to purchase homes when values were very low from 2009 through to about 2014. At the same time, homebuying by investors rose dramatically. One result of all of this was a large transfer of property ownership from Black homeowners to investors. While Black homebuying began to increase significantly in the latter half of the 2010s, the foreclosure crisis widened the Black-white homeownership gap.

Metropolitan Atlanta saw a significant decline in its homeownership rate after the foreclosure crisis, but the decline was more significant among Black households. The Urban Institute has shown that from 2005, before the foreclosure crisis, to 2019, the Black homeownership rate declined by 2.4 percentage points, from 50.6 to 48.2 percent, while the white rate declined by only 1.4 percentage points, from 78.7 to 77.3 percent.[7] The result was that the Black-white homeownership gap widened over this period to reach 29.1 percentage points in 2019.

Neighborhoods with more Black homeowners before the foreclosure crisis saw many of the largest declines in homeownership from 2000 to 2017. Map 16 shows changes in homeownership rates from 2000 to 2017 using 2000 Decennial Census and American Community Survey five-year 2015–2019 data. Declines in homeownership over this period were largest across a sizeable U-shaped swath of the region running from the western suburban Paulding and Douglas counties, southeast through south Fulton and the southwest side of the city, through Clayton and Henry counties to the south, southeast DeKalb and up into Gwinnett County. Some neighborhoods in the favored quarter also saw significant declines in homeownership, especially along expressways and arterials where significant multifamily rental housing was developed during this period. However, many of the reductions in ownership in western, southern, and eastern suburbs were driven by the conversion of single-family homes into rental housing during and after the foreclosure crisis. Many of the neighborhoods experiencing the largest declines in ownership rates were areas with increasing or already larger Black populations, including parts of Douglas, Clayton, Henry, and Gwinnett counties. Many of these same areas—especially working- and middle-class suburban neighborhoods—were

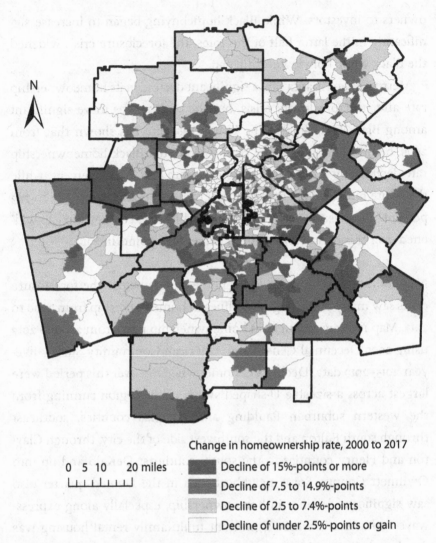

Change in homeownership rate, 2000 to 2017

0   5 10   20 miles

■ Decline of 15%-points or more
■ Decline of 7.5 to 14.9%-points
■ Decline of 2.5 to 7.4%-points
□ Decline of under 2.5%-points or gain

Map 16. Change in the homeownership rate, 2000 to 2017

Data Source: 2000 Decennial Census in 2010 tracts via Social Explorer; American Community Survey 2015–2019 5-year estimates (centered on 2017).

targets of institutional real estate investors who entered the market in 2012 to purchase foreclosed homes and convert them to rental properties, as described in Chapter 4.

In the latter half of the 2010s, Black homebuying began to increase. However, in 2020 as COVID-19 home-price acceleration took hold, more

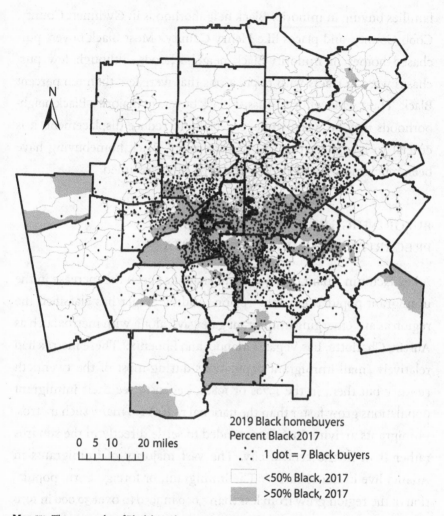

N

0 5 10   20 miles

2019 Black homebuyers
Percent Black 2017
∴ 1 dot = 7 Black buyers

☐ <50% Black, 2017
■ >50% Black, 2017

Map 17. The geography of Black homebuyers in 2019

Data source: Home Mortgage Disclosure Act data. Home purchase loans to owner-occupiers.

rapid increases in home prices began to lock many Black families out of homeownership once again. Before COVID-19, in 2019, Black homebuying in the region, though still disproportionately located in Black neighborhoods, was much more diffuse than it had been in earlier decades. Map 17 illustrates these patterns of Black homebuying, with many Black families buying in minority-Black neighborhoods in Gwinnett County, Cobb County, and places like Henry County.[8] Most Black buyers purchased homes in minority-Black neighborhoods, although few purchases were in tracts with populations that were less than ten percent Black. Thus, while efforts to assist Black buyers in majority-Black neighborhoods may be worthwhile, especially to reduce displacement, it is crucial to recognize that recent patterns of Black homebuying have been much more spatially diverse than is often assumed.

BUFORD HIGHWAY AND THE HOUSING PRECARITY OF IMMIGRANT ATLANTA

A key factor in Atlanta's growing diversity has been the increase in the immigrant population in the region. Audrey Singer has classified the region as an "emerging immigrant gateway," along with metros such as Austin, Charlotte, Las Vegas, Orlando, and Phoenix.[9] These metros had relatively small immigrant populations during most of the twentieth century but then, in the 1970s or 1980s, began to see their immigrant populations grow faster than the national rate. As in many such metros, immigrants arriving in Atlanta tended to settle directly in the suburbs rather than in the central city. The vast majority of immigrants in Atlanta live in the suburbs.[10] The immigrant, or foreign-born, population of the region grew from less than 5,000 in 1950 to over 50,000 in 1970 and then to over 250,000 by 1990, according to estimates that were adjusted for likely census undercounts.[11] The growth of the airport, the 1996 Olympics, and the increased presence of refugee resettlement agencies have been cited as reasons for Atlanta's growth in immigrant populations.[12] By 2019, the immigrant population of metro Atlanta had exceeded 850,000, or more than fourteen percent of the overall population. More than twenty-eight percent of this population had entered the U.S. since 2010, with more than fifty-six percent having arrived since 2000. The origins of Atlanta's immigrants are diverse, with forty-four percent coming from Latin America, thirty-four percent from Asia, and eleven percent from Africa. The leading countries of origin were Mexico (17%), India (11%), Vietnam (5%), Jamaica (5%), and China (4%).

Perhaps no place in the Atlanta region is more emblematic of its growing multiethnic diversity than the area known as Buford Highway. State Route 13 runs about thirty miles from the junction of I-85 and State Route 400 to the city of Buford at the northeastern tip of Gwinnett County. The area surrounding the approximately seven-mile stretch that runs through the suburbs of Brookhaven, Chamblee, and Doraville in northern DeKalb County is what many Atlantans think of as the Buford Highway "area" or "corridor" (see Map 18). It is a place that has dramatically transformed over the last forty-plus years from a quintessential 1970s auto-dominated arterial lined by car dealers and repair shops, nondescript strip malls, and other white working- and middle-class consumer uses, to one of a rich multiethnic mix of restaurants, retail, and service businesses (see Figure 7). As Marian Liou, who founded the We Love Buford Highway organization in 2015, put it, the growth of multiethnic and often immigrant-owned businesses along the corridor has given Buford Highway its "identity and vitality," despite the road being an "unsafe, underdeveloped, and underutilized corridor designed to move cars and trucks."[13] Liou has argued that Buford Highway is central to understanding the evolution of a multiethnic Atlanta, one that has moved beyond a Black-white image of the region. She makes the point that "the image of Atlanta as the birthplace of the civil rights movement is not up to date unless you talk about Buford Highway. That's how it completes our story and it is modernized."[14]

While some have referred to the area as Atlanta's "Chinatown," the term is a poor fit. The area is home to businesses owned by and catering to a wide variety of immigrants and ethnicities. Mexican and Bangladeshi establishments are mixed in with Chinese and Korean ones. Even back in 2002, Susan Walcott found that among just the twenty-six immigrant-owned businesses she interviewed, the owners came from

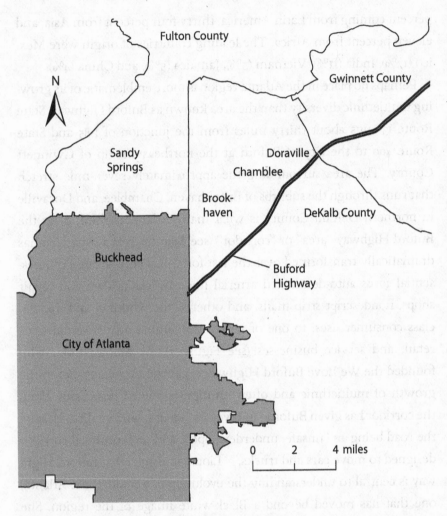

Map 18. The Buford Highway corridor and nearby communities

thirteen different ethnic backgrounds, some immigrating directly from their birth country, while others had moved from California.[15] Recent estimates suggest that the Buford Highway area is home to more than 1,000 immigrant businesses owned by individuals from various ethnic backgrounds and birthplaces.[16]

Brookhaven is the most affluent of the three DeKalb County suburbs through which the Buford Highway corridor runs. As of 2017, its

Figure 7. Along the Buford Highway corridor

median household income was over $93,000 (in 2021 dollars), with a median home value of over $490,000 (again in 2021 dollars), and its homeownership rate was fifty-one percent.[17] Chamblee and Doraville are much less affluent. Chamblee's median household income was about $63,000 (2021 dollars) in 2017, its median home value was $287,000, and its homeownership rate was thirty-seven percent. Doraville had the lowest median income of the three suburbs, at just over $52,000, with a forty-eight percent homeownership rate and a median home value of about $180,000. Chamblee and Doraville, especially, had been viewed as bastions of relatively more affordable housing in the region for some time. However, gentrification and development pressures have been mounting over the last decade.

Doraville and Chamblee are highly diverse suburbs home to many immigrants. Some might call them "ethnoburbs," although Susan Walcott has argued that they do not fit that definition well because they are not home to just one predominant ethnic group.[18] Some have called such places "global neighborhoods."[19] Doraville is a majority-Latinx city, with non-Hispanic whites comprising less than twenty-two percent of the population as of 2017. Asians comprise sixteen percent and Latinx comprise fifty-five percent. Chamblee is also very diverse, with a population that is thirty-seven percent Latinx, eight percent Asian, sixteen percent Black, and thirty-six percent white. Brookhaven is a mostly affluent, majority-white suburb with significant numbers of Latinx (22%), Black (11%), and Asian (6%) residents.

As of 2017, Doraville and Chamblee both had large immigrant populations at forty-six percent and thirty-two percent, respectively, although Chamblee's immigrant share has dropped significantly over time, at least partly because of its major annexations.[20] Brookhaven also has a significant foreign-born population at twenty-two percent. In Doraville and Chamblee, about two-thirds of the immigrant population is comprised of people born in Latin America; Brookhaven's Latin American share is closer to half. Chamblee's largest immigrant groups include those born in Mexico (36%), Guatemala (20%), Ethiopia (7%), Bangladesh (7%), and Honduras (5%). Doraville's largest immigrant groups include those born in Mexico (32%), Guatemala (19%), Vietnam (8%), Bangladesh (8%), China (7%), and El Salvador (6%).

The communities along the Buford Highway corridor face multiple challenges, including traffic, poor walkability, and dangerous conditions for pedestrians and cyclists. Buford Highway has been called the "most dangerous road" in the region.[21] Much of the corridor lacks sidewalks and many residents and workers in the area are dependent on walking, cycling, or public transit. High speeds, a lack of cycling infrastructure, inadequate bus stops, insufficient safe crossings, and frequent curb cuts combine to make travel in the area more hazardous than it should be.

Another major concern is that the area has, especially after 2012, been the locus of strong gentrification and displacement pressures. All three suburbs along the corridor have seen substantial declines in low-cost rental housing. Older apartment buildings, many built before 1990, have been purchased, and the sites redeveloped into new, more expensive rental housing or into townhomes or retail and commercial space.

Comparing the 2014 to the 2019 five-year American Community Survey estimates shows that the number of low-cost rental units (those with rents under $800 per month) declined in all three of the DeKalb County Buford Highway suburbs over this timespan, with each city losing at least half of its low-cost rental stock.[22] Brookhaven lost sixty-one percent of its low-cost units, while Chamblee lost fifty-two percent, and Doraville lost eighty-four percent. Together, these three suburbs saw a net loss of more than 1,900 low-cost rental units over these five years, representing over sixty-two percent of their combined low-cost stock at the beginning of the period. Over the same period, rental units priced at over $2,000 per month more than tripled, from 480 units to more than 1,500.

In June 2016, a group of religious leaders in Brookhaven wrote a letter to the City Council urging it to act on the issue of gentrification and affordable housing in the suburb.[23] As a result, an Affordable Housing Task Force was appointed in September of 2016 and produced a set of recommendations in the summer of 2017. One of the recommendations included considering enacting a mandatory inclusionary zoning ordinance for new higher-density developments. In November of 2018, the city adopted an inclusionary zoning ordinance triggered whenever a special land use permit or rezoning was approved. The rule required that ten percent of the units of such developments be leased at rents affordable to households with incomes less than than eighty percent of the metropolitan median income. However, because many low-income renters in the existing low-cost apartments earn well under this income level, it was unclear to what extent such a measure, by itself, would reduce displacement or provide the sort of affordable housing needed by lower-income residents.

Nonprofits such as the Center for Pan Asian Services, the Latin American Association, We Love Buford Highway, Los Vecinos de Buford Highway (a nonprofit focused on assisting tenants in the corridor), and others have been sounding the alarm about rising rents and redevelopment-induced-displacement for some time. During the later 2010s, the problems appeared to accelerate.[24] Rebekah Cohen-Morris, a cofounder of Los Vecinos, told a journalist in 2019, "We're seeing a lot more people just kind of open their homes and apartments and allow [in] families that lost their homes to it being torn down. We've seen other people start living together, like two or three families in a one, two or three-bedroom unit."[25]

Unfortunately, Buford Highway, or at least its lower-income renters, are the victims of the corridor's success—at least success as measured by new development and real estate values. The area is close to many high-income parts of the region, offers many of the best international dining options in the metro, and has contained a good deal of older, low-cost real estate—especially older apartment buildings ripe for redevelopment and "repositioning" for a different type of tenant or land use. While some planning efforts have focused on anti-displacement and affordability, it's unclear whether these localities have the willingness, or perhaps the wherewithal, to take meaningful steps to preserve lower-cost housing options in their communities. It is also unclear how many of their residents or elected officials feel that they can or should do so. The mayor of Brookhaven stated in a public meeting in 2017 that affordability and displacement along Buford highway were "something I constantly struggle with." At the same time, the mayor admitted that the city's economic development department had developed a pitch to Amazon to locate their new headquarters in the city, a move that, if it had been successful, would likely have acted as a sort of displacement bomb. It is important to note that this was in a mostly affluent suburb, with no threats of economic decline on the horizon.

One might ask whether affordable housing task forces and weak inclusionary zoning ordinances are more than performative measures, initiatives that give the appearance of taking affordability issues seriously rather than doing something more substantive. At the end of the day, will the "success" of Buford Highway come without radically reshaping it? Can the fortunes of the immigrants along Buford High-way and the fortunes of the street itself "both rise together," as Marian Liou has asked?[26]

SECESSION AS RACIAL AND ECONOMIC EXCLUSION

During the first two decades of the twenty-first century, there were two principal responses to the growing suburbanization of poverty and the increasing racial and ethnic diversity in many majority-white suburbs, especially those in the northern favored quarter of the region, bounded mostly by I-75 to the west and I-85 to the east. The first was secession, or "cityhood," involving the legal incorporation of previously unincorporated suburban communities to gain more local control, especially over zoning and policing. By gaining control of local zoning and building codes, newly incorporated cities could discourage affordable rental housing and thus impede the in-movement of lower-income families. The second type of response, which will be discussed below, was the redevelopment of parts of a community that housed many lower-income families, predominantly households of color, to be replaced by higher-cost housing and commercial development.

In Georgia, counties had historically been the dominant local government unit, with most of the metropolitan population living in unincorporated parts of counties. It was no surprise that the first suburban communities to incorporate in the new century were majority-white and affluent. In the twentieth century, the Atlanta metro had not been as municipally fragmented as many older northern metros, such as Pittsburgh, St. Louis, Kansas city, Minneapolis, or Columbus, Ohio.[27] Municipal fragmentation, which can increase local power over zoning, policing, code enforcement, and other regulatory authorities and services, can be a powerful tool to further inter-jurisdictional segregation by both income and race. Outside of a moderate number of older municipalities, however, the Atlanta metro was, before 2005, comprised mostly of larger county governments that handled most local responsibilities. However, things began to change rapidly after 2004, when Republicans had gained control of both legislative chambers and the governor's office.

In the 1960s, city of Atlanta leaders, including former Mayor William Hartsfield, who had successfully annexed much of the northern part of the city, including Buckhead, in 1952, had their eye on Sandy Springs, a predominantly white, affluent community north of Buckhead, as an annexation target. But the suburb fought hard to resist annexation. In 1975, Eva Galambos and other advocates of cityhood formed the Committee for Sandy Springs.[28] Galambos had earned the nickname "the Dragon Lady" from her fights to enforce code enforcement against businesses with signage that she didn't like and to restrict growth in the suburb. The Committee circulated materials that argued that Sandy Springs' residents were being "ripped off" by taxes paid to the county for "Grady Hospital (the main public hospital, located in the city of Atlanta), the courts, welfare, and social and health services."[29]

Opponents of Sandy Springs' incorporation were regularly able to fend off serious action during the rest of the twentieth century. However, after the full Republican takeover of state government in 2004, the city of Sandy Springs was incorporated in 2005. After Sandy Springs broke off, several majority-white suburbs followed, including Milton, Johns Creek, Chattahoochee Hills, Dunwoody, and Brookhaven. All of these, except for Chattahoochee Hills, are in the favored northern quarter.[30] These communities could segregate a substantial portion of their relatively high tax base—Sandy Springs is home to many Fortune 500 companies—from the rest of the county. Galambos became the city's mayor, and fellow incorporation advocate Oliver Porter became city manager. Porter claimed that incorporation had little to do with racial exclusion, but he told researcher Sam Rosen that a principal motivation behind the move was zoning and, in particular, Fulton County's refusal to limit multifamily housing in Sandy Springs to forty percent of all units. "Mainly there was a concern that apartment-dwellers are not as devoted to the community as people who buy homes, pay property taxes, and all . . . Apartments also tend to—and this is not true of all—but tend to have a greater impact on public safety . . . There's more crime—again, because of the transient nobody-knows-who-I-am sort of thing."[31] As Rosen has pointed out, the bulk of Black and Latinx households in the city were renters. If zoning was a key factor in the cityhood push, it is certainly difficult to suggest that the motivations did not involve race. One effect of limiting rental housing is certainly racial exclusion.

The secession movement has not ended. Following the 2020 election, several Cobb County suburbs began making moves towards possible incorporation, including East Cobb, West Cobb, Mableton, and Vinings. In May of 2021, a website promoting the city of "Lost Mountain" in West Cobb argued that "overdevelopment, industrial zoning, and increased high-density housing inevitably lead to declining property values, increased road traffic, reduced green space, and overcrowded schools. Before long, everything we've come to know and love about West Cobb will be transformed."[32] This refrain was reminiscent of the earlier secessionist campaigns of Sandy Springs, Dunwoody, and other suburbs.

The secessions led to new suburban municipalities that could use their newfound zoning and regulatory powers to exclude rental and, especially, affordable housing even more effectively than they had been able to in the past. In 2017, Sandy Springs changed its building code to require apartment buildings over three stories or more than 100,000 square feet to be built with concrete construction, raising multifamily construction costs on the order of twenty-five percent or more for such properties.[33] Even market-rate construction became difficult under such rules. Affordable development became almost impossible because affordable housing developers must work to keep total development costs low to garner scarce, competitive subsidy dollars. According to

HR&A, the consultant that prepared the city's housing needs assessment in 2020, multifamily development of any sort in the city declined from an average pace of 1,000 units permitted per year from 2011 to 2016 to only nineteen units total permitted from 2017 to 2020.[34] The city had adopted a policy to effectively shut down multifamily development, apparently deciding that it had seen enough growth in even high-end apartments.

In late 2018, the city of Dunwoody, an affluent suburb in northern DeKalb County with a population that was about eighty percent white, adopted a six-month moratorium on multifamily construction in the middle of an apartment development boom. This was mainly in response to the state legislature's preempting its ban on wood construction in larger multifamily properties.[35] This occurred after the city had initiated its Affordable Housing Task Force to explore the need for "workforce housing." The task force was controversial, with the mayor and several City Council members opposing its efforts. The mayor condemned the idea of increasing workforce housing development, comparing it to stigmatized housing projects in St. Louis and Chicago. "They are all failures. In St. Louis, they built multistory brick buildings and then bulldozed them all down."[36] One City Council member who supported the task force responded by saying, "This is not public housing! The government is not involved in (workforce housing)."[37] The verbal gymnastics necessary to entertain the possibility of affordable housing even for moderate-income families was on full display. The city had been sued earlier in the decade based on the Fair Housing Act for repeatedly filing code enforcement complaints against older apartment buildings after plans to demolish the buildings to build a park had fallen through, although the suit was eventually dropped.[38]

In the wake of the protests following the murder of George Floyd in 2020, Dunwoody established a "racial dialog" to address issues of racial inequities in the suburb. During a forum in the fall, the mayor, who had been one of the City Council members to advocate for workforce housing in 2018, objected to the notion that race was involved in the suburb's move to incorporate in 2008. A City Council member claimed that race "had nothing to do with anything when it comes to (incorporation) . . . It was about efficiency of taxes and that we could do the services better. End of story."[39] At the same forum, the mayor claimed that motivations for incorporation included gaining control of policing and zoning, hardly topics devoid of racial implications. The mayor stated, "The development that DeKalb was allowing was consistently a five-story apartment complex all over."[40] A key point of context here was that the incorporation effectively wrested control of zoning and policing activities away from a county governed by Black leadership.

In late 2020, the secession issue moved into the city of Atlanta proper. With crime, including some high-profile shootings, rising in some parts of predominantly white, affluent Buckhead area, talk of secession from the city arose. This was not the first time such talk had occurred, but this time the threat of secession appeared more serious. Proposals to allow ADUs and for modest levels of increased density in the area also helped to fuel the secessionist clamor. A group calling itself the Buckhead Exploratory Committee wrote in an *AJC* op-ed that "new zoning laws currently being forced by the city of Atlanta's leadership targeting Buckhead will negatively impact the overall quality of life and sense of community."[41]

Buckhead includes a large amount of high-value residential and commercial properties, including many single-family homes valued at well over $1 million, as well as large office buildings, shopping malls, restaurants, and high-rise luxury apartment buildings. Breaking off from the city of Atlanta would have a severe and devastating impact on the city's tax base, which, as discussed earlier, is already suffering from significant public finance dysfunction. A consultant to a group opposing Buckhead secession, the Committee for a United Atlanta, estimated that Buckhead separating from Atlanta would cost city government $252 million in revenue, about thirty-eight percent of the city's total local revenues, while saving the city somewhere between $135 million and $172 million, for a net annual loss to the city of between $80 and $116 million.[42] These figures do not include revenue or expenses related to public schools, which would likely fall into the domain of Fulton County Public Schools if secession were to occur.

Later, in 2021, the secession initiative appeared to gain steam, but with relatively little support from state legislators who served Buckhead. Rather, political support seemed to come from outside the city, including Republican state legislators from the northern suburbs.[43] Moreover, the lead organizer of the "Buckhead City Committee," as the key group advocating for secession came to be called, was a relatively recent resident of the city, having moved to Atlanta and Buckhead only in 2018. Bill White was a former fundraiser for Hilary Clinton who switched sides after Clinton's loss and raised millions for the 2020 Trump campaign. As of October 2021, White's group had raised almost $1 million for the secession campaign.

Besides the fiscal impact on the city, the breaking away of Buckhead would return the city, at least for a while, to majority-Black status. Buckhead's population of about 90,000, a bit under one-fifth of the city at this point, has a median household income of about $140,000, more than double that of the rest of the city, and the area is about three-quarters white.[44] Given its significant concentration of office and retail space, Buckhead would also constitute a new source of competition for jobs and tax base for the city of Atlanta.

As of this writing, it is difficult to say how likely the loss of Buckhead is. The process requires a legislative vote and gubernatorial approval to put a referendum on the ballot. Secession advocates hope these will occur in 2022. The current governor has not indicated whether he would support such a move. Still, it seems likely he would since Buckhead is the one bastion of Republican voters in the city of Atlanta, and he will be running for reelection in 2022 in what is expected to be a close race. In what strikes many observers as unfair, only voters in

Buckhead itself will have an opportunity to vote in the referendum, should it occur, despite the severe financial ramifications this would have for the entire city. The *AJC* conducted a poll in which fifty-four percent of Buckhead residents indicated support for cityhood. However, there would be at least a year and lots of politicking left before the earliest possible vote in November 2022.[45]

DISPLACE-AND-REPLACE SUBURBAN REDEVELOPMENT

The second type of response by some suburbs to the suburbanization of poverty and growing diversity was the planned physical displacement of lower-income, Latinx and Black families through the redevelopment of older, lower-cost rental housing. Incorporation gave the new cities greater local control of development finance (floating development bonds, creating tax increment financing districts, etc.) and planning, which enabled local officials to promise homeowner associations and real estate interests new abilities to engage in twenty-first century suburbanized slum clearance projects that would reduce the numbers of poor residents in their cities and schools. These projects were reminiscent of federally funded urban renewal programs employed in postwar cities, except this time funded by new sorts of locally funded, but state and federally enabled and sometimes subsidized, development finance tools. The targets of such development were often "tired" or "dated" suburban strips populated with many older apartment buildings that housed lower-income, Latinx and Black families.

These two responses to growing metropolitan diversity and the suburbanization of poverty—increased exclusionary zoning and building codes facilitated by secession and displace-and-replace redevelopment— were not mutually exclusive. Affluent suburbs used them to practice racial and economic exclusion and displacement simultaneously, to stem the inflow of lower-income families while simultaneously hastening the exodus of such families out of their communities.

Combined with the growing exclusion of lower-income families of color from the city of Atlanta, these practices resulted in such households also being excluded from more-affluent suburbs such as Sandy Springs. Unlike some other affluent suburbs that had obtained control of local zoning much earlier and so were able to exclude multifamily rental development more effectively in the latter decades of the twentieth century, Sandy Springs had a substantial stock of multifamily housing by 2000, much of it built before 1990, mainly clustered along major arterials such as Roswell Road. In fact, Fulton County's refusal to limit multifamily housing to forty percent of Sandy Springs' housing stock was cited by incorporation advocates as a major reason to form the new municipality. Due in part to the construction of apartment buildings, the locality's homeownership rate had dropped from fifty-seven percent to below forty-six percent from 1980 to 2000, while the median home value remained among the highest in the region.

Sandy Springs' redevelopment efforts took off after the foreclosure crisis, when capital began flowing rapidly again into real estate markets, especially into multifamily residential and mixed-use developments. The city focused on two major projects, City Springs and Sandy Springs Gateway, both near the major north-south arterial, Roswell Road, around which many older apartment buildings were clustered. In 2012, the Sandy Springs City Council approved a plan to develop an area near the suburb's center into City Springs. This would be the site of a new city hall and performing arts center and a place that city leaders would refer to as "everybody's neighborhood," a gathering place for residents from all segments of the city's diverse population. Mayor Rusty Paul described it as a "place to be a community" and "care about each other."[46] The project was funded by almost $230 million in local bonds.

The Gateway project, at the southern end of the suburb as it meets Atlanta's northern border, involved the Sandy Springs Development Authority issuing $100 million in bonds in 2014 to fund a twenty-one-acre mixed-use redevelopment. Mayor Paul told the local paper that "people want a more integrated lifestyle—one where they can work, live, eat out and shop all within proximity to one another."[47] Real estate websites portrayed the project as demolishing "outdated" rental buildings to replace them with "first-rate" apartment living and commercial properties.[48]

The Gateway redevelopment involved the demolition of four apartment buildings that included almost 1,100 rental units, displacing an estimated 3,000 or more residents, over eighty percent of whom were estimated to be Latinx or Black.[49] These apartments housed many lower-income families with children. The demolitions were tied to sharp decreases in enrollment and reductions in staff at local elementary schools, including enrollment declines of as much as thirty-four and forty-one percent in two schools.[50]

Like many Atlanta suburbs, Sandy Springs had become somewhat more diverse since the 1970s. The non-Hispanic white share of the population had dropped from over ninety-six percent in 1980 to seventy-three percent by 2000, with renters accounting for over eighty-six percent of the town's Black and Latinx population.[51] Non-whites comprised forty-six percent of the renter population in 2000, compared to just over seven percent of the homeowner population. With large single-family lots and high home values dominating the owner-occupied stock, the city was increasingly polarized both racially and economically. Despite renters accounting for about half of the population, wealthier homeowners and real estate interests maintained political power, especially when it came to development decisions.

But Sandy Springs did not reject renters of all stripes, at least not until 2017, when it adopted a more exclusionary building code. The suburb not only engaged in publicly financed redevelopment projects that demolished lower-cost rental housing, displacing their tenants, it also welcomed new, much more expensive apartment buildings. In the redevelopment area, the apartment replacement ratio was about one for one, with almost 1,200 multifamily units replacing the roughly 1,100 lost to demolition from 2010 to 2020, according to the city's housing needs assessment performed by the real estate consultant HR&A.[52] However, from 2012 to 2018, the city saw a decline of over 1,700 apartments priced at rents affordable to families earning below eighty percent of the region's median income, and rents increased faster than incomes for residents with less than a college education.

The replacement of older, more affordable apartments with new, more expensive ones was a classic example of displace-and-replace suburban redevelopment. The overall decline in more-affordably priced apartments was almost precisely the same as the decline of approximately 1,800 households in the city earning less than $50,000. By the end of the decade, Sandy Springs faced a deficit of more than 5,000 rental housing units affordable to renters earning less than fifty percent of the area median income. This was despite the fact that, in 2014, Mayor Paul told researcher Elisa Lanari that "there is a lot of nervousness about (affordable housing) . . . but that's not an issue today. In fact, we have an overabundance of low-income housing in this city."[53] Apparently, the city's own housing consultant, HR&A, did not agree, at least by the end of the decade.

Sandy Springs was far from the only Atlanta suburb engaging in a displace-and-replace redevelopment strategy in the face of suburbanizing poverty and changing racial dynamics. Other suburbs, many of them located in the affluent favored quarter, engaged in redevelopment projects that involved the demolition of older apartment buildings and redevelopment into mixed-use projects involving higher-end residential and commercial space. Scott Markley has estimated that over 9,000 people living in apartments were displaced by redevelopment projects in the suburbs of Marietta, Smyrna, Roswell, Sandy Springs, and Brookhaven from 2010 to 2017.[54] He estimated that Latinx families comprised almost sixty percent of the displaced population despite accounting for about one-third of the renter population in these areas. In these five suburbs, Markley estimated that ten percent of

Latinx renters lived in apartment buildings in 2010 that would be demolished by 2017, a remarkable statistic of physical displacement and exclusion.

The city of Marietta, which falls just outside the favored quarter, lying just southwest of I-75, about twenty miles to the northwest of downtown Atlanta, received perhaps the most media attention for its publicly financed displace-and-replace efforts. This is partly due to the language used by the political leaders and advocates for the redevelopment. In 2013, the city proposed a $68 million bond to redevelop the 1.2-mile Franklin Road corridor, home to older apartment buildings and retail and a significant Black and Latinx population. Community leaders stigmatized the road for being a high-crime area. Even U.S. Senator Johnny Isakson was quoted by the *Marietta Daily Journal* as saying, "I go by Franklin Road as fast as I can every day."[55] Two local politicos active in Republican Cobb County politics, including a former chief of staff of Senator Isakson, formed an advocacy group, Revitalize Marietta, to push for the redevelopment scheme and the bond.[56] Voters approved the bond in November of 2013.

After the approval, the Cobb County chairman said that the project would help "improve the conditions of the Marietta school system."[57] Senator Isakson's former chief of staff told the *Marietta Daily Journal* that ". . . we see communities that ignore problems and eventually suffer the loss of identity and the loss of economic activity and the loss of the middle class, and we saw that happening in Marietta. When bad government policies create high concentrations of slum-like housing, it takes the government to step in and to help fix the problem."[58] Some in the community saw racism in the plans. One resident told the paper, "They want to eliminate the poor people on Franklin Road . . . It's blatant discrimination against the school children who live over there."[59] Marietta's mayor's language as the buildings were demolished seemed to support this view. He told the local paper in 2015 as the buildings were demolished that "It's almost like a dream. It's almost like it's 1970 again."[60] The mayor blamed the area's problems on federal fair housing policy that protected families with children from housing discrimination, arguing that the 1988 expansion to the Fair Housing Act was the reason for the area's deterioration. "Without children, you had less problems. And with the change in the law, the apartments began to slide."[61] The mayor attempted to finish off his erasure of the Franklin Road stigma by renaming the street "Gateway," but at least one local community organization objected, and the City Council settled on a compromise, renaming the street "Franklin Gateway" in 2016.[62]

These suburban displace-and-replace projects were driven by logics that combined the exclusion of the poor and near-poor with a reimagining of the city populated by an increasingly affluent population, one attracted to a denser, more walkable suburb, and a "live, work, play" identity. This involved not just new, higher-rent residential development but the sorts of retail and commercial development that would be supported by such residents, which in turn is intended to support the publicly financed debt that enables the redevelopment in the first place. New development was valued over renovating older apartment buildings that serve the needs of existing lower-income residents.

One commonality to many of these redevelopment schemes are New Urbanist design principles and rhetoric that promote remaking the traditional car-centric and strip-mall-oriented fabric of the suburbs with mixed-use, walkable development where people can walk to shopping, restaurants, and possibly even their jobs. New Urbanism advocates tout the compact form as supporting environmental sustainability, but it has been criticized for not always providing for racial or income diversity, affordability, or social sustainability. Research on suburban Atlanta from 2000 to 2013 suggests that New Urbanist developments have resulted in declining racial diversity, and in particular, declining Latinx populations and increasing white populations in neighborhoods where they are developed.[63] Indeed, for environmental sustainability purposes, compact development, especially if connected to public transportation, is a laudable goal. However, such developments appear to require—and perhaps are sometimes even aimed at—displacing lower-income residents of color, precisely the residents most likely to use public transit and walk to shopping and work.

Public finance and the private profits enabled via publicly financed projects are inextricably implicated in these redevelopment schemes. Investors in the bonds financing these projects expect tax revenues to increase to allow local governments to absorb their new debt service obligations. Investors and bond underwriters expect the locality to do what is necessary, both before and after the development, to ensure an increased property tax base.[64] This can mean working towards ends that will promote higher rents, higher home prices, and exclusion. Just as the city of Atlanta's scheme to finance the Beltline through a TAD, itself premised on rising land values, created conflicts with promoting housing affordability and working against displacement, so too have many suburban redevelopment schemes.

The case of Marietta provided perhaps the most vivid illustration of bringing state power to add value to the redevelopment process. The suburb's mayor described one of the city's roles as the physical displacer of existing, lower-income renters on Franklin Road, so developers did not have to get their fingers dirty in such affairs. He told the *Marietta Daily Journal* that a "good developer can buy land still in metropolitan Atlanta and not have to worry about what to do with 400 families. We basically took that step out to do it."[65] Suburban governments, like the city of Atlanta counterpart in HOPE VI redevelopments, can "clear the way" for the revaluing of property once lower-income residents, and their perceived stigmas, are expelled from the area.

Two key aspects of suburban governments' displace-and-replace actions were the relative lack of visibility of these actions in the broader metropolitan media and the scarcity of affordable housing advocates active in the suburbs. Major Atlanta media, including the *AJC* and public radio, spent much more time covering development and affordable housing issues in the city than in the suburbs, even though the bulk of the region's population and a majority of low-income renters live in suburban communities. Media attention to most suburban development initiatives was usually limited to local, suburban newspapers. Many nonprofit affordable housing providers and the small number of affordable housing advocates tended to focus disproportionately on issues concerning the city of Atlanta. As a result, advocacy on behalf of lower-income renters and homeowners was often even more limited in the suburbs than in the city proper. As the suburbs continue to diversify and poverty suburbanizes, there appears to be some progress towards more advocacy in the suburbs. Groups like the Coalition for a Diverse DeKalb in DeKalb County, the Coalition for a Diverse Decatur in the inner, eastern suburb of Decatur, and Sandy Springs Together in Sandy Springs, all sprouted up in the last decade. However, regionally, funding for affordable housing advocacy is scarce, and many advocacy efforts that do receive funding remain focused primarily on the city of Atlanta. Geographically expanded advocacy efforts are going to be critical not only to bring about local change and support for affordable housing but also to build a broader coalition that can speak to a larger and more geographically diverse set of state legislators to advocate for tenants' rights, affordable housing, and other issues at the state level.

Sandy Springs once again provides an example, this time of growing local advocacy for affordable housing and lower-income tenants, and resistance to the planned displacement and exclusion in which suburban local governments often engage. In April 2017, the city held a public event to meet its community development block grant requirements.[66] Only a small number of lower-income residents could attend the meeting, but they complained about the worsening affordable housing problem in the city. This event took place in the wake of the city-sponsored demolition of over a thousand lower-cost rental units. Given the traditional lack of housing groups in Sandy Springs, nonprofit social service providers who work with low-income renters began acting as advocates for affordable housing. The director of a local social service agency argued that the city needed to provide deeper subsidies for lower-income families and not focus solely on "workforce" or middle-income housing.[67] The director warned of an "exodus" of thousands of lower-income residents, a trend that had already begun in the wake of the demolitions.

In 2015, a group of Sandy Springs residents concerned about the displacement of lower-income families from the suburb began meeting to address the need for affordable housing.[68] Led by local philanthropists, Melanie Noble-Couchman and David Couchman, the group explored policies and practices adopted in other places and presented their findings to the mayor and City Council in July 2017, where the Couchmans requested that the city appoint an affordable housing task force.

Rather than forming an affordable housing task force, in March 2018, the city formed the North End Revitalization Task Force to consider the future of a four-square-mile North End Revitalization Area, which contained four shopping centers as well as a substantial amount of older, lower-cost multifamily rental housing. The mayor asked the Couchmans to co-chair the Task Force, led by a chair who was a City Council member. The Task Force included fourteen members, nine of whom were involved in the real estate industry but did not include any residents of the threatened apartment buildings or any people of color.[69] The Task Force met eight times over six months. Two of the meetings were open to the public. Hundreds of residents, including renters and homeowners, attended the first public meeting, vocalizing a wide variety of opinions, including many arguing for providing for economically inclusive redevelopment. In the second public meeting, however, input was allowed only through participants being allowed to place colored dots next to their issues or concerns, which created significant frustration among participants. The Task Force's final report was published with a general consensus on five of six initiatives, including support for a community center and a "greenline trail," although concerns were raised over the displacement that might accompany some of these five initiatives. There was more significant disagreement over a critical first recommendation that called for a major, initial redevelopment initiative.

The majority's Task Force recommendations included a sixty- to eighty-acre "catalyst project" that would involve the demolition of 1,200 lower-cost apartments. The replacement housing would include only owner-occupied housing priced from almost $300,000 to as much as $1.5 million. This initiative's two key advocates were partners at two different real estate development firms, North American Properties and S.J. Collins.[70] When the affordable housing proponents on the committee argued for preserving, and renovating when needed, the existing rental housing, these two Task Force members pushed back, with one arguing, "We are not the North End Task Force of Preservation. We hope it is new."[71] In response to concerns that the development would lead to rising housing costs, this same developer argued that "after the spark, then you can govern the change."[72] Given the state preemption of rent control in Georgia and the failure of the city of Atlanta to address the spillover gentrification associated with large redevelopment projects like the Beltline, the argument that the city could in fact "govern the change" after the redevelopment seemed more than dubious.

Three committee members, including the Couchmans and an affordable housing expert, objected to this key first initiative in the Task Force report. They insisted on an appendix that detailed their problems with the initiative and offered their own alternative proposals. The appendix included recommendations that the city conduct a housing needs assessment and that it consider using an underutilized shopping center and an industrial park as a location for affordable housing.

The Couchmans criticized the North End plan as one "essentially replacing our essential workers for a more affluent worker and disrupting the socioeconomic and racial diversity of the area."[73] They added that the composition of the Task Force was a "clear indication, from the beginning, where this process was headed."[74] Within a few months of the plan's publication, in early 2019, the Couchmans launched Sandy Springs Together to oppose the redevelopment plan as produced by the developers on the Task Force. The city, however, proceeded with the formal planning process for the redevelopment, including hiring architectural and financial consultants and beginning a community engagement process, including forming a "North End Revitalization Committee." By the fall of 2020, members of the committee were pushing the project towards a greater amount of single-family development in the plans and away from schemes calling for tall apartment buildings. One comment complained, "more apartments, there are more than enough in Sandy Springs, let alone in the North End . . . Adding more apartments will only decrease our property values and not help to improve our schools."[75] The Couchmans and Sandy Springs Together continue to advocate for affordable housing in the redevelopment and the city more broadly.

The stories of displacement and the loss of affordable housing in suburban spaces such as Sandy Springs and Buford Highway speak to the growing need for metropolitan and statewide organizing around affordable housing, tenants' rights, and local development policies. While low-income families increasingly reside in suburban communities, they have not gained comparable political power. Many housing advocates in the region have remained focused primarily on city of Atlanta housing, zoning, and related policies, even though a large majority of low-income households now live in the suburbs. Some of this is due to historical inertia, as affordable housing issues have been a significant focus of contention and debate in the city proper since at least the middle part of the twentieth century. The concentration of the early public housing programs in the city, low suburban poverty rates, and the political polarization between city and suburb account for much of this historical legacy. The fact that the regional media, including the *AJC* and public radio stations, focus much more on the city is also a contributing factor.

Another factor has been that a critical locus of affordable housing attention at a regional basis has been the Atlanta Regional Commission's "Regional Housing Forum" and related ARC regional housing task forces and advisory committees. While ARC has done significant work in generating data and analyses on housing issues and convening periodic regional housing forum events, the agency is a politically cautious, quasi-governmental regional planning organization. It is not an affordable housing advocacy organization that engages in lobbying or even proposing policies that advance things like tenants' rights, public spending for affordable housing, or other needed changes in state and local policies. ARC's leadership is generally dominated by suburban government officials and corporate leaders, including those from the real estate industry. At the time of this writing, the chair since 2014 was a partner with a major real estate developer, Pope and Land. Before him, it was someone who now leads a business improvement district, and before that a well-known Republican politician from Cobb County. According to journalist Maria Saporta, ARC has had only one non-white chair—in the late 1980s—and no female chairs in its fifty-year history.[76]

Without more robust and broader regional and statewide coalitions focused on affordable housing, tenants' rights and protections, fair housing, and related issues, these topics are unlikely to rise to the top of the agendas of suburban officials, state legislators, and governors. Even Democratic legislators have rarely prioritized these issues. Optimistically, it is possible that wider, fundamental political change in the state legislature and the governor's office could alter this situation, as lawmakers sympathetic to these issues would likely see such policy initiatives becoming more politically viable.

Over the last three decades, the Atlanta suburbs have become increasingly diverse, both racially and economically. Many suburbs have seen larger nonwhite and larger low- and moderate-income populations. At the same time, many more affluent and whiter suburbs, especially those located in the favored quarter, have pushed back against the growing diversity they have seen within and near their borders. Wealthier homeowners and local politicians have sought increased ability to exclude via secession and the greater zoning and policing powers it brings. They have also actively worked with developers and others to subsidize the redevelopment of parts of their communities that house lower-income, Black and Latinx households, predominantly renters, resulting in large-scale displacement and exclusion. The city of Atlanta is not the only part of the metro where racial and economic exclusion has been planned and subsidized. This is a larger phenomenon that includes similar sorts of large "place-making" projects aimed ostensibly at maintaining or improving a community's tax base, but that also work to exclude many current and future nonwhite, lower-income families. This is not a process of some unfettered market, or the result purely of traditional exclusionary zoning, although both "markets" and exclusionary zoning play a role. Rather, this trajectory has relied upon the use of public redevelopment power and finance to resist the encroachment of a more diverse region. Instead of this path, policymakers and planners could choose to embrace racial and economic diversity head-on. They could use public resources and planning power to rehabilitate older apartment buildings for the residents who live in them, rather than redevelop them for a new, wealthier, and whiter residential base.

This chapter also points to the particular challenges of organizing against exclusion and in favor of affordable, fair, and stable housing in suburban communities. Resources and activism in these arenas, limited as they are, remain focused heavily on the city of Atlanta. Yet, more than ever, a large majority of lower-income, Black, and Latinx households, including renters, live in the suburbs. Moreover, state government resources and regulatory power are needed, both in the suburbs and in the city, to provide more affordable and stable housing and reduce exclusion. To achieve these resources and power, political change at the state level will be critical.

CONCLUSION

THE ATLANTA REGION HAS GONE through tremendous changes since the 1990s, both in the central city and throughout the suburbs. It has pivoted from a region where the core city was often perceived, especially by suburbanites and outsiders, as declining, losing population, and plagued with concentrated poverty and urban "dysfunction" to one in which the city is clearly gentrifying, a desired point of location for technology firms, and a place where buying a home is becoming increasingly difficult for middle-income families. The Atlanta suburbs, not at all a monolithic group, have transformed from being viewed as, at least north of Interstate 20, predominantly places of whiteness and conservative Republican politics, into a much more difficult-to-describe landscape of variegated localities, some more racially and economically diverse than others, some more tolerant than others, and some more politically contested than others. While most suburban communities are more diverse than they were twenty-five years ago, and especially forty or fifty years ago, any notion that racial and economic diversity is welcome everywhere is sorely misguided. In many majority-white suburbs, increasing diversity has been met with strong and often successful attempts to exclude and sometimes even remove lower-income, often nonwhite families. Poverty remains disproportionately constrained to certain parts of the region. Some communities have managed to keep their poverty rates and Black populations below ten percent, well below that of many nearby communities and the region as a whole. Many of these suburbs have worked hard to remain majority-white and mostly affluent. There are also suburbs that are more racially and ethnically diverse but still quite exclusionary by class.

RACIAL AND ECONOMIC EXCLUSION IN
THE FACE OF GROWING REGIONAL DIVERSITY

The city of Atlanta underwent a fundamental change in its demographic trajectory during the 1990s that continued and accelerated in later decades, especially in the 2010s. The city has become more affluent and less Black, with many relatively high-paid college-educated in-movers in recent years, putting enormous stress on the city's housing costs and land values. Widespread, racialized gentrification in the city began in earnest in the 1990s, continued in the 2000s, and then surged after the foreclosure crisis.

Nationally, gentrification in the wake of the housing crisis was not isolated to a few large coastal cities, as the national media and some observers often suggest, but occurred in a good number of central cities in metropolitan areas experiencing job growth, especially in the south and southwest. This does not mean that sprawl hasn't also continued; it certainly has in Atlanta and many other metros. The two are not mutually exclusive phenomena, especially in growing regions. This most recent wave of gentrification has been called "fifth wave gentrification" by some scholars.[1] It has been enabled and facilitated by high-wage job growth spreading beyond traditional "superstar" cities and by the rush of global capital pouring into real estate markets after the global financial crisis.

The data discussed in Chapter 3 demonstrate the degree of gentrification in the city of Atlanta since 1990, and especially since 2012. The population grew from under 400,000 in 1990 to about 500,000 by 2019. Most of this growth occurred after 2012 as real estate markets recovered and the construction of multifamily apartments in the city boomed, with more than 30,000 apartments permitted in just six years from 2013 through 2018.[2] Many of these rental units were added in the traditional multifamily corridors in Midtown and Buckhead but also in formerly poorer parts of the city, including near the Beltline. In inflation-adjusted 2021 dollars, the city's median family income almost doubled, from just over $50,000 in 1990 to over $96,000 by 2019, while the family poverty rate in the city dropped by thirty-seven percent over this period, from 24.7 percent to 15.5 percent. The share of adults in the city with a college education went from just over one out of four to more than one of two. A key statistic is the ratio of the city's median family income to that of the larger metropolitan area. In 1990 this ratio was only 0.60. By 2007 it had increased to 0.85 and held steady across the foreclosure crisis and the Great Recession, so that it was 0.87 in 2012. But over the next seven years, this ratio increased to 1.10, an increase of more than twenty-six percent over only seven years. The city had gone from being significantly lower income than its suburbs to being substantially higher income. All signs are that these trends will continue.[3]

The data above could be viewed as primarily good news by some city boosters and civic leaders. Indeed, many of the trends of the seventies and eighties in the central city were problematic. But the gentrification of the city has brought substantial social and economic costs, especially to lower-income families and households of color. Over the 1990 to 2019 period, the number of families below the poverty line in the city fell by almost thirty percent. After 2012, the gentrification trends that had begun during the 1990s accelerated, fracturing social networks and displacing residents. Rents and housing prices increased sharply. From 2010 to 2019, the city lost over 7,000 low-cost rental units, while housing prices skyrocketed, especially in lower-income neighborhoods on the south, southwest, and west sides, making the city increasingly unaffordable for lower-income families.[4] Critically, from 2012 to 2019, the city shifted from being a majority-Black to a majority-non-Black city. Over the longer three-decade period, the city had gone from being two-thirds Black in 1990 to less than half-Black by 2019, with the trends pointing to an even smaller Black share in the future.

The city was not the only locus of significant change over the last couple of decades. The metro's population had grown by almost fifty percent from 2000 to 2019, with the great bulk of that growth occurring in the suburbs.[5] The metro went from being a majority-white one in 2000 to a majority-nonwhite one in 2019, with non-Hispanic whites accounting for forty-six percent of the population. While Latinx and Asian populations grew at the fastest percentage rates, Black households comprised the single-largest share of the region's growth, accounting for almost one out of two net new residents. Latinx and Asian households, combined, accounted for another one out of three net new residents. Atlanta has established itself as a multiethnic region.

While most Black households had already lived in the suburbs by 1990, the share increased from sixty percent to eighty-eight percent by 2019. Only about one out of eight Blacks lived in the city by 2019. Majority-Black suburban neighborhoods, which had traditionally been constrained to the south of I-20, moved north of the expressway into Douglas County, South Cobb, and South Gwinnett. By 2017, twenty-seven percent of census tracts in the region were majority-Black. Despite the spread of Black suburbs and the overall growth of the Black population in the region, many suburban communities continued to house few Black families. As of 2017, one out of four neighborhoods in the region were less than ten percent Black, despite Black people accounting for over one-third of the region's population. Many of these neighborhoods were located in northern suburbs of North Fulton, East Cobb, Cherokee, and Forsyth counties, as well as in some other communities scattered around the region.

The vast majority of Latinx and Asian households live in the suburbs. The growing Latinx population resulted in more neighborhoods that were at least twenty-five percent Latinx. These neighborhoods more than doubled from 2000 to 2017, reaching one out of ten census tracts. The number of majority-Latinx tracts, while still modest, also increased. There were no neighborhoods with Asian populations of at least twenty-five percent in 1990, but the number grew to thirty-five by 2017. Many of these were located in northern and northwest suburbs in North Fulton, North DeKalb, South Forsyth, and North Gwinnett.

While suburban poverty is not a new phenomenon, it has been increasing in Atlanta. The suburban poverty rate grew from 7.8 percent to 9.7 percent from 2000 to 2019. Moreover, eighty-five percent of poor individuals lived in the suburbs by 2019, up from seventy-five percent in 2000. Higher poverty suburban neighborhoods are disproportionately concentrated in parts of south-central DeKalb County, Clayton County, Douglas County, central Cobb, and central Gwinnett Counties, and many parts of fringe, exurban counties.

The region's homeownership rate fell from 2000 to 2019 but fell disproportionately among Black households and neighborhoods with larger and newer Black populations due to the foreclosure crisis and the region's uneven recovery. Homeownership rates dropped from 2000 to 2017 across a large U-shaped ribbon running from western suburban Paulding and Douglas counties, southeast through south Fulton and the southwest side of the city, through Clayton and Henry counties to the south, through southeast DeKalb, and then up into Gwinnett County. Many of these neighborhoods were areas with increasing or already large Black populations.

POINTS OF INFLECTION: MISSED OPPORTUNITIES TO REDUCE RACIAL AND ECONOMIC EXCLUSION

The city and the region have faced various inflection points over the last thirty years, periods during which they were at the cusp of change and had critical opportunities to affect the nature and trajectory of future growth and development. Too often, policy and planning choices facilitated, fostered, and subsidized development patterns that prioritized the interests of landowners, capital, and more-affluent households. These choices fostered a heavily racialized exclusion of lower-income families rather than more inclusive development that would allow such households to participate in and benefit from local growth.

In the city of Atlanta, the first point of inflection, chronicled in Chapter 1, was the 1990s and early 2000s during and after the 1996 Olympics. After more than two decades of growing poverty and inequality, the Atlanta urban regime viewed the Olympics as a key opportunity to reinvent the city. The regime reimagined Atlanta as a "world-class" city that could attract a whiter, more affluent residential base and the commercial development expected to accompany that population. As the Olympics were ending, Mayor Campbell and CODA created the Atlanta Renaissance program chaired by the head of Coca-Cola, one of the stalwart members of the traditional regime. The Renaissance program retained the services of McKinsey to do their research and generate policy options. The group settled primarily on a goal of attracting more middle-income residents to move into the city, with less attention to what this would mean for the housing costs and options faced by lower-income Atlantans. The city's preparation for the Olympics and its continued reimagining afterward unleashed the urban regime's long-held desires to redevelop public housing in the city. Going back to at least the 1970s, corporate leaders with real estate assets and workers located near projects like Techwood Homes floated various proposals to get rid of public housing developments. But the Olympics, together with the advent of the federal HOPE VI program, provided the perfect opportunity to begin the "transformation" of public housing in the city. Without serious efforts to replace most of the demolished low-income units, the demolition of these stigmatized properties helped clear the way for new, higher-end housing developments in key locations. Moreover, by removing public housing, land in nearby neighborhoods became more valuable and primed for development. Far from being seen as problematic and possibly leading to increased displacement and exclusion of lower-income Black families, such broader neighborhood transformations seemed precisely the goal.

During the 1990s and early 2000s, little effort was made to develop new deeply affordable housing in the city that would provide a substantial, long-term base of housing stability to lower-income residents. Moreover, no provisions were made to address the rising rents or property taxes that would be precipitated in surrounding neighborhoods by mixed-income housing projects such as those replacing Techwood or East Lake Meadows. The housing authority instead moved primarily to being an issuer of housing vouchers, which, though desperately needed by families, depended on the whim and biases of landlords willing to accept them. Over time, as apartments in the city could draw higher market rents, only landlords in poorer neighborhoods, where neighborhood market rents were low, were likely to accept vouchers. In addition, as neighborhoods gentrified, landlords could easily opt out of the voucher system, requiring tenants to look elsewhere.

In 2001, the city's Gentrification Task Force issued a report outlining a long set of recommendations to slow the city's emerging gentrification trends or at least adapt to them by providing a stronger affordable housing response. Despite a few suggestions finding their way into city ordinances, enforcement and implementation fell away, and many recommendations were not acted upon at all.

In the mid-2000s, a critical missed opportunity was the policy architecture of the Atlanta Beltline. While advocates managed to insert affordable housing language into the 2005 ordinance that authorized the TAD, the funding set-aside requirement was structured in a way that allowed ABI to spend far too few resources on affordable housing. No serious efforts to acquire land for affordable housing were made early on, and early Beltline efforts paid little attention to the issue. The great bulk of resources were devoted to building trails and parks, precisely the investments that real estate speculators were hoping for, and that caused land values to accelerate as the city came out of the foreclosure crisis.

A third key inflection period came in the wake of the foreclosure crisis from about 2009 to 2012. Property values fell precipitously in many parts of the region, especially in Black and more diverse neighborhoods, in both the city and suburbs. Vacant housing pockmarked many Black neighborhoods and slowed housing market recovery in affected areas. While the federal NSP provided limited resources for local governments to purchase some of these homes or help homeowners purchase them, the program provided far too few dollars to acquire a substantial share of vacant homes. State and city governments did little to bring their own resources to bear on this opportunity. Most simply saw their role as spending the federal dollars and following the rules about how they could do so. While there were some successful efforts to reclaim vacant homes, renovate them, and sell them to lower-wealth, often Black, homebuyers, there were very few initiatives aimed at acquiring large numbers of properties to repurpose as long-term affordable housing to prepare for an eventual rise in home prices and rents.

This was a huge missed opportunity, especially in the city of Atlanta. The city proper contained thousands of vacant homes during this period, with some neighborhoods experiencing vacancy rates of over fifty percent.[6] Resources going to building trails and parks around the Beltline could have been focused first on purchasing homes and land to combat the speculation occurring during this time of low values and prepare for the inevitable resurgence of higher rents and prices. The evidence of the Beltline's impact on land values had been made clear in the years before the crisis, yet this lesson was effectively ignored.

In the suburbs, except for the more affluent ones, with mortgage markets remaining very tight for years after the crisis, many foreclosed homes flowed to investors and were converted into long-term rental properties. Then, beginning in 2012, large-scale private-equity investment firms identified metropolitan Atlanta as a "strike zone" for single-family rentals, and federal policymakers encouraged them to enter this market. The result was that the region became the number one metro for Wall Street investment in single-family rentals. Over time, many middle- and working-class suburban neighborhoods—especially many racially diverse and Black ones—shifted significantly towards lower homeownership rates. Under different policy choices, including federal ones, many of these homes could have been acquired by modest-wealth homebuyers when prices were low. Others could have been acquired and converted into long-term affordable housing. Instead, the crisis resulted in a significant transfer of property and land ownership from individual, working- and middle-class families to real estate investors.

As real estate markets heated up beginning in 2012, local governments returned to established paths of facilitating private capital in ways that led to gentrification and suburban exclusion. Large redevelopment projects in both the city and suburbs used ample planning and public finance support to remake places. This placemaking was done on top of, and often not for the benefit of, already existing communities, including many lower-income families and residents of color. These projects were not the result of some fictitious free market being unleashed to magically rediscover the locational advantages of these places. Instead, they resulted from heavily organized, planned, and subsidized public-private partnerships that placed the desires of developers, affluent homeowners, and future higher-income residents above the simple housing needs of modest-income families and communities.

A CHANGING CITY, A CHANGING REGION, AND EVOLVING URBAN REGIMES AND POWER

During the last quarter-century, the city and its more affluent suburbs adopted policies and planning approaches that displaced and excluded lower-income families, usually households of color. Of course, they used exclusionary zoning to do so, especially in the most affluent parts of the city and in the suburbs. This reflected the traditional role of "homevoter" power, the political power of homeowners, especially affluent ones, to maintain exclusionary housing policies that minimize the ability of lower-income families to enter a community.[7] But local governments also achieved racial and economic exclusion via displace-and-replace redevelopment projects. They provided public finance and redevelopment assistance to developers and other real estate actors who profited from the revaluing—the revalorization—of places that had suffered from wealth extraction and disinvestment for decades.[8] The private parties to the public-private partnership, the "structural speculators" to use a term coined by John Logan and Harvey Molotch, gained access to critical planning, public finance, and redevelopment tools such as revenue or general obligation bonds, tax increment financing, and community improvement districts that only local government could provide.[9]

Racialized displacement and exclusion are not recent phenomena in Atlanta. As Chapter 1 demonstrates, the development of the city of Atlanta includes a long string of displace-and-replace efforts aimed at mostly lower-income Black Atlantans. Such efforts included the use of local, state, and federal redevelopment programs and highway construction to constrain or remove Black communities when it suited real estate investors' and white homeowners' interests. From tolerating anti-Black violence to allowing the building of Black subdivisions only in acceptable places, to demolishing Black neighborhoods and public housing, the Atlanta urban regime, together with its state and federal enablers, worked to protect the interests of corporations, real estate investors, and white homeowners, who often shared similar views about what was good for the future of the city. These interests were served well by the Atlanta "biracial" white-Black corporatist regime, as a part of what is now often called "the Atlanta Way," allowing the regime to retain political and economic power while Black Atlantans gained voting rights.

As the region grew, the corporate and philanthropic players involved in the city regime changed, with some being more globalized. As the real estate interests and corporate power itself became increasingly suburbanized, the role of the urban regime in the city has become somewhat less important to the region overall. The state of Georgia and the ARC grew in importance. The state never gave the ARC strong regional planning powers that would enable it to constrain regional growth, compel more compact development, or set affordable housing goals for local governments, despite some glimmers that it might move in at least some of these directions under Governor Jimmy Carter. The pro-business, pro-jobs, and limited-government ideologies were deep in the DNA of most Georgia politicians. Under Democratic Governor Joe Frank Harris, the state turned away from more robust growth management that would direct the ARC to steer development more strongly towards goals of sustainability and social equity. Instead, the ARC catered to the interests of suburban developers and exclusionary suburban governments, accommodating and supporting sprawling new single-family subdivisions and spatial inequality. When anti-government, anti-planning Republicans took control of both the legislature and the governor's office in the early 2000s, things only moved further in this direction. Unless local governments wanted to adopt progressive measures such as rent control or fair housing laws that would benefit lower-income residents and households of color, control of economic and housing development was mostly left to localities. Local governments in turn, catered mostly to the desires of affluent homeowners and to private developers who sought opportunities to build farther out or to "retrofit" older parts of suburbs in ways that would bring in more-affluent residents and generate higher property values and lucrative development fees.

Because most affluent suburbs continue to have minority-Black populations, their local power structures tend not to resemble that of the traditional urban regime that persisted in the city of Atlanta. The Atlanta region contains many distributed but somewhat networked suburban redevelopment machines. At least when it comes to redevelopment decisions, affordable housing debates, and land-use decision-making, these suburban redevelopment machines are often dominated by a combination of vocal, middle- and upper-income homeowners, a cohort of active real estate developers and landowners, and elected officials, who tend to respond well to the interests of these other parties. The power of affluent homeowners and developers in supporting the funding and planning of such projects, together with the fact that many of the lower-income renters tend to be families of color with less political influence, give these processes a racial power dynamic that is reminiscent of Louise Seamster's description of "hegemonic whiteness as also working, behind the scenes . . . to maintain the racial order."[10] Occasionally however, as evidenced by the media coverage of the redevelopment of Franklin Road in Marietta, described in Chapter 5, racial dominance in the planning process was not entirely kept "behind the scenes."

In the city, the corporate-led urban regime did not go away but evolved in terms of which players became more or less important. Corporate groups, often led by predominantly white business executives, such as the Atlanta Committee for Progress, the Metro Atlanta Chamber of Commerce, and the Council for Quality Growth, as well as individual corporations and real estate developers, remain active and heavily involved with city policymaking. The ARC, the Chamber, the Community Foundation of Greater Atlanta, and the United Way continue to steer resources towards some nonprofit activities more than others. Few resources get devoted to advocacy efforts that could offer serious challenges to the existing power structure. Coalitions aimed at issues like affordable housing tend to seek the blessings and buy-in of corporate and real estate interests and have been reluctant to push efforts that these interests are likely to oppose, such as stronger tenant protections. The city of Atlanta regime has retained a biracial mix, although as the city becomes less Black, the power of the Black "junior partners" in the regime is likely to weaken.

A NEW POLITICS IN GEORGIA? PROSPECTS FOR CHANGE FOLLOWING A HISTORY OF EXCLUSION

The 2020 fall elections put Georgia on the front pages of national newspapers, and the 2022 elections likely will as well. By 2020, Georgia had become a swing state, both in the presidential election and with its all-important two U.S. Senate seats. Eventually, the state went for President Biden and elected two Democrats to the Senate, taking it to a 50–50 tie, with Vice-President Harris providing the tie-breaking vote to put the chamber barely under Democratic control. While some state legislative gains were also made in 2018, with the Democrats gaining thirteen seats in the 180-seat House of Representatives, they only managed to pick up one more seat in 2020, leaving themselves at a still sizable 76 to 103 minority. The Republicans also control the state senate as of 2021 with a 34 to 22 majority. The challenge to gain Democratic control of state government appears to be even steeper than the challenge to maintain Democratic wins in national elections. This is in large part due to the fact that Republicans have been able to gerrymander both legislative boundaries to maintain dominance despite the electorate having approached a near 50–50 Republican-Democratic split statewide.

At the same time, the demographics and the political organizing strength in the state point in a more progressive direction for at least statewide elections. As of 2019, the Atlanta metro now accounts for approximately fifty-seven percent of the statewide population. That share is likely to continue growing so that the political center of gravity will continue to shift towards the region. Statewide, the non-college white voter turnout rate increased in the 2020 election, which worked against Democrats, but this group's share of the statewide eligible voting population is declining.[11] The Black turnout rate increased from 2016 to 2020, while the Latinx turnout rate dropped a bit, but the raw number of Latinx voters has been increasing. Moreover, because voters of color still tend to turn out at lower levels than college-educated whites, this suggests the potential for more organizing among less-educated, younger voters of color. They are precisely the types of voters most likely to be affected by issues such as the lack of affordable housing, exclusion, and housing instability.

Gwinnett County provides an example of the political transformation of many suburbs in the region. From 1990 to 2019, the share of Gwinnett that was non-Hispanic white fell by almost exactly half, from just under ninety percent to about forty-five percent. This massive change contributed significantly to electoral changes in the county. George W. Bush won the county by thirty-two points in 2004, while President Biden won it by eighteen points. In between, President Obama lost the county by nine points as late as 2012. But only six years later, Stacy Abrams won the county by more than fourteen points in her narrow loss in the governor's race. Fast-changing demographics played a vital role in Gwinnett and the suburbs more generally, but to dismiss the power of stronger organizing, both in getting people registered and getting them to vote, would be a major mistake, as suggested by historian James Cobb.[12] More robust voter registration and turnout efforts by groups like Fair Fight, the New Georgia Project, and many others, were well-funded and arguably as strong as any in the nation. The question is not whether the electoral changes are primarily the result of demographic shifts or stronger organizing. The two forces are interactive and multiplicative. More organizing works better as greater diversity occurs, and more diversity is much more powerful when accompanied by more organizing.

While federal policy is essential in terms of funding affordable housing, a great deal of policy and planning that affects affordable housing, redevelopment, and racial and economic exclusion fall under state and local control. In Georgia, state government has been generally unhelpful, or downright hostile, to local efforts such as reducing exclusionary housing policies, requiring landlords to accept housing vouchers, enacting local fair housing ordinances, or regulating real estate markets in ways that would help protect low-income families from exclusion and displacement. For example, the state enacted a statute preempting local rent control ordinances in 1984. More recently, during the foreclosure crisis in 2010, when DeKalb County enacted an ordinance to require owners of vacant properties, including banks, to register them and pay a modest fee, the legislature quickly passed state preemption of such ordinances.[13] When a few legislators proposed reforming the property tax appeals process that was a pivotal contributor to the under-taxation of large commercial properties in the city of Atlanta, as discussed in Chapter 3, the bill went nowhere. Efforts to create new funding streams to fund affordable housing or steer existing ones towards such uses often require changes to state law. Similarly, a proposal simply to provide tenants with a "right-to-cure" period before a landlord can formally file for eviction, as in most other states, was introduced in the legislature in 2021 but did not advance.

The prospects for increasing support for affordable housing, strengthening Georgia's weak tenant protections, or reforming the property tax system so that local growth benefits lower-income residents, are all hindered by state policymakers who care little about exclusion, displacement, and housing instability and who cater to the short-term interests of real estate investors, whom they often consider as the most important component of "free markets." This is not to say that local governments have no role; they certainly do. For one thing, they can stop putting the force of local planning and subsidy behind displace-and-replace and other exclusionary projects and, instead, use such power and resources to build affordable housing in their communities. They can also resist pressures to retain or expand exclusionary zoning or building codes that make it challenging to build affordable housing in their communities.

In the fall of 2022, the gubernatorial election offers the potential for the beginnings of substantive change in the state capitol. As of this writing, the Democratic candidate for governor will almost certainly be Stacey Abrams, the nationally known voting rights advocate. Abrams lost to former Secretary of State Brian Kemp in the governor's race in 2018 by only 1.4 percentage points. Critics on the Democratic side, including some from Abrams' team, accused the Republican side of various forms of voter suppression, including the purging of voter rolls before the election.[14]

Demographic changes continue to bode well for Democrats in 2022, with the state adding approximately 1.3 million registered voters between 2018 and late 2021, about half of whom are voters of color and many moving into metro Atlanta.[15] Between just 2018 and 2020, Asian voters grew from 1.7 percent to 2.5 percent of statewide voters, and Latinx voters grew from 2.3 percent to 3 percent.[16] What may be as important as these demographic changes, however, is the increased power of Abrams' and others' voter mobilization operations, which are credited with being a major force in the Democrat's major victories in the state in 2020. That apparatus will certainly gear up again and receive substantial support from outside the state. Even in 2018, before Abrams was such a well-known national figure, she was able to outraise Kemp significantly in contributions with her campaign spending more than $27 million on the race.[17] Since then, her group, Fair Fight Action, had, as of late 2021, raised over $100 million.

At the same time, demographics are not political destiny, and the increased organizing power of the Democrats will be confronted with increased voter suppression efforts by the Republicans. In March 2021, the Republican legislature passed, and Governor Kemp signed, a bill that rolled back efforts to enable easier voting. The bill shortened the time allowed to request and return absentee ballots, required state ID to request the ballot, restricted access to drop boxes, imposed stronger oversight of local election boards, and made it a crime to offer food or water to voters waiting in line.[18] Whether organizing efforts and demographic changes that favor Democrats are enough to counter these and possibly other efforts at voter suppression remains to be seen.

Even if Stacey Abrams manages to move into the governor's office in 2023, state-level policy change will not come rapidly. The legislature will almost certainly remain fully or partly under the control of Republicans. Moreover, even Democratic control would not result in a legislature that is immune to the power of landlords, exclusionary local governments, and other forces that are resistant to progressive change. However, a change in control of the state's executive branch could be a significant, if incremental, first step towards a different, more inclusive future for the Atlanta region.

While partisan changes may be at play at the state level in 2022, in late 2021, the city of Atlanta saw the election of a new mayor, Andre Dickens. Dickens, who had introduced the city's two inclusionary zoning ordinances in 2017, was no stranger to issues of affordable housing in the city and ran on a campaign of continuing working towards some of Mayor Bottoms' affordable housing goals. As important as the election of a new mayor in 2021 was the election of a number of new City Council members who were viewed as less of a rubber stamp for the mayor's office and perhaps more likely to push for progressive policies such as funding affordable housing and resisting excessive developer subsidies. Whether these changes might lead to larger changes in the governance of the city and the weakening of the Atlanta Way and the corporate-led regime, it is too early to say as of this writing.

AVOIDING "MARKET-INEVITABILITY" FATALISM: URBAN AND SUBURBAN FUTURES AS POLITICAL CHOICE

Some witnessing the sorts of racial and economic exclusion described in this book argue that these patterns are inevitable in growing cities and regions like Atlanta. Where the conditions are ripe, they suggest, rampant gentrification is pre-ordained, a product of market forces that cannot be altered or slowed. These observers are also likely to argue that suburban redevelopment in a revanchist, racialized displace-and-replace fashion is unavoidable. Local and state governments can do little to constrain the appetite of capital for identifying places with "underutilized" potential and fuel redevelopment that recasts a community into one that will attract a wealthier and likely whiter constituency. Such responses are perhaps understandable, especially without grasping the mechanisms of how urban and suburban places get reimagined, reshaped, and remade. They reflect a failure to understand the reality that, like it or not, government is responsible for establishing and regulating many of the institutional structures within which markets operate and so bears a significant share of responsibility for the racialized exclusion and displacement of poor communities.

The changes in Atlanta over the last twenty-five years, much like the changes throughout the twentieth century, are not the result of apolitical, impersonal, anonymized market forces. The city is a politically and socially constructed space, and its trajectories are the products of policy decisions. No single change in policy or planning will, by itself, reverse the trends of exclusion that bear down hardest on those whose lives are the most precarious. Yet changes to how major projects get done, how they are financed, and whether planners and dealmakers are forced to consider the immediate and longer-term questions of who benefits and who is harmed from the next big "place-making" project can and do make a difference. Many of the policy choices that have been made in the Atlanta region since the 1990s could have been made differently, in ways that would have led to less gentrification and displacement, more housing stability and affordability for low-income families, and less reshuffling of poor families—mostly households of color—from one place to another. There is always an opportunity to do substantially better the next time.

Notes

1. This book will generally provide demographic figures for metropolitan areas as defined by the Atlanta metropolitan statistical area (MSA), as designated by the U.S. Census Bureau. In 2019 this included twenty-nine counties. The MSA is not a static definition, however, and has increased over time as the region has grown and sprawled. Most of the regional maps used in the book do not correspond precisely to the 2019 MSA, but they are very close. They include twenty-nine counties: twenty-eight of the twenty-nine counties in the 2019 MSA plus Hall County, at the northeast tip of the region, which includes a significant amount of urbanized area stemming off of Gwinnett County and is in the Metropolitan North Georgia Water Planning District. One small exurban/rural county that is in the MSA but is not shown in the regional maps is Morgan County, which lies to the east of Newton County. It had less than 20,000 residents as of 2019, while Hall County had just under 205,000. The MSA population in 2019 was just over six million in 2019, so the population of the twenty-nine-county region in Map 1

is slightly larger, at about 6.2 million, less than four percent more than the MSA. The differences in demographics between the two twenty-nine-county areas are not significant for the purposes of the analyses in the book.

2. Frederick Allen, *Atlanta Rising: The Invention of an International City, 1946–1996* (Atlanta, GA: Longstreet Press, 1996), ix.

3. The data in this section come from the 2000 U.S. Decennial Census and the 2019 American Community Survey one-year estimates. No attempts are made to adjust for changes in metropolitan statistical area definitions or annexations for central cities.

4. These two studies ranked Atlanta as the fifth- and fourth-fastest gentrifying cities in the country, respectively. Michael Maciag, "Gentrification in America Report." *Governing Magazine,* January 23, 2015, https://www.governing.com /archive/gentrification-in-cities-governing-report.html; and Quentin Brummet and Davin Reed, "The Effects of Gentrification on the Well-Being and Opportunity of Original Resident Adults and Children," Federal Reserve Bank of Philadelphia, WP19–30, July 2019, https://www.philadelphiafed.org/-/media/frbp /assets/working-papers/2019/wp19-30.pdf?la = en.

CHAPTER 1. BUILDING THE RACIALLY SEGREGATED SOUTHERN CAPITAL

1. Marthasville was apparently in honor of the daughter of a former governor. The name Atlanta was purportedly a feminine version of Atlantic, the name given at first to the city's railroad depot. Andy Ambrose, "Atlanta," *New Georgia Encyclopedia.* March 15, 2004. https://www.georgiaencyclopedia.org /articles/counties-cities-neighborhoods/atlanta.

2. Charles Rutheiser, *Imagineering Atlanta: The Politics of Place in the City of Dreams* (New York: Verso, 1996), 18.

3. Ibid., 140.

4. Lee Ann Lands, *The Culture of Property: Race, Class, and Housing Landscapes in Atlanta, 1880–1950* (Athens, GA: University of Georgia Press, 2009), 19.

5. Rutheiser, supra, note 2, 28.

6. Maurice Hobson, *The Legend of the Black Mecca: Politics and Class in the Making of Modern Atlanta* (Chapel Hill: University of North Carolina Press, 2017), 13.

7. Ibid., 18.

8. John Logan and Matthew Martinez, "The Spatial Scale and Spatial Configuration of Residential Settlement: Measuring Segregation in the Postbellum South," *American Journal of Sociology* 123, no. 4 (2018): 1161–1203.

9. Lands, supra, note 4, 18.

10. Rutheiser, supra, note 2, 141.

11. Douglas Blackmon, *Slavery by Another Name: The Re-enslavement of Black Americans from the Civil War to World War II* (New York: Anchor Books, 2009), 341, 347–350.

12. Lands, supra, note 4, 21, 25, 61.

13. Ronald Bayor, *Race and the Shaping of Twentieth-Century Atlanta* (Chapel Hill: University of North Carolina Press, 2000), 7; Tomiko Brown-Nagin, *Courage to Dissent: Atlanta and the Long History of the Civil Rights Movement* (Oxford: Oxford University Press, 2012) 46; Lands, supra, note 4, p. 32.

14. Lands, supra, note 4, 39; Richard Lloyd, "Urbanization and the Southern United States," *Annual Review of Sociology,* 38 (2012): 483–506.

15. Logan and Martinez, supra, note 8.

16. The most common measure of residential segregation is the dissimilarity index. This is a number that ranges from 0 to 1 for a city or metropolitan area, with 1 representing complete spatial segregation between two racial groups and 0 representing a complete lack of segregation. In this case, the number represents the share of a city's Black residents who would have to move into a different geographical unit (neighborhood, street, or building) in order for the share of Black residents in every unit within the city to be made equal, thereby achieving a uniform spatial distribution across the units. If a city has a segregation index of 0, no Black residents would have to relocate because a level of perfect uniformity across the geographic units would have already been achieved. But measures of segregation like this are sensitive to the geographic unit at which segregation is measured, and tend to increase when measured at finer geographic scales. Therefore, traditional measures of residential segregation, which tend to use census tracts, or fairly large notions of "neighborhood," may mask finer levels of segregation.

17. Logan and Martinez, supra, note 8.

18. Logan and Martinez, supra, note 8.

19. Alton Hornsby Jr., *"Black Power in Dixie: A Political History of African Americans in Atlanta,"* Gainesville: University Press of Florida, 2009), 45.

20. Rebecca Burns, "To Understand the Mob Violence at the US Capitol, Remember the 1906 Atlanta Race Riot," January 12, 2021, https://www.atlantamagazine.com/news-culture-articles/to-understand-the-mob-violence-at-the-u-s-capitol-remember-the-1906-atlanta-race-riot/.

21. Clarence Stone, *Regime Politics: Governing Atlanta, 1946–1988.* (Lawrence: University Press of Kansas, 1989), 11; Hornsby, supra, note 19, 28, 30.

22. Lands, supra, note 4, 89; Hornsby, supra, note 19, 49.

23. Bayor, supra, note 13, 54; Lands, supra, note 4, 76, 143, 152.

24. Lands, supra, note 4, 155.

25. Quoted in Lands, supra, note 4, 147.

26. Lands, supra, note 4, 54, 55, 176.

27. Kevin Kruse, *White Flight: Atlanta and the Making of Modern Conservatism.* (Princeton: Princeton University Press, 2007), 14, 23, 45.

28. Ibid., 46, 47.

29. Kruse, supra, note 27, 54.

30. Katherine Hankins and Steve Holloway, "Suburbanization and the Making of Atlanta as the 'Black Mecca'," in *The Life of North American Suburbs* (Toronto: University of Toronto Press, 2020), 223–244.

31. Kruse, supra, note 27, 29; Andrew Wiese, *Places of Their Own* (Chicago: University of Chicago Press, 2009), 176.

32. Wiese, supra, note 31, 183.

33. Lands, supra, note 4, 167.

34. Wiese, supra, note 31, 178.

35. Lands, supra, note 4, 198.

36. Lands, supra, note 4, 18.

37. Kruse, supra, note 27, 12.

38. Data in Map 3 are from: Steven Manson, Jonathan Schroeder, David Van Riper, Tracy Kugler, and Steven Ruggles, *IPUMS National Historical Geographic Information System: Version 15.0*, Minneapolis, MN: IPUMS, 2020, http://doi.org/10.18128/D050.V15.0.

39. Lands, supra, note 4, 194.

40. These observers include Keating, Stone, Hobson, Hornsby, and Bayor, among others.

41. Bayor, supra, note 13, 59; Brown-Nagin, supra, note 13, 54; Wiese, supra, note 31, 181.

42. Stone, supra, note 21, 33; Brown-Nagin, supra, note 13, 57.

43. Testimony of Robert C. Stuart, Director, Metropolitan Planning Commission, US Conference on Civil Rights, House Hearings, April 10, 1959, 481. Cited in Brown-Nagin, supra, note 13, 45.

44. US Commission on Civil Rights, "Report of the US Commission on Civil Rights," 1959, 426, https://www.hsdl.org/?abstract&did = 473401#:~:text = This%201959%20report%20from%20the,of%20the%20United%20States%20government.&text = The%20Constitution%20of%20the%20United,stands%20against%20such%20a%20division.

45. Lands, supra, note 4, 137.

46. Atlpm0389, Planning Atlanta City Planning Maps Collection, Georgia State University.

47. Kruse, supra, note 27, 37.

48. Atlpp0005_22, Planning Atlanta City Planning Maps Collection, Georgia State University.

49. AJCP142–026c, Atlanta Journal-Constitution Photographic Archive. Special Collections and Archives, Georgia State University.

50. Stone, supra, note 21, 30.

51. Keating, Larry. 2001. *Atlanta: Race, Class and Urban Expansion*. (Philadelphia: Temple University Press, 93); Bayor, supra, note 13, 70.

52. Robert Nelson and Edward Ayers, editors, "Renewing inequality," American Panorama, accessed March 27, 2021. https://dsl.richmond.edu/panorama/renewal/#view = -25/-57/1&viz = cartogram&city = atlantaGA&loc = 12/33.7559/-84.4052.

53. Keating, supra, note 51, 93.

54. L. Keating and C. Flores, "Sixty and Out: Techwood Homes: Transformed by Enemies and Friends." *Journal of Urban History* 3 (2000): 275–311, 277.

55. Stone, supra, note 21, x.

56. Bayor, supra, note 13, p. 61.

57. Keating, supra, note 51, 48.

58. Kruse, supra, note 27, 167, 245.

59. Kruse, supra, note 27, 245.

60. All figures in this paragraph are from the author's calculations of data from the US Census Bureau's Decennial Densus, accessed from Socialexplorer.com.

61. All figures in this paragraph are from the author's calculations of data from the US Census Bureau's decennial census, accessed from Socialexplorer.com.

62. Hankins and Holloway, supra, note 30.

63. All figures in this paragraph are from the author's calculations of data from the US Census Bureau's decennial census, accessed from Socialexplorer.com.

64. Data in this paragraph are from the US Department of Housing and Urban Development, State of the Cities Data System, accessed, June 11, 2021, https://www.huduser.gov/Portal/datasets/socds.html.

65. Keating, supra, note 51, 14.

66. Stone, supra, note 21, 80; Hornsby, supra, note 19, 135.

67. Jon Nordheimer, 1973, "Race is Factor in Runoff Vote for Atlanta Mayor Tomorrow," *New York Times,* October 15, 1973, 22, https://www.nytimes.com /1973/10/15/archives/race-is-factor-in-runoff-vote-foratlanta-mayor-tomorrow-city-52-per.html.

68. Hornsby, supra, note 19, 151.

69. Akira Drake Rodriguez, *Diverging Space for Deviants: The Politics of Atlanta's Public Housing* (Athens: University of Georgia Press, 2021), 138.

70. Stone, supra, note 21, 86.

71. Stone, supra, note 21, 95; Hornsby, supra, note 19, 181.

72. Hobson, supra, note 6, 144–145.

73. Rutheiser, supra, note 2, 161.

74. Stone, supra, note 21, 110.

75. Stone, supra, note 21, 136.

76. Stone, supra, note 21, 74, 97.

77. Quoted in Kruse, supra, note 27, 249.

78. Hornsby, supra, note 19, 132.

79. Hornsby, supra, note 19, 192.

80. Keating, supra, note 51, 123.

81. Keating, supra, note 51, 21.

82. Rutheiser, supra, note 2, 229.

83. Hobson, supra, note 6, 1; Rutheiser, supra, note 2, 3.

84. For discussion of the benefits and costs of the 1996 Olympics, see Keating, supra, note 51, 154; and Michael Dobbins, Leon Eplan, and Randall Roark,

Atlanta's Olympic Resurgence: How the 1996 Games Revived a Struggling City, (Charleston, SC: The History Press), 100–101.

85. Seth Gustafson, "Displacement and the Racial State in Olympic Atlanta." *Southeastern Geographer* 53, no. 2 (2013): 198–213.

86. Hobson, supra, note 6, 183.

87. Dobbins, Eplan, and Roark, supra, note 84, 91, 99.

88. Ibid., 119, 120.

89. Ibid., 120.

90. Hobson, supra, note 6, 90.

91. Gail Radford, "The Federal Government and Housing during the Great Depression," in J. Bauman, R. Biles, and K. Szylvian, eds., *From Tenements to the Taylor Homes*. (University Park: Penn State University Press, 2000)

92. Rodriguez, supra, note 69, 3.

93. Ed Goetz, *New Deal Ruins: Race, Economic Justice and Public Housing Policy* (Ithaca: Cornell University Press, 2013), 40–47, 102.

94. Hornsby, supra, note 19, 189.

95. US Department of Housing and Urban Development, "Final Report of the National Commission on Severely Distressed Public Housing," August 1992, https://www.hud.gov/sites/documents/DOC_9836.PDF.

96. Goetz, supra, note, 93, 101–103.

97. Keating and Flores, supra, note 54.

98. Keating and Flores, supra, note 54.

99. Lawrence Vale, *Purging the Poorest: Public Housing and the Design Politics of Twice-Cleared Communities* (Chicago: University of Chicago Press, 2013), 113, 119, 126.

100. Goetz, supra, note 93, 103.

101. Griff Tester, Erin Ruel, Angela Anderson, Donald C. Reitzes, and Deirdre Oakley, "Sense of Place among Atlanta Public Housing Residents," *Journal of Urban Health* 88, no. 3 (2011): 436–453.

102. Rodriguez, supra, note 69, 188.

103. Vale, supra, note 99, 136.

104. Carlton Basmajian, *Atlanta Unbound: Enabling Sprawl Through Policy and Planning*. (Philadelphia: Temple University Press, 2013), 44, 110.

105. Rutheiser, supra, note 2, 94.

106. Keating, supra, note 51, 52.

107. Peter Applebome, "A Suburban Eden Where the Right Rules," *New York Times*. April 14, 1994, https://www.nytimes.com/1994/08/01/us/a-suburban-eden-where-the-right-rules.html.

108. Basmajian, supra, note 104, 24.

109. "Now . . . for Tomorrow" plan quoted in Basmajian, supra, note 104, 26.

110. Basmajian, supra, note 104, 3, 13.

111. Basmajian, supra, note 104, 87, 89.

112. Basmajian, supra, note 104, 86.

113. Basmajian, supra, note 104, 91.

114. Data in this section come from the 1980 and 2000 US Decennial Census.

115. Keating, supra, note 51, 202.

116. Rutheiser, supra, note 2, 5, 73.

117. Rutheiser, supra, note 2, 72.

118. Rutheiser, supra, note 2, 72.

119. Hornsby, supra, note 19, 32.

120. Ivan Allen, Jr., as quoted in Kruse, supra, note 27, 28.

121. Lee Ann Lands, "Emmaus House and Atlanta's Anti-Poverty Movements," *Atlanta Studies*, April 28, 2015, https://www.atlantastudies.org/2015/04/28/emmaus-house-and-atlantas-anti-poverty-movements/.

122. Hornsby, supra, note 19, 247.

123. Brown-Nagin, supra, note 13, 2.

124. Stone, supra, note 21, 192.

125. Keating, supra, note 51, 82.

126. Jack Spalding, "Where Now, Atlanta?" *Atlanta Constitution*, September 5, 1971, 18A.

127. Keating, supra, note 51, 2.

128. Jim Higdon, as quoted in Basmajian, supra, note 104, 119.

129. Basmajian, supra, note 104, 12.

130. Basmajian, supra, note 104, 183.

131. As an example, see the edited volume by this name, Robert Bullard, Glenn Johnson, and Angel Torres, *Sprawl City: Race, Politics and Planning in Atlanta* (Washington, DC: Island Press, 2000).

CHAPTER 2. THE BELTLINE AS A PUBLIC-PRIVATE GENTRIFICATION PROJECT

1. An example is Mark Pendergrast's *City on the Verge: Atlanta and the Fight for America's Future* (New York: Basic Books, 2017).

2. Reliable data on demographics is not available for years between 1990 and 2000, as the American Community Survey did not begin until the mid-2000s. Data in this paragraph come from the 1990 and 2000 Decennial Census and the 2007 American Community Survey one-year estimates.

3. Larry Keating and Frank Alexander, "A City for All: The Report of the Gentrification Task Force," Atlanta City Council, September 17, 2001.

4. Georgia Institute of Technology, "Current Gentrification in Atlanta Contrasts to Previous Waves of Restoration," September 4, 2003, https://www.eurekalert.org/pub_releases/2003–09/giot-cgi090403.php.

5. Atlanta Development Authority, "Beltline Redevelopment Plan," September 2005, 77; Atlanta Beltline, Inc., "*2030 Strategic Implementation Plan Final Report*," December 2015, 6, 7.

6. Pendergrast, supra, note 1, 13–15; Ryan Gravel, "Addendum to the Beltline Thesis," December, 2005, https://beltline.org/wp-content/uploads/2012/04/Gravel-Thesis-Addendum-2005.pdf.

7. Pendergrast, supra, note 1, 21.

8. Ethan Davidson, "The Atlanta Beltline: A Green Future," *Public Roads* Vol 75, No 2. September/October 2011.

9. Woolard's reference to a "very big train" referred to some proposals for running new heavy rail through the neighborhood. Maria Saporta, "Existing Web of Rail Lines Key to Creating a Better Transit System," *Atlanta Journal-Constitution*, April 1, 2002, F4.

10. Pendergrast, supra, note 1, 29.

11. David Pendered, "How Does the Beltline Grow? Cousins Network Helps Developer's Associates Cultivate Project," *The Atlanta Journal-Constitution*, July 18, 2005, E1.

12. Adam Goldstein, "A Purposely Built Community: Public Housing Redevelopment and Resident Replacement at East Lake Meadows," *Atlanta Studies*, March 17, 2017, https://www.atlantastudies.org/2017/03/14/a-purposely-built-community-public-housing-redevelopment-and-resident-replacement-at-east-lake-meadows/.

13. Pendered, supra, note 11.

14. Gravel, supra, note 6.

15. David Pendered, "Beltline Still Faces Big Obstacles," *Atlanta Journal-Constitution*, April 11, 2005, E5.

16. Alex Garvin and Associates, Inc., 2004. *The Beltline Emerald Necklace: Atlanta's New Public Realm*. Alexander Garvin and Associates, Inc., December 15, 2004, p. 6.

17. Ibid., 12.

18. Ibid., 53.

19. Pendergrast, supra, note 1, 26–27.

20. Pendered, supra, note 11.

21. David Pendered, "City grapples with Beltline Housing Prices," *Atlanta-Journal Constitution*, October 31, 2005, B1.

22. Thomas Wheatley, "The 22-mile Life Preserver," *The Next American City*. Issue 21 (Winter 2008), 28–33.

23. Paul Donsky, "Funding Lawsuit Ties Up Beltline," *Atlanta Journal-Constitution*, December 27, 2007, D6; and Bill Torpy and Matt Kempner, "Beltline Lawyer Ruling Lawyer and Enigmatic Litigant," *Atlanta Journal-Constitution*, February 24, 2008, D1.

24. David Pendered, "Land Donor Snubbed in Belltine plan," *Atlanta Journal-Constitution*, September 27, 2005, B1.

25. Alycen Whiddon, "Beltline Plan Incorporates Trees, Transit . . . and Cars," *Atlanta Journal-Constitution*, June 16, 2005, A19.

26. Paul Donskey, "Unequal Spending Likely for Beltline: $45 million due: Third of Bond Issue Needed to Pay Off Loan or Project Will Lose Mason's Land, Earnest Money," *Atlanta Journal-Constitution*, July 9, 2008.

27. Thomas Wheatley, "Critics Question Beltline about Land Deal," *Creative Loafing*, December 17, 2008.

28. Beltline Transit Panel. 2005, "The Atlanta Beltline: Transit Feasibility White Paper," September 29, 2005.

29. Paul Donsky, "Panel Doubts Beltline Transit Goals," *Atlanta Journal-Constitution*, September 30, 2005, E1.

30. Paul Donsky, "Bus Transit Looks Like the Ticket for Beltline," *Atlanta Journal-Constitution*, 2006, D1. Also see URS Corporation, "Detailed Screening

Results and Selection of Locally Preferred Alternative. Prepared for MARTA," January 2007.

31. All quotes are from URS Corporation, "Detailed Screening Results and Selection of Locally Preferred Alternative. Prepared for MARTA," January 2007, D-30, D-32, D-33, D-34, D-36, D41.

32. The term "great inversion" is a reference to Alan Ehrenhalt, *The Great Inversion the Future of the American City* (New York: Vintage, 2013).

33. Pendered, supra, note 21.

34. Atlanta Beltline, Inc., "2030 Strategic Implementation Plan Final Report," December 2013, 46.

35. Dan Immergluck, "The Beltline and Rising Home Prices: Residential Appreciation Near the Beltline Tax Allocation District and Policy Recommendations to Minimize Displacement," Atlanta: Georgia Stand-Up, September 2007, https://www.forworkingfamilies.org/sites/default/files/publications /archive/ga/ TheBeltlineAndRisingHomePrices.pdf. The findings on home values are also found in: Dan Immergluck, "Large redevelopment initiatives, housing values and gentrification: The case of the Atlanta Beltline," *Urban Studies* 46, no. 8 (2009): 1723–1745.

36. The method used to do this is called hedonic price analysis. It involves employing actual sales data and characteristics of houses to identify relationships between the characteristics and the prices. The logic of such methods is that the price of a house is a function of a set of physical characteristics (e.g., square footage of the building, lot size, number of bedrooms and bathrooms, basement type, exterior construction, etc.), a set of neighborhood characteristics (e.g., poverty rate, owner-occupancy rate, etc.), location variables (e.g., distance from the central business district), and the date of the sale.

37. Immergluck, supra, note 35.

38. Lower-income neighborhoods are defined here as census tracts whose median family incomes are below eighty percent of the metropolitan median family income, a common definition of low- and moderate-income neighborhoods and one used by federal bank regulators. Upper-income homebuyers are those whose income is above 120 percent of the metropolitan median family income. Immergluck, supra, note 35.

39. Georgia Stand-Up, "Georgia Stand-Up: Organizing for an Equitable Atlanta," Center for Working Families, December 20, 2007, https://www.forworkingfamilies.org/blog/georgia-stand-organizing-equitable-atlanta.

40. Drafts were released in 2017. The paper was eventually published as Dan Immergluck and Tharunya Balan, "Sustainable for Whom? Green Urban Development, Environmental Gentrification, and the Atlanta Beltline," *Urban Geography* 39, no. 4 (2018): 546–562.

41. Tax allocation districts are what tax increment financing districts are called in Georgia.

42. Molly Bloom, "After Years of Conflict, Mayor Kasim Reed and APS reach Beltline deal," *Atlanta Journal-Constitution*, January 29, 2016, http://www.myajc.com/news/local-govt—politics/after-years-conflict-mayor-kasim-reed-and-aps-reach-beltline-deal/Wm6CxnlSwUmsVu78pcNsaK/.

43. Thomas Wheatley, "Ryan Gravel and Nathaniel Smith Resign from Beltline's Fundraising Arm over Affordability Concerns," *Creative Loafing*, September 27, 2016, https://creativeloafing.com/content-267202-ryan-gravel-and-nathaniel-smith-resign-from-beltline-s-fundraising-arm.

44. Atlanta Beltline Inc., "Atlanta Beltline Closes $155 million 2016 Bond Issue to Advance Affordable Housing, Capital Construction, and Economic Development," Atlanta Beltline, Inc., January 22, 2017, http://beltline.org/2017/01/22/atlanta-beltline-closes-155-million-2016-bond-issue-to-advance-affordable-housing-capital-construction-and-economic-development/.

45. Willoughby Mariano, Lindsey Conway, and Amastachia Ondieki, "Beltline Falls Short on Housing Promise," *Atlanta Journal-Constitution*, July 16, 2017, A1.

46. Ibid.

47. Ibid.

48. Leon Stafford and Willoughby Mariano, "Beltline CEO Quits Amid Housing Rift," *Atlanta Journal-Constitution*, August 24, 2017, A1.

49. Atlanta Beltline, Inc., "Integrated Action Plan for Economic Development, Housing & Real Estate," Atlanta Beltline, Inc., December 2015, http://beltlineorg.wpengine.netdna-cdn.com/wp-content/uploads/2016/03/IAP-Report-Final.pdf, 7.

50. Housing Justice League and Research/Action Cooperative, "Beltlining: Gentrification, Broken Promises, and Hope on Atlanta's Southside." October

2017, https://static1.squarespace.com/static/59da49b712abd904963589b6/t/59dedb
75f7e0ab47a08224b5/1507777424592/Beltlining+Report+-+HJL+and+RA+Oct+9
.pdf.

51. The original Beltline Redevelopment plan specified that 5,600 affordable
housing units would be created in the TAD funded by the "Workforce Housing Fund." Affordable homeownership units could be sold at prices affordable
to buyers with incomes up to 100 percent of area median income. Affordable
rental units would be those rented at rates affordable to those with incomes up
to sixty percent area median income. Atlanta Development Authority, Inc.,
"Atlanta Beltline Redevelopment Plan," November 2005, https://beltline.org
/wp-content/uploads/2019/03/BeltLine-Redevelopment-Plan.pdf.

52. The Beltline regularly included rental units priced at up to 80 percent of
area median income in its progress reports toward its goals. Atlanta Beltline,
Inc., accessed June 27, 2021, "Affordable Housing Pipeline," https://beltline
.org/the-project/affordable-housing-on-the-beltline/goals-progress/.

53. Atlanta Beltline, Inc., "2020 Annual Report," 2021. https://beltline.org
/flipbook/2020-annual-report/.

54. Atlanta Beltline, Inc., "2019 Annual Report," Atlanta Beltline, Inc., 2020,
https://beltline.org/wp-content/uploads/2020/04/ABL-2019-Annual-Report-Web
.pdf.

55. Atlanta Beltline, Inc., supra, note 53.

56. Old 4th Ward Economic Security Task Force, https://www.econsecurity-
atl.org/, accessed May 12, 2021. Atlanta Regional Commission, "Neighborhood
Statistical Area M02: Old Fourth Ward, Sweet Auburn," accessed May 12,
2021, http://documents.atlantaregional.com/NN/Profiles/AtlantaProfiles/M02
.pdf.

57. Edward Hatfield, "Auburn Avenue (Sweet Auburn)," *New Georgia Encyclopedia*, June 2, 2006, https://www.georgiaencyclopedia.org/articles/counties-
cities-neighborhoods/auburn-avenue-sweet-auburn.

58. U.S. Department of Housing and Urban Development, "Atlanta, GA FY
2005 HOPE VI Revitalization Grant Awards," Accessed May 16, 2021, https://
www.hud.gov/sites/documents/DOC_10100.PDF.

59. Historic Old Fourth Ward Park Conservancy, "History of the Area
and Park," http://www.h4wpc.org/history-of-the-area-park/, accessed May 12,
2021.

60. Kevin Mara, "Large-Scale Mixed-Use Developments as Catalytic Real Estate Projects: Evaluating the Narrative of Neighborhood Revitalization," Georgia Institute of Technology, April 26, 2017, https://smartech.gatech.edu/bitstream/handle/1853/58530/kevin_mara_large_scale_mixed-use_developments_as_catalytic_real_estate_projects.pdf.

61. Ibid.

62. Douglas Sams, "Atlanta Office Space Breaks $50 a Square Foot Rent Barrier," *Atlanta Business Chronicle*, March 24, 2017, http://www.bizjournals.com/atlanta/news/2017/03/24/atlanta-office-spacebreaks-50-a-foot-rent-barrier.html.

63. Douglas Sams, "Ponce City Market Developer Seeks Minority Partner, Could Spark One of Atlanta's Largest Real Estate Deals," *Atlanta Business Chronicle*, February 22, 2021, https://www.bizjournals.com/atlanta/news/2021/02/21/ponce-city-market-owner-jamestown-seeks-partner.html.

64. Mara, supra, note 60.

65. Details in this paragraph on the financing of Ponce City Market are from Mara, supra, note 60.

66. The property tax information for the primary PCM parcel was obtained from the Fulton County Tax Assessor's online system, accessed June 28, 2021, https://iaspublicaccess.fultoncountyga.gov/datalets/datalet.aspx?mode = profileall&sIndex = 0&idx = 1&LMparent = 20. Details on Georgia's Preferential Property Tax Assessment Program are from Georgia Department of Community Affairs "Preferential Property Tax Assessment Program," accessed June 28, 2021, https://www.dca.ga.gov/georgia-historic-preservation-division/tax-incentives-grants/state-tax-incentives/preferential.

67. These calculations are from the Atlanta Regional Commission, supra, note 56, and are based on the 2000 Decennial Census and the 2015–2019 five-year American Community Survey.

68. Zillow data for all-sales home value index downloaded from https://www.zillow.com/research/data/, accessed May 12, 2021. The 15 listings over one million dollars figure is from Josh Green, "Before/After: A Decade of Changes in Atlanta's Old Fourth Ward," *Urbanize Atlanta*, May 11, 2021, https://urbanize.city/atlanta/post/gentrification-development-old-fourth-ward-beltline-apartments-housing.

CHAPTER 3. PLANNING, SUBSIDY, AND HOUSING PRECARITY IN THE GENTRIFYING CITY

1. Author's calculations using data from the U.S. Census Bureau's LED Extraction Tool, accessed May 23, 2021, https://ledextract.ces.census.gov/static /data.html.

2. Author's calculations from the U.S. Census Bureau's LED Extraction Tool, ibid.

3. Maria Saporta and Amy Wenk, "NCR Corp. Relocating to Midtown, Bringing 3,500 to 4,000 Jobs into the City," *Atlanta Business Chronicle*, January 14, 2015, https://www.bizjournals.com/atlanta/real_talk/2015/01/ncr-corp-relocating-to-midtown-bringing-3–500-to-4.html.

4. CBRE, "CBRE's Annual Scoring Tech Talent Report: Atlanta Lands at Number Nine," CBRE, July 15, 2020, https://www.cbre.us/people-and-offices /corporate-offices/atlanta/atlanta-media-center/ cbres-annual-scoring-tech-talent-report-atlanta.

5. Jonathon Shieber, "How Did Atlanta Become a Breeding Ground for Billion Dollar Startups in the Southeast?" *Tech Crunch*, May 2, 2021, https:// techcrunch.com/2021/05/02/how-did-atlanta-become-a-top-breeding-ground-for-billion-dollar-startups-in-the-southeast/.

6. Atlanta Committee for Progress, "About," accessed May 24, 2021, http:// atlprogress.org/about.php.

7. Maria Saporta, "Atlanta Committee for Progress Laying Foundation for Next Mayor," March 27, 2017, https://saportareport.com/atlanta-committee-progress-laying-foundation-next-mayor/.

8. Atlanta Committee for Progress, "Atlanta Committee for Progress Releases "Go-Forward Priorities" for city of Atlanta," October 13, 2017, http:// atlprogress.org/_pdf/ACP_Press_Release_10–13–17.pdf.

9. Grantmakers for Southern Progress, "As the South goes: Philanthropy and social justice in the US South," February 2013, http://www.p-sj.org/files /As%20the%20South%20Goes-%20Full%20Report.pdf.

10. The first four waves of gentrification occurred from the 1950s through the 2000s. The first two waves were characterized by predominantly private actors, including individual homebuyers and small real estate firms. The third and fourth wave, which began in the 1990s and 2000s, were characterized more

by a stronger role of government in leading or catalyzing gentrification. The fifth wave including public sector roles but also included a stronger role for financialized capital. Derek Hyra, Mindy Fullilove, Dominic Moulden, and Katharine Silva, "Contextualizing Gentrification Chaos: The Rise of the Fifth Wave," Metropolitan Policy Center at American University, May 6, 2020, https://www.american.edu/spa/metro-policy/upload/contextualizing-gentrification-chaos.pdf.

11. The city of Atlanta annexed an area containing Emory University and the offices of the Centers for Disease Control in December 2017. According to the *Atlanta Journal-Constitution,* the annexed area added an estimated 6,376 people to the city's population. Mark Niesse, "Atlanta Expands Eastward by Completing Annexation of Emory and CDC," December 4, 2017, https://www.ajc.com/news/local-govt—politics/atlanta-expands-eastward-completing-annexation-emory-and-cdc/nnLePc3xFxV989npP7MfNK/. A large majority of this increase should be college students, and the city's group quarters population increased by just over 4,800 from 2017 to 2018 ACS one-year estimates. The changes in the ACS figures from 2012 to 2019 as described in this section were not materially affected by this small annexation. The median family income (in 2021 dollars) in the city increased from $63,889 to $83,046 from 2012 to 2017, before the annexation, and then stayed basically flat after the annexation at $83,710 in 2018, but then increased to $96,268 in 2019. The annexation accounts for just over fifty percent of the 2017 to 2018 increase in the estimated city population, and just over ten percent of the 63,000 increase from 2012 to 2019. Since students are in group quarters, they are not included in calculations of median family incomes or poverty rates.

12. Ibid.

13. The term, "great inversion" is from Alan Ehrenhalt, *The Great Inversion and the Future of the American City* (New York: Vintage, 2013).

14. All figures in this paragraph are calculated from the American Community Survey, one-year estimates for 2010 and 2019 for the city of Atlanta. Inflation factors are CPI less shelter figures for the Atlanta CBSA from the Federal Reserve Bank of St. Louis at https://fred.stlouisfed.org/series/CUUSA319SA0L2.

15. Quentin Brummet and Davin Reed, "The Effects of Gentrification on the Well-Being and Opportunity of Original Resident Adults and Children," Federal Reserve Bank of Philadelphia, WP19–30, July 2019, https://www.philadelphiafed.org/-/media/frbp/assets/working-papers/2019/wp19–30.pdf?la = en.

16. Maggie Lee, "Atlanta Board OKs Controversial Cash, Tax Breaks for Major Companies," *Saporta Report*, November 19, 2020, https://saportareport .com/atlanta-board-oks-controversial-cash-tax-breaks-for-major-companies /sections/reports/maggie/#:~:text = BlackRock%2C%20the%20world%27s% 20largest%20asset,business%20retention%20and%20 expansion%E2%80%9D%20grant.

17. J. Scott Trubey, "Atlanta Kroger Redevelopment May Get Tax Break," *Atlanta Journal-Constitution*, October 19, 2016, https://www.ajc.com/news /local/atlanta-kroger-redevelopment-may-get-tax-break/ i9X6ISJpCMRQFK9FDImqvN/.

18. Maggie Lee, "Developer Property Tax Breaks in Hot Atlanta Neighborhoods Raising Questions," *Saporta Report*, July 29, 2019, https://saportareport .com/developer-property-tax-breaks-in-hot-atlanta-neighborhoods-raising-questions/columnists/maggie-lee/maggie/.

19. Maggie Lee, "Fulton Agency Approves Nearly $100 Million in Property Tax Abatements," *Saporta Report*, January 22, 2019, https://saportareport.com /fulton-agency-approves-nearly-100-million-in-property-tax-abatements/sections /reports/maggie/#:~:text = Fulton%20agency%20approves%20nearly%20% 24100%20million%20in%20property%20tax%20abatements,-Maggie%20Lee%20 January&text = Fulton%20County%27s%20development%20agency%20on, .%27s%20mega%20Midtown%20development.

20. Maggie Lee, "Commercial Property Tax Discounts in Atlanta," *Saporta Report*, December 8, 2020, https://saportareport.github.io/tax-discounts/.

21. J. Scott Trubey and Ben Brasch, "Fulton Commissioners Shelve Development Authority Nominee," *Atlanta Journal-Constitution*, June 2, 2021, https:// www.ajc.com/news/investigations/fulton-commissioners-shelve-development-authority-nominee/OFLUOZTZQBFPZHKWPCMFIZMJXE/.

22. Arielle Kass and J. Scott Trubey, "Fulton Tax Officials Often Undervalue Atlanta Commercial Properties," *Atlanta Journal-Constitution*, November 15, 2018, https://www.ajc.com/news/local-govt—politics/fulton-tax-officials-often-undervalue-atlanta-commercial-properties/hv9BNyRMoEJLOzCnsxvXcJ/.

23. Office of the County Auditor, Fulton County, "Tax Assessors Office Review of Commercial Properties," Fulton County, Georgia, July 17, 2019.

24. J. Scott Trubey and Arielle Kass, "Commercial Properties in Atlanta Undervalued for Taxes, Report Says," *Atlanta Journal-Constitution*, November

20, 2019, https://www.ajc.com/news/local/atlanta-report-shows-commercial-properties-undervalued-for-taxes/8Fj6BjvCEtkjIVfZIQPvrN/.

25. Julian Bene, "Fixing Commercial Under-Assessment is Worth Hundreds of Millions of Dollars per Year," unpublished memo, November 11, 2019.

26. Maggie Lee, "Georgia Skyscraper Owners Need to Open Up to Tax Assessors, Say Some Lawmakers," *Saporta Report,* March 9, 2020, https://saportareport.com/georgia-skyscraper-owners-need-to-open-up-to-tax-assessors-say-some-lawmakers/sections/reports/maggie/.

27. The chronology in this paragraph is taken largely from Arielle Kass and Vanessa McCray, "Fulton County, Atlanta Tax Proposals Would Bring Relief, Consequences," *Atlanta Journal-Constitution,* November 5, 2018, https://www.ajc.com/news/local-govt—politics/fulton-county-atlanta-tax-proposals-would-bring-relief-consequences/nGyT3jWiBBqkgyAVS6llnM/.

28. Ben Brasch, "After COVID-19, Will Taxpayer-funded Venues Go Back to Normal?" *Atlanta Journal-Constitution,* February 26, 2021. https://www.ajc.com/news/atlanta-news/after-covid-19-will-taxpayer-funded-venues-go-back-to-normal/T255FNPK5ZEMBJS7IS5DDPMJZE/.

29. Tim Tucker, "New Stadium Lures 2019 Super Bowl to Atlanta," *Atlanta Journal-Constitution,* September 3, 2016, https://www.ajc.com/sports/football/new-stadium-lures-2019-super-bowl-atlanta/kJKUJdLlOwzOmoVAMkEFkO/.

30. Alex Delany, "Hot Dogs Are $2.00 at the New Atlanta Falcons Stadium," *Bon Appetit,* September 18, 2017,https://www.bonappetit.com/story/atlanta-falcons-stadium-cheap-concessions.

31. Leon Stafford, "Fort McPherson sale to Perry approved," *Atlanta Journal-Constitution,* September 23, 2016, https://www.ajc.com/news/breaking-news/fort-mcpherson-sale-perry-approved/8JMN6CP3S2I93gtPId2FZL/.

32. Larry Copeland, "Some Question Atlanta's Land Deal with Tyler Perry," September 10, 2014, https://www.usatoday.com/story/news/nation/2014/09/10/atlanta-land-deal-with-tyler-perry/15126323/.

33. Maria Saporta, "An Open Letter to Atlanta Mayor Kasim Reed about Fort McPherson," *Saporta Report,* May 18, 2015, https://saportareport.com/an-open-letter-to-mayor-kasim-reed-about-fort-mcpherson/.

34. J. Scott Trubey, Kelly Yamanouchi, and Stephen Deere, "Reed, City Concealed Secret $147K Payout to Fired Atlanta Airport Boss." *Atlanta Journal-

Constitution, January 10, 2019, https://www.ajc.com/news/local-govt—politics/reed-city-concealed-secret-147k-payout-fired-atlanta-airport-boss/kuhbVghD3N3FnxAxZxzBnI/.

35. Christina Maxouris, "Becker Talks USAS, Why CBA is Not Feasible," *Georgia State Signal,* March 28, 2017, https://georgiastatesignal.com/becker-talks-usas-cba-not-feasible/.

36. Ricky Bevington, "Turner Field Neighbors Divided Over Community Benefits Agreement," *GPB Radio,* May 12, 2017, https://www.gpb.org/news/2017/05/12/turner-field-neighbors-divided-over-community-benefits-agreement.

37. City of Atlanta, "Frequently Asked Questions: The Gulch Development Project," accessed May 15, 2021, https://www.atlantaga.gov/home/showpublisheddocument?id = 38456.

38. J. Scott Trubey, "The Atlanta Gulch Deal Explained," *Atlanta Journal-Constitution,* November 7, 2018, https://www.ajc.com/news/local-govt—politics/the-gulch-deal-explained-what-you-need-know-about-the-proposal/YVhVQeTzOl9ginjCrm5VrO/.

39. Vanessa McCray and J. Scott Trubey, "Atlanta School Chief Sets Gulch Conditions," *Atlanta Journal-Constitution,* October 6, 2018, A1.

40. Mike Dobbins, William Boone, J. C. Bradbury, Dan Immergluck, and Julian Bene, "Independent Review of the City-Gulch Proposal on Behalf of the Residents of the city of Atlanta," Unpublished memo. October 23, 2018.

41. Ibid.

42. Author's calculations using Proquest Central database of *AJC* articles.

43. Laura Kusisto, "Luxury Apartment Building Boom Fuels Rent Squeeze," *Wall Street Journal,* May 21, 2015, A2.

44. Terri Lee, "Affordable Housing Key Goal," *Atlanta Journal Constitution,* June 5, 2015, A12.

45. Maria Saporta, "Mayor Reed to Work to Keep City "Equitable" in 2016," *Saporta Report,* February 9, 2016. https://saportareport.com/mayor-reed-work-keep-city-equitable-2016/sections/abcarticles/maria_saporta/.

46. Dan Immergluck, Ann Carpenter, and Abram Lueders, "Declines in Low-Cost Rented Housing Units in Eight Large Southeastern Cities," Community & Economic Development Discussion Paper, No. 03–16, Federal Reserve Bank of Atlanta, May 2016.

47. Tasnim Shamma, "Atlanta Passes Ordinance for More Affordable Housing," *WABE Radio*, May 3, 2016, https://www.wabe.org/atlanta-passes-ordinance-more-affordable-housing/.

48. Matthew Cardinale, "Atlanta Moves Forward with Mandatory Inclusionary Zoning," *Atlanta Progressive News*, December 12, 2017, http://atlantaprogressivenews.com/2017/12/12/atlanta-moves-forward-with-mandatory-inclusionary-zoning/.

49. City of Atlanta, Ordinance 17–0–1542 Z-17–73, approved November 29, 2017, accessed May 19, 2021, https://www.atlantaga.gov/home/showpublisheddocument?id = 38768.

50. City for All, "Ten Essential Priorities," accessed May 21, 2021, https://www.cityforall.org/#:~:text = The%20City%20for%20All%20Coalition,for%20housing%20affordability%20and%20accessibility.

51. J. Scott Trubey and Stephen Deere, "Plan Tackles Challenge of Affordable Housing," Atlanta Journal-Constitution, June 25, 2019, A1.

52. House ATL, "Who is Involved?" Accessed May 18, 2021, https://houseatl.org/who-is-involved/.

53. House ATL, "Recommendations," accessed May 19, 2021, https://houseatl.org/recommendations/.

54. J. Scott Trubey and Stephen Deere, "Plan Tackles Challenge of Affordable Housing," Atlanta Journal-Constitution, June 25, 2019, A1.

55. City of Atlanta, Housing Affordability Action Plan, June 2019, https://www.atlantaga.gov/government/mayor-s-office/projects-and-initiatives/housing-affordability-action-plan.

56. City of Atlanta, "Mayor Keisha Lance Bottoms Signs $50 Million Housing Bond Legislation," January 11, 2021, https://www.atlantaga.gov/Home/Components/News/News/13559/.

57. Maria Saporta, "Atlanta Mayor Kasim Reed and AHA's Renee Glover Never Built a Workable Partnership," *Saporta Report*, October 16, 2011, https://saportareport.com/atlanta-mayor-kasim-reed-never-connected-with-ahas-renee-glover/columnists/mariasmetro/maria_saporta/.

58. Willoughby Mariano, "Housing Agency's Land May Go for Upscale Use," *Atlanta Journal-Constitution*, March 12, 2017, A1.

59. Willoughby Mariano, "Atlanta Housing Agency: $120M Windfall for Developer in Disputed Deal," *Atlanta Journal-Constitution*, October 12, 2017,

https://www.ajc.com/news/local/atlanta-housing-agency-120m-windfall-for-developer-disputed-deal/IsgZDjqIp3M9n1139lJXjL/.

60. Maria Saporta, "Atlanta Developer Egbert Perry Fires Back at Mayor Kasim Reed, Atlanta Housing Authority," *Atlanta Business Chronicle*, November 7,2017,https://www.bizjournals.com/atlanta/news/2017/11/07/atlanta-developer-egbert-perry-fires-back-at-mayor.html.

61. The details in this paragraph are taken from Atlanta Housing, Inc. and Integral Development, LLC, "Settlement Agreement and Release," December 18, 2019. Unpublished document.

62. The housing authority had pegged the value of the parcels at over \$130 million, relying on estimates from a consultant. Even if the housing authority's estimate was too high, and there is reason to expect that it was, the option price was likely a fraction of what the land was actually worth at the time of the settlement. Hopefully the profit-share agreement in the settlement will improve the financial equity of the arrangement. This may depend on whether the authority shares equally in all the sources of effective profits, including development fees.

63. Stephannie Stokes, "Battle Over Empty Land Touches on Atlanta's Approach to Affordable Housing," *WABE Radio*, January 19, 2018, https://www.wabe.org/battle-empty-land-touches-atlantas-approach-affordable-housing/.

64. Mariano, supra, note 58.

65. Max Bau, "Atlanta's Housing Authority Stopped Building Rental Units for Nearly a Decade," *Atlanta Magazine*, November 13, 2018, https://www.atlantamagazine.com/news-culture-articles/atlantas-housing-authority-stopped-building-rental-units-for-nearly-a-decade-can-it-make-up-for-lost-time/.

66. Data in this paragraph were derived from data in: National Housing Preservation Database, accessed May 25, 2021, https://preservationdatabase.org/.

67. Austin Harrison, Dan Immergluck, Jeff Ernsthausen, and Stephanie Earl, "Housing Stability, Evictions, and Subsidized Rental Properties: Evidence from Metro Atlanta, Georgia," *Housing Policy Debate* (2020): 1–14.

68. Gregory Preston and Vincent J. Reina, "Sheltered from Eviction? A Framework for Understanding the Relationship Between Subsidized Housing Programs and Eviction." *Housing Policy Debate* (2021): 1–33.

69. Calculations of data obtained from Princeton University's EvictionLab .org.

70. The analysis discussed in this paragraph is based on an ordinary-least-squares regression using data from EvictionLab.org for 1,306 census block groups in the five core counties of the Atlanta region (Clayton, Cobb, DeKalb, Fulton, and Gwinnett). The dependent variable was the eviction (judgement) rate per 100 rental units. The independent variables included: percent Black, percent Hispanic, percent Asian, poverty rate, percent renters, median gross rent, median household income, median home value, and the portion of renters who were cost-burdened. Details not shown, but available from the author.

71. Megan Hatch, "Statutory Protection for Renters: Classification of State Landlord–Tenant Policy Approaches," *Housing Policy Debate* 27, no. 1 (2017): 98–119.

72. Than Merrill, "A Guide to the Most Landlord-Friendly States," *Fortune Builders*, accessed on May 5, 2021 at https://www.fortunebuilders.com /landlord-friendly-states/.

73. Elora Lee Raymond, Ben Miller, Michaela McKinney, and Jonathan Braun, "Gentrifying Atlanta: Investor Purchases of Rental Housing, Evictions, and the Displacement of Black Residents," *Housing Policy Debate* (2021): 1–17.

74. The figures in this sentence are from author's calculations of data obtained from Princeton University's EvictionLab.org.

75. City of Atlanta Planning Department, "Atlanta Zoning Ordinance Update, Phase 11," accessed May 20, 2021, https://citycouncil.atlantaga.gov /Home/ShowDocument?id = 1366. Michael Dobbins, former city of Atlanta planning commissioner, quoted in Taylor Berry, "Atlanta Zoning Rewrites Could Bring Transit, Parking Changes," *University Wire*, April 4, 2016.

76. City of Atlanta, Ordinance 18-0–1581, adopted January 22, 2019, accessed June 23, 2021, https://library.municode.com/ga/atlanta/ordinances/code_of_ ordinances?nodeId = 939835.

77. The twenty-two percent figure was calculated by the author from shape files obtained from the Atlanta Department of City Planning. The sixty percent figure is from Atlanta Department of City Planning, "Atlanta City Design Housing," March 15, 2021.

78. Eric Bethany, "Why ADUs are So Hard to Build, and How Atlanta Could Make It Easier," Atlanta: Kronberg Urbanists Architects, October 29,

2020, https://www.kronbergua.com/post/why-adus-are-so-hard-to-build-and-how-atlanta-could-make-it-easier.

79. Tim Keane and Terri Lee, "Intentionally Shaping a Better Housing Future in Atlanta," *Atlanta Journal-Constitution*, December 20, 2020, A20.

80. Ben Hirsch, "Atlanta Mayor Endorses Sweeping Rezoning That Would Impact Buckhead," *Buckhead*, December 23, 2020, https://www.buckhead.com/atlanta-mayor-proposes-sweeping-rezoning-that-would-impact-buckhead/.

81. Sean Keenan, "Atlanta Mayor Says Density-Focused Zoning Changes Could Be Scaled Down," *Saporta Report*, April 15, 2021, https://saportareport.com/atlanta-mayor-says-density-focused-zoning-changes-could-be-scaled-down/atlanta-civic-circle/housing-affordability/seankeenan/.

82. The 37,000 figure includes condominium buildings with more than five units, but very few of those were developed over this period in the city of Atlanta. Data were calculated from U.S. Department of Housing and Urban Development State of the Cities Data System Build Permits Database, accessed June 22, 2021, https://socds.huduser.gov/permits/.

CHAPTER 4. SUBPRIMED ATLANTA

1. Keeanga-Yamahtta Taylor, *Race for Profit: How Banks and the Real Estate Industry Undermined Black Homeownership* (Chapel Hill: University of North Carolina Press, 2019), 5.

2. Dan Immergluck, "The Local Wreckage of Global Capital: The Subprime Crisis, Federal Policy and High-Foreclosure Neighborhoods in the US," *International Journal of Urban and Regional Research* 35, no. 1 (2011): 130–146.

3. Dan Immergluck, *Foreclosed: High-Risk Lending, Deregulation, and the Undermining of America's Mortgage Market* (Ithaca: Cornell University Press, 2009), 72–84.

4. Kathe Newman, "Post-industrial Widgets: Capital Flows and the Production of the Urban. *International Journal of Urban and Regional Research* 33 no. 2 (2009): 314–331.

5. For a fuller discussion of the subprime boom and the resulting foreclosure crisis, see Immergluck, supra, note 3.

6. The case of the Georgia Fair Lending Act is told in more detail in Immergluck, supra, note 3, 172–173, 178–179.

7. The Financial Crisis Inquiry Commission, "Financial Crisis Inquiry Report." February 25, 2011, https://www.govinfo.gov/content/pkg/GPO-FCIC/pdf/GPO-FCIC.pdf, pp. 123, 124.

8. High-cost mortgages are defined in the Home Mortgage Disclosure Act regulations as those where the annual percentage rate on a loan is at least three percentage-points higher than interest rate on treasury securities of the same maturity, and are a common measure of subprime loans. For more information, see https://www.federalreserve.gov/pubs/bulletin/2006/hmda/default.htm.

9. Dan Immergluck and Marti Wiles, "Two Steps Back: The Dual Mortgage Market. Predatory Lending, and the Undoing of Community Development," (Chicago: The Woodstock Institute, 1999).

10. Carolina Reid, Debbie Bocian, Wei Li, and Roberto G. Quercia, "Revisiting the Subprime Crisis: The Dual Mortgage Market and Mortgage Defaults by Race and Ethnicity," *Journal of Urban Affairs* 39, no. 4 (2017): 469–487.

11. Ibid.

12. Data on foreclosure notices were calculated by the author from data from the Atlanta Regional Council, derived from foreclosure notices published in county legal organs. The available data consistent over this period cover thirteen counties in the region, including the five core counties of Fulton, DeKalb, Cobb, Gwinnett, and Clayton, and account for a large majority of single-family mortgages in the broader metropolitan area.

13. Dan Immergluck, *Preventing the Next Mortgage Crisis: The Meltdown, the Federal Response, and the Future of Housing in America* (Lanham: Rowman and Littlefield), 52–53.

14. Some neighborhoods, including some majority-Black ones, had too few sales in 2011 (or occasionally 2006) to calculate a home price index, so that a change in home values from 2006 to 2011 could not be calculated. These tracts are shown by the cross-hatched areas on the left-side map of Map 11.

15. Peter Dreier, Saqib Bhatti, Rob Call, Alex Schwartz, and Greg Squires. "Underwater America," Haas Institute, 2014, https://belonging.berkeley.edu/sites/default/files/haasinsitute_underwateramerica_publish_0.pdf.

16. These figures were calculated from using the Federal Housing Finance Agency repeat sales index at the census tract level, accessed April 21, 2021, https://www.fhfa.gov/DataTools/Downloads/Pages/House-Price-Index-Datasets.aspx, and 2010 Decennial Census data.

17. Elora Raymond, Kyungsoon Wang, and Dan Immergluck. "Race and Uneven Recovery: Neighborhood Home Value Trajectories in Atlanta Before and After the Housing Crisis." *Housing Studies* 31, no. 3 (2016): 324–339.

18. Author's calculation from USPS vacancy data compiled by census tract by the U.S. Department of Housing and Urban Development, accessed November 22, 2019, https://www.huduser.gov/portal/datasets/usps.html.

19. This and the following discussion on the initial (2007, 2008) regional response to the foreclosure crisis relies largely on: Todd Swanstrom, Karen Chapple, and Dan Immergluck, "Regional Resilience in the Face of Foreclosures: Evidence from Six Metropolitan Areas," University of California Berkeley Institute of Urban and Regional Development. May 27, 2009, https://escholarship.org/uc/item/23s3q06x.

20. Dan Immergluck, "Too Little, Too Late, and Too Timid: The Federal Response to the Foreclosure Crisis at the Five-Year Mark," *Housing Policy Debate* 23, no. 1 (2013): 199–232.

21. Ibid.

22. Ibid.

23. Alan Judd, "Foreclosures: No Rush on Debt Relief in Georgia," *Atlanta Journal-Constitution*. June 1, 2008, A1.

24. Ibid.

25. Ruling quoted in Greg Bluestein, "Foreclosures Too Easy, Georgia Supreme Court Says," *Atlanta Journal-Constitution*, May 30, 2013.

26. Katie Leslie. "Funds for at-Risk Homeowners Idle: Mortgage Assistance Program's Marketing, Eligibility Rules Get Flak," *Atlanta Journal-Constitution*, April 5, 2012. A.1.

27. Office of the Special Inspector General of Troubled Asset Relief Program, "Georgia's State Housing Finance Agency Has Mismanaged the Hardest Hit Fund Program," October 13, 2017, https://www.sigtarp.gov/sites/sigtarp/files/Audit_Reports/Georgia_HHF_Audit_Press_Release.pdf.

28. Ibid.

29. Dan Immergluck, "Distressed and Dumped: Market Dynamics of Low-Value, Foreclosed Properties During the Advent of the Federal Neighborhood Stabilization Program," *Journal of Planning Education and Research* 32, no. 1 (2012): 48–61.

30. Harriet Newberger, "Acquiring Privately Held REO Properties with Public Funds: The case of the Neighborhood Stabilization Program," Washington, DC: Federal Reserve Board of Governors, September 1, 2010, https://www.bostonfed.org/publications/one-time-pubs/reo-vacant-properties-strategies-for-neighborhood-stabilization.aspx.

31. Immergluck, supra note 29.

32. For some discussion of this, see Dan Immergluck and Jonathan Law, "Investing in Crisis: The Methods, Strategies, And Expectations of Investors in Single-Family Foreclosed Homes in Distressed Neighborhoods," *Housing Policy Debate* 24, no. 3 (2014): 568–593.

33. Eric Stirgus, "City Up Against Deadline for Funds," *Atlanta Journal-Constitution*, January 26, 2010, A1.

34. Michael Pell, "Housing Rehab Effort Struggles to Lift Areas," *Atlanta Journal-Constitution*, November 29, 2012, A1.

35. Atlanta Regional Commission. "A Region Responds Neighborhood Stabilization Program Overview of NSP 1 Implementation and Best Practices in Metro Atlanta," Atlanta: Atlanta Regional Commission, 2012, https://files.hudexchange.info/resources/documents/ AtlantaNSPOverviewBestPractices.pdf.

36. Atlanta Neighborhood Development Partnership, "Impact of Rehab Investments on Neighborhood Home Values in Douglas County, GA," Atlanta: Atlanta Neighborhood Development Partnership, September 2015, https://e96d8fd0–8057–4990–8ee2-f9ddd1doc1da.filesusr.com/ugd/9bcf20_a01ba95f-86b14bbobb2334d33966cc1a.pdf/. Also see Atlanta Neighborhood Development Partnership, "Creating Homeownership and Economic Opportunity," Atlanta: Atlanta Neighborhood Development Partnership, August 2019, https://e96d8fd0–8057–4990–8ee2-f9ddd1doc1da.filesusr.com/ugd/. 9bcf20_08do464e3af140739d46799f441a8424.pdf.

37. Pell, 2012, supra, note 34.

38. A community land trust (CLT) is a form of land trust in which a modest-income homebuyer buys only the structure, while the land beneath is owned by

the CLT. It is a form of "shared-equity homeownership" in that appreciation gains to the homeowner are contractually limited and the home is generally required to be sold, under similar terms, to another modest-income homebuyer.

39. Dan Immergluck, "The Beltline and Rising Home Prices: Residential Appreciation Near the Beltline Tax Allocation District," Atlanta: Georgia Stand Up. September 2007, https://www.forworkingfamilies.org/sites/default/files/publications/archive/ga/TheBeltlineAndRisingHomePrices.pdf.

40. Atlanta Land Trust, "A Timeline of Our Progress," accessed April 21, 2021. https://atlantalandtrust.org/who-we-are/history/.

41. Russell Grantham. "Investors Scoop Up Omni homes," *Atlanta Journal-Constitution*, March 28, 2010, D1.

42. Russell Grantham and Scott Trubey, "Housing Collapse Leaves Trail of Blight," *Atlanta Journal Constitution*, October 28, 2012, A1.

43. Ta-Nehisi Coates, "The Case for Reparations," *The Atlantic*, June 2014, https://www.theatlantic.com/magazine/archive/2014/06/the-case-for-reparations/361631/ and Beryl Satter, *Family Properties: Race, Real Estate and the Exploitation of Black Urban America* (New York: Picador, 2009).

44. Jeremiah Battle, Sarah Mancini, Margo Saunders and Odette Williamson, "Toxic Transactions: How Land Installment Contracts Once Again Threaten Communities of Color," Washington, DC: National Consumer Law Center. July 2016, https://www.nclc.org/images/pdf/pr-reports/report-land-contracts.pdf.

45. Dan Immergluck, "Old Wine in Private Equity Bottles? The Resurgence of Contract-For-Deed Home Sales in US Urban Neighborhoods," *International Journal of Urban and Regional Research* 42, no. 4 (2018): 651–665. And see Matthew Goldstein, Matthew and Alexandra Stevenson, "Market for Fixer-Uppers Traps Low-Income Buyers. *The New York Times*. February 21, 2016, A1.

46. Atlanta Legal Aid, "2018 Harbour Portfolio," accessed April 21, 2021, https://atlantalegalaid.org/portfolio-item/2018-harbour-portfolio/.

47. All of the numbers in this paragraph are from, Dan Immergluck, "Renting the Dream: The Rise of Single-Family Rentership in the Sunbelt Metropolis," *Housing Policy Debate* 28, no. 5 (2018): 814–829.

48. Ibid.

49. Sandeep Bordia, "U.S. Single Family Rental—An Emerging Institutional Asset Class," Urban Institute Data Talk Presentation, Washington, DC:

Urban Institute, September, 26, 2017, https://www.urban.org/sites/default/files/2017/09/26/final_presentations_-_single-family_rentals_2.pdf.

50. Joshua Beroukhim, "The Story and Lessons Behind Invitation Homes," Behind the Deals, March 15, 2017, https://behindthedeals.com/2017/03/15/the-story-and-lessons-behind-invitation-homes-blackstones-acquisition-of-50000-single-family-homes-for-10-billion-between-2012-and-2016/.

51. Quoted in Francesca, Mara, "A $60 Billion Housing Grab by Wall Street," *The New York Times Magazine*, March 4, 2020, https://www.nytimes.com/2020/03/04/magazine/wall-street-landlords.html.

52. Suzanne Lanyi Charles, "The Financialization of Single-Family Rental Housing: An Examination of Real Estate Investment Trusts' Ownership of Single-Family Houses in the Atlanta Metropolitan Area," *Journal of Urban Affairs* 42, no. 8 (2020): 1321–1341.

53. Ibid.

54. Board of Governors of the Federal Reserve System, "The U.S. Housing Market: Current Conditions and Policy Considerations," Washington, DC: Board of Governors of the Federal Reserve System, January 4, 2012, https://www.federalreserve.gov/publications/other-reports/files/housing-white-paper-20120104.pdf.

55. Ibid., 25.

56. I somehow managed to be invited to two of these in the Atlanta area in 2012.

57. Brett Christophers, "The Role of the State in the Transfer of Value from Main Street to Wall Street: US Single-Family Housing after the Financial Crisis," *Antipode* (2021). https://doi.org/10.1111/anti.12760.

58. Alex Crippen, "Warren Buffet on CNBC: I'd Buy Up a Couple Hundred Thousand' Single Family Homes if I Could," CNBC, February 27, 2012, https://www.cnbc.com/id/46538421.

59. Kerry Curry, "Invitation to a Housing Revolution," *D Magazine*, April 2018, https://www.dmagazine.com/publications/d-ceo/2018/april/invitation-homes-rental-dallas/.

60. Arielle Kass, "Big-scale Buyers Drive Housing Sales," *Atlanta Journal-Constitution*, March 17, 2013, D.1.

61. Board of Governors of the Federal Reserve System, supra, note 54, p. 13.

62. Aaron Smith and Stephen Gande, "Blackstone CEO Schwarzman's $223 Million Year," *Money*, February 29, 2012, https://money.cnn.com/2012/02/29/news/companies/blackstone_schwarzman/ index.htm#:~:text = That%20includes%20Schwarzman%27s%202011%20salary,It%20also%20includes%20his%20dividends. And Reuters, 2016, "Blackstone CEO Took Home $810.6 million in 2015," Reuters, February 26, https://www.reuters.com/article/us-blackstone-group-schwarzman/blackstone-ceo-took-home-810–6-million-in-2015-idUSKCN0W004N.

63. Rob Call, Denechia Powell, and Sarah Heck, "Blackstone: Atlanta's Newest Landlord," Atlanta: Homes for All Atlanta and The Right to the City Alliance, April 2014, https://homesforall.org/wp content/uploads/2014/04/BlackstoneReportFinal0407141.pdf.

64. Alana Semuels, 2019, "When Wall Street is Your Landlord," *The Atlantic*, February 13, https://www.theatlantic.com/technology/archive/2019/02/single-family-landlords-wall-street/582394/.

65. Elora Raymond, Richard Duckworth, Ben Miller, Michael Lucas, and Shiraj Pokharel, "From Foreclosure to Eviction: Housing Insecurity in Corporate-Owned Single-Family Rentals," *Cityscape* 20, no. 3 (2018): 159–188.

66. Todd Frankel and Dan Keating, "Eviction Filings and Code Complaints: What Happened When a Private Equity Firm Became One City's Biggest Homeowner," *Washington Post*, December 25, 2018, https://www.washingtonpost.com/business/economy/eviction-filings-and-code-complaints-what-happened-when-a-private-equity-firm-became-one-citys-biggest-homeowner/2018/12/25/995678d4–02f3–11e9-b6a9–0aa5c2fcc9e4_story.html.

67. Emily Mahoney and Ben Wieder, "Multi-millionaire French Heirs to Hermes Fortune Own Stake in Tampa Rental Houses," February 19, 2021, https://www.tampabay.com/news/real-estate/2021/02/19/multi-millionaire-french-heirs-to-hermes-fortune-own-stake-in-tampa-rental-houses/.

68. Semuels, supra, note 64.

69. Michelle Conlin, "Spiders, Sewage and a Flurry of Fees—The Other Side of Renting a House from Wall Street," *Reuters*, July 27, 2018, https://www.reuters.com/investigates/special-report/usa-housing-invitation/.

70. Semuels, supra, note 64.

71. Mara, supra, note 51.

72. The exception here is California, where SFR firms have been active in some metros. The size of the market is so large that it may have been hard to avoid.

73. Ryan Dezember and Nick Timiraos, "Fannie Mae Expands Role to Backing Home Rentals," *Wall Street Journal*, January 26, 2017, B5.

74. Lorraine Woellert, "Fannie Mae's $1 Billion Blackstone Deal Draws Fire," *Politico*, February 1, 2017.

75. Elina Tarkazikis, "FHFA Halts Program Expanding GSEs' Role in Rental Market," *American Banker*. August 22, 2018.

76. Laurie Goodman, Jun Zhu, and Taz George, 2014, "Where Have All the Loans Gone? The Impact of Credit Availability on Mortgage Volume," *Journal of Structured Finance* 20: 45–53.

77. Dan Immergluck, Stephanie Earl, and Allison Powell, "Black Homebuying after the Crisis: Appreciation Patterns in Fifteen Large Metropolitan Areas," *City & Community* 18, no. 3 (2019): 983–1002.

78. Ibid.

79. Atlanta Neighborhood Development Partnership, "Creating Homeownership and Economic Opportunity," Atlanta: Atlanta Neighborhood Development Partnership, August 2019, https://e96d8fd0–8057–4990–8ee2-f9ddd1d0c1da.filesusr.com/ugd/. 9bcf20_08d0464e3af140739d46799f441a8424.pdf.

80. ANDP also analyzed the gains of the thirty-two borrowers who had resold their homes. The average among these owners sold after 3.6 years and realized appreciation of thirty-one percent over their ownership period.

CHAPTER 5. DIVERSITY AND EXCLUSION IN THE SUBURBS

1. These figures are from the 2000 Decennial Census and the 2019 American Community Survey one-year estimates. The figures are for the metropolitan statistical area as defined by the Office of Management and Budget and the Census Bureau at the two different points in time and does not use a constant geographic area. The expanded number of counties reflects the growing geographic scope of the region. However, the nine counties added the Atlanta MSA from 2000 to 2019 only accounted for 3.1 percent of the 2019 MSA population, so the boundary changes do not have a substantial influence on the large changes that occurred in the region. The population growth and demographic

changes are due almost to changes in the counties that comprised the 2000 definition of the region.

2. Truman Hartschorn and Keith Ihlandfeldt, "The Dynamics of Change: An Analysis of Growth in Metropolitan Atlanta over the Past Two Decades," Research Atlanta, 1993, https://digitalcollections.library.gsu.edu/digital/collection/research ATL/id/9618.

3. Katherine Hankins and Steve Holloway, "Suburbanization and the Making of Atlanta as the 'Black Mecca'," in *The Life of North American Suburbs* (Toronto: University of Toronto Press, 2020), 223–244.

4. Dan Immergluck, Stephanie Earl, and Allison Powell. "Black Homebuying after the Crisis: Appreciation Patterns in Fifteen Large Metropolitan Areas." *City & Community* 18, no. 3 (2019): 983–1002.

5. The analysis of tract-level changes uses a constant-geography for both the region and the neighborhoods. It uses 2010 census tracts. Tract-level data for 2000 are estimated for 2010 census tracts per SocialExplorer.com. The latest tract-level data available at the time of writing was five-year ACS data for the years 2015 through 2019. While this is often referred to as "2019 5-year data," the midpoint of the survey period is 2017, so is referred to as 2017 data here.

6. I used a similar approach to that of other scholars studying concentrated affluence. The threshold for defining very affluent neighborhoods was a tract median income that was at least double the median of the metropolitan area. For example, in the 2015 to 2019 American Community Survey, the metropolitan median household income was just over $68,000, so if a tract has a median income over $136,000, it was classified as very affluent for 2017. For a similar approach, but using the national median income as the base instead of the metropolitan median income, see Edward Goetz, Anthony Damiano, and Rashad A. Williams. "Racially Concentrated Areas of Affluence," *Cityscape* 21, no. 1 (2019): 99–124.

7. Michael Neal, Cait Young, and Jung Choi, "Housing Wealth Equity Initiative: Racial and Ethnic Homeownership Gaps in Atlanta," Urban Institute. Presentation. April 19, 2021.

8. These data are from the 2019 Home Mortgage Disclosure Act data and include only owner-occupied homebuyers using a mortgage, so they exclude all cash buyers as well as investors using mortgages.

9. Audrey Singer, "Metropolitan Immigrant Gateways Revisited, 2014," Washington, D.C.: The Brookings Institution (2015).

10. Paul McDaniel, Darlene Xiomara Rodriguez, and Anna Joo Kim, "Receptivity and The Welcoming Cities Movement: Advancing a Regional Immigrant Integration Policy Framework in Metropolitan Atlanta, Georgia," *Papers in Applied Geography* 3, no. 3–4 (2017): 355–379.

11. Susan Walcott, "Overlapping Ethnicities and Negotiated Space: Atlanta's Buford Highway," *Journal of Cultural Geography* 20, no. 1 (2002): 51–75.

12. AJ Kim, "A Welcoming (and Sometimes Not) America: Immigrant Integration in the New South", *Metropolitics*, 1, November 2016, https://metropolitics.org/A-Welcoming-and-Sometimes-Not.html; Kathryn Wilson, "Atlanta: Immigrant Gateway of the Globalized South," National Council on Public History, February 19, 2020, https://ncph.org/history-at-work/atlanta-immigrant-gateway-globalized-south/.

13. Marian Liou, "Opinion: A vision for Buford Highway," *Brookhaven Reporter*, June 11, 2016, https://reporternewspapers.net/2016/06/11/opiniona-vision-buford-highway/.

14. Adam Newman, "Rethinking Buford Highway: An Interview with Marian Liou," *Atlanta Studies*, April 13, 2017, https://www.atlantastudies.org/2017/04/13/rethinking-buford-highway-an-interview-with-marian-liou/.

15. Walcott, supra, note 11.

16. Tia Mitchell, "Region's Culture: Buford Highway," *Atlanta Journal-Constitution*, March 4, 2018, A1.

17. All figures in this paragraph are from the 2015–2019 five-year American Community Survey. 2017 is the midpoint year of the survey and so these figures are considered estimates for 2017. All dollar figures are adjusted by the consumer price index to 2021 dollars.

18. Walcott, supra, note 11.

19. John Logan and Charles Zhang. "Global Neighborhoods: New Pathways to Diversity and Separation," *American Journal of Sociology* 115, no. 4 (2010): 1069–1109.

20. The Census Bureau uses the term "foreign-born" to categorize immigrants. Thus, immigrants here are those born in other countries, including those who moved to an area from another part of the U.S. The data here are from the 2015–2019 American Community Survey, and so the center date of 2017 is used.

21. Angie Schmitt, "The Campaign to Fix Atlanta's Most Dangerous Street and Preserve Its Immigrant Cultures," *Streetsblog*, September 21, 2017, https://usa.streetsblog.org/2017/09/21/the-campaign-to-fix-atlantas-most-dangerous-street-and-preserve-its-immigrant-cultures/.

22. These data were calculated from the 2000–2014 and 2015–2019 five-year American Community Survey and are for gross rents. While the relatively large ACS rent categories do not allow for adjusting rents by inflation, the cumulative consumer price index (CPI for expenses less shelter) for the Atlanta metro over this period was less than three percent, so non-housing inflation did not account for an appreciable amount of these declines.

23. City of Brookhaven, "City of Brookhaven Affordable Housing Task Force Report and Recommendations," July 25, 2017, https://www.brookhavenga.gov/sites/default/files/fileattachments/community_development/page/16983/executive_summary_recommendations.07.25.2017.pdf.

24. Dyana Bagby, "Coalition Forms to Address Affordable Housing on Buford Highway," *Brookhaven Reporter*, May 13, 2018, https://reporternewspapers.net/2018/05/13/coalition-forms-to-address-affordable-housing-on-buford-highway/.

25. Adina Solomon, "The Uncertain Future of North Atlanta's Most Affordable Cities," *Curbed Atlanta*, March 11, 2019, https://atlanta.curbed.com/atlanta-development/2019/3/11/18253838/chamblee-doraville-atlanta-development-affordability.

26. Liou, supra, note 13.

27. Michael Maciag, Michael, "How Many Local Governments is Too Many?" *Governing*, May 7, 2019, https://www.governing.com/topics/politics/gov-most-local-governments-census.html.

28. Arlinda Smith Broady, "Drive for New Cities Began in Sandy Springs," *Atlanta Journal-Constitution*, March 19, 2020, https://www.ajc.com/news/local/drive-for-new-cities-began-sandy-springs/WxLnVdtWFFidI2PsQmSSZL/.

29. Michan Andrew Connor, "Metropolitan Secession and the Space of Color-Blind Racism in Atlanta." *Journal of Urban Affairs* 37, no. 4 (2015): 436–461.

30. In the second half of the 2010s, some less-affluent suburbs began to incorporate, including two predominantly Black suburbs, Stonecrest and South Fulton.

31. Sam Rosen, "Atlanta's Controversial 'Cityhood' Movement: Recent Border Battles Have Once Again Redrawn the Lines of the Metro Area," *The Atlantic*. April 27, 2017, https://www.theatlantic.com/business/archive/2017/04/the-border-battles-of-atlanta/523884/.

32. Stephen Deere, "Cityhood Movements Grow After Cobb County's Blue Wave," *Atlanta Journal-Constitution*, May 25, 2021. https://www.ajc.com/news/atlanta-news/cityhood-movements-grow-following-cobb-countys-blue-wave/WLDLYONCOBAC3CPITMGLEOSVUE/.

33. The state legislature, at the behest of the powerful Georgia lumber industry, stepped in to preempt such bans of lumber construction in 2018. See Everett Catts, "Bill nullifying part of Sandy Springs' building code OK'd," *Northside Neighbor*, March 20, 2018, https://www.mdjonline.com/neighbor_newspapers/northside_sandy_springs/bill-nullifying-part-of-sandy-springs-building-code-okd/article_2c1b9a8e-2c60–11e8-b151–3b858a7ac20e.html. The city left its ban in place, however, effectively daring developers to challenge it in court. Reportedly, developers did not seek permits for projects going against the ban even after the state preemption was enacted.

34. HR&A, "Sandy Springs Housing Needs Assessment," city of Sandy Springs, December 2020, https://www.sandyspringsga.gov/home/showpublisheddocument/23970/637431003597830000.

35. Sean Keenan, "Dunwoody Halts Apartment, Condo Development for Six Months," *Curbed Atlanta*, November 26, 2018, https://atlanta.curbed.com/2018/11/26/18112347/dunwoody-apartment-condo-development-moratorium.

36. Dyana Bagby, "Dunwoody to Form and Affordable Housing Task Force," *Dunwoody Reporter*, March 2, 2018, https://reporternewspapers.net/2018/03/02/dunwoody-form-affordable-housing-task-force/.

37. Ibid.

38. Bill Torpy, "Apartments Focus of Controversy in Dunwoody," *Atlanta Journal-Constitution*, August 31, 2013, https://www.ajc.com/news/apartments-focus-controversy-dunwoody/qJ1TmvHoifd6Pz7kHcqbFK/.

39. Erin Schilling, "On Racial Dialog, Dunwoody Takes a Different Course from Other Local Cities," *Dunwoody Reporter*, October 10, 2020, https://reporternewspapers.net/2020/10/10/on-racial-dialogue-dunwoody-takes-different-course-from-other-local-cities/.

40. Ibid.

41. Sam Lenaeus, "The Case and Reasons for De-Annexing to Create Buckhead City," Atlanta Journal-Constitution, May 1, 2021, https://www.ajc.com /opinion/opinion-the-case-and-reasons-for-de-annexing-to-create-buckhead-city /TJLYAJIKGVGMTG7XLY23TFSU44/.

42. KB Advisory Services, "Buckhead De-Annexation Fiscal Analysis," August 2021, https://static1.squarespace.com/static/60ad1429731b6a1179d5a5ba /t/6142492756eec74b629ff3d8/1631734060061/Buckhead+De-Annexation+Fiscal+ Impact.pdf.

43. Brett Pulley and Brentin Mock, "Atlanta's Wealthiest and Whitest District wants to Secede," Bloomberg, October 1, 2021, https://www.bloomberg. com/news/features/2021-10-01/buckhead-cityhood-vote-district-wants-to-secede-from-atlanta.

44. Ibid.

45. Ibid.

46. Elisa Lanari, "Envisioning a New City Center: Time, Displacement, and Atlanta's Suburban Futures," City & Society, Volume 31, no. 3 (2019): 365–391.

47. Anne Marie Quill, "Demolition Under Way for the Gateway Project," Sandy Springs Reporter, March 20, 2014, https://reporternewspapers.net/2014/03 /20/demolition-way-gateway-project/.

48. Josh Green, "Behold The 21-Acre 'Sandy Springs Gateway' Project," Curbed Atlanta, March 21, 2014, https://atlanta.curbed.com/2014/3/21/10128764 /behold-the-21acre-sandy-springs-gateway-project.

49. These estimates were generated from two documents. First was the housing needs assessment performed by a housing consultant for the city of Sandy Springs in 2020, HR&A, supra, note 34. HR&A identified 1,073 apartment units in four buildings that were demolished from 2013 to 2015 in the Gateway project area. In a comment on the city's fair housing analysis of impediments document, Melanie and David Couchman detail figures from Scott Markley, a researcher at the University of Georgia, who identified properties demolished in the city, including three of the properties identified in the HR&A study, in: Melanie Noble-Couchman and David Couchman, "Comments on 2020 Draft Analysis of Impediments to Fair Housing," March 6, 2020, https://sandyspringstogether.org/wp-content/uploads/2020/03/SSTs-Public-Comments-on-CDBG-2020.pdf. Three of the buildings from the two documents overlap. Markley identified 865 units that were demolished, but some of

the unit counts were higher in the HR&A analysis. Markley estimated that 2,589 residents lived in the 865 apartments that he identified as demolished. Thus, assuming that the 1,073 apartments identified as demolished by HR&A have similar numbers of residents per unit, they are expected to contain over 3,200 residents. Markley uses census block-level data to estimate the racial composition of the five buildings and estimates that sixty-five percent of the displaced tenants were Latinx and another seventeen percent were Black, with the Latinx shares especially being much higher than the overall Sandy Springs Latinx population.

50. Noble-Couchman and Couchman, supra, note 49.

51. Figures in this paragraph are calculated from the U.S. Decennial Census for 1980 and 2000.

52. HR&A, supra, note, 34.

53. Elisa Lanari, "Excluded from 'Everybody's Neighborhood? Constructing Sandy Springs New City Center," Atlanta Studies, February 9, 2017, https://www.atlantastudies.org/2017/02/09/excluded-from-everybodys-neighborhood-constructing-sandy-springs-new-city-center/.

54. Scott Markley, "From Exclusion to Expulsion: Demolition, Displacement, and Race in Atlanta's Northern Suburbs," Atlanta Studies, October 30, 2018, https://www.atlantastudies.org/2018/10/30/from-exclusion-to-expulsion-demolition-displacement-and-race-in-atlantas-northern-suburbs/.

55. Marietta Daily Journal Staff, "Mayor: We're on Schedule for Success: Tumlin Confident in Franklin Road Redevelopment Bond," Marietta Daily Journal, June 28, 2015, https://www.mdjonline.com/news/mayor-we-re-on-schedule-for-success-tumlin-confident-in/article_3f75b84a-50a4-5276-8eaf-96d28bb96502.html.

56. Tal Wright, "The Renaissance of Franklin Road," Gateway Marietta Community Improvement District, November 26, 2018, https://www.gatewaymarietta.org/news/linkhttps/insideradvantagecom/2018/11/15/the-renaissance-of-franklin-road.

57. Marietta Daily Journal Staff, "$68M Redevelopment Bond Passes," Marietta Daily Journal, November 6, 2013, https://www.mdjonline.com/news/68m-redevelopment-bond-passes/article_ee8879d7-7d85-5807-bboc-f5088be7f278.html.

58. Ibid.

59. Ibid.

60. Marietta Daily Journal Staff, "Franklin Falls, Hope Rises as Talks Heat Up," *Marietta Daily Journal*, June 6, 2015, https://www.mdjonline.com/opinion/mdj_editorials/franklin-falls-hopes-rise-as-talks-heat-up/article_cafc61fc-bbb3–508f-a19f-8c0b8fbe3819.html.

61. Marietta Daily Journal Staff, supra, note 55.

62. Carolyn Cunningham, "Marietta's Franklin Road to be Franklin Gateway," *Atlanta Journal-Constitution*, August 16, 2016, https://www.ajc.com/news/local/marietta-franklin-road-franklin-gateway/cEg5IX8eau101qWWWYxvUO/.

63. Scott Markley, "New Urbanism and Race: An Analysis of Neighborhood Racial Change in Suburban Atlanta." *Journal of Urban Affairs* 40, no. 8 (2018): 1115–1131.

64. For more discussion of the real estate and planning pressures that public finance tools such as bonds and tax increment financing can pose for cities, see Rachel Weber, "Selling City Futures: The Financialization of Urban Redevelopment Policy," *Economic Geography* 86, no. 3 (2010): 251–274.

65. Marietta Daily Journal Staff, supra, note 55.

66. John Ruch, "As Sandy Springs Rents Rise, a Working-class 'Exodus' Begins," *Sandy Springs Reporter*, April 14, 2017, https://reporternewspapers.net/2017/04/14/sandy-springs-rents-rise-working-class-exodus-begins/.

67. Ibid.

68. Sandy Springs Together, "Task Force Timeline," Sandy Springs Together, accessed June 1, 2021, https://sandyspringstogether.org/task-force/timeline/.

69. Sandy Springs Together, "Questions and Answers," Sandy Springs Together, accessed June 1, 2021, https://sandyspringstogether.org/our-community/questions-answers/.

70. City of Sandy Springs, "Plan for the North End," accessed June 1, 2021, https://www.sandyspringsga.gov/home/showpublisheddocument?id = 20406.

71. Evelyn Andrews, "Housing Policy Debate Continues as Sandy Springs' North End Task Force Winds Down," *Sandy Springs Reporter*, November 15, 2018, https://reporternewspapers.net/2018/11/15/housing-policy-debate-continues-as-sandy-springs-north-end-task-force-winds-down/.

72. Ibid.

73. Evelyn Andrews, "Sandy Springs' North End Redevelopment Concepts Head to City Council," *Sandy Springs Reporter*, December 14, 2018, https://

reporternewspapers.net/2018/12/14/sandy-springs-north-end-redevelopment-concepts-head-to-city-council/.

74. Ibid.

75. Bob Pepalis, "Sandy Springs North End Shopping Center Concepts Review Favors Mixed-Use with Single-family Homes," *Sandy Springs Reporter,* October 5, 2020, https://reporternewspapers.net/2020/10/05/sandy-springs-north-end-shopping-center-concepts-review-favors-mixed-use-with-single-family-homes/.

76. Maria Saporta, "As Region Becomes More Diverse, Atlanta Regional Commission Trying to Catch Up," *Saporta Report,* April 19, 2021, https://saportareport.com/as-region-becomes-more-diverse-atlanta-regional-commission-trying-to-catch-up/columnists/maria_saporta/.

CONCLUSION

1. Derek Hyra, Mindy Fulliove, Dominic Moulden, and Katharine Silva, "Contextualizing Gentrification Chaos: The Rise of the Fifth Wave," Metropolitan Policy Center at American University, May 6, 2020, https://www.american.edu/spa/metro-policy/upload/contextualizing-gentrification-chaos.pdf.

2. The figures in this paragraph come mostly from Chapter 3 and are explained in more detail there. The U.S. Department of Housing and Urban Development State of the Cities Data Systems shows over 31,000 housing units permitted in the city of Atlanta from 2013 through 2018 in buildings with five or more units. U.S. Department of Housing and Urban Development, accessed June 21, 2021, https://socds.huduser.gov/permits.

3. The city of Atlanta's population grew from July 2019 to July 2020 by 1.1 percent. While this is slightly below the previous two year's growth rates, the 2018 to 2019 growth of 1.7 percent was partly the result of an annexation that brought in about 6,400 additional residents. Without the annexation, the city's 2018–2019 growth rate would have been about one percent, roughly the same as the 2019 to 2020 rate. Data are U.S. Census Bureau estimates taken from this publication and associated data: William Frey, "America's Largest Cities Saw the Sharpest Population Losses During the Pandemic, New Census Data Shows," Brookings Institution, June 8, 2021, https://www.brookings.edu/research/the-largest-cities-saw-the-sharpest-population-losses-during-the-pandemic-new-census-data-shows/.

4. Again, the figures in this paragraph all come from Chapter 3 and are explained in more detail there.

5. The figures in the remainder of this section are from Chapter 5 and are explained in more detail there.

6. Dan Immergluck, "The Cost of Vacant and Blighted Properties in Atlanta: A Conservative Analysis of Service and Spillover Costs," Center for Community Progress, January 27, 2016, https://www.communityprogress.net /filebin/Cost_of_Vacant_and_Blighted_Immergluck_FINAL_02.17.16.pdf.

7. William Fischel, *The Homevoter Hypothesis: How Home Values Influence Local Government Taxation, School Finance, and Land-Use Policies* (Cambridge: Harvard University Press, 2005).

8. Bernadette Hanlon and Whitney Airgood-Obrycki. "Suburban Revalori- zation: Residential Infill and Rehabilitation in Baltimore County's Older Suburbs." *Environment and Planning A: Economy and Space* 50, no. 4 (2018): 895–921.

9. John Logan and Harvey Molotch, *Urban Fortunes: The Political Economy of Place* (Berkeley, CA: University of California Press, 1987), 30–31.

10. Louise Seamster, "The White City: Race and Urban Politics," *Sociology Compass* 9, no. 12 (2015): 1049–1065.

11. William Frey, "Turnout in 2020 Election Spiked Among Both Demo- cratic and Republican Voting Groups, New Census Data Shows," *Brookings Institution*, May 5, 2021, https://www.brookings.edu/research/turnout-in-2020- spiked-among-both-democratic-and-republican-voting-groups-new-census-data- shows/.

12. James C. Cobb, "Why a Key Georgia County Flipped from Red to Blue—and What it Means for Democrats," *Fortune*, December 27, 2020, https:// fortune.com/2020/12/27/georgia-election-2020-gwinnett-county-flipped/.

13. Timothy Davis, "A Comparative Analysis of State and Local Govern- ment Vacant Property Registration Statutes," *The Urban Lawyer* 44, no. 2 (Spring 2012): 399–427.

14. Tim Craig and Vanessa Williams, "As Stacey Abrams Enters Governor's Race, Georgia Becomes a Key 2022 Battleground," *The Washington Post*, Decem- ber 4, 2021, https://www.washingtonpost.com/national/stacey-abrams-brian- kemp-faceoff/2021/12/04/441de08a-5464-11ec-8927-c396fa861a71_story.html.

15. Ibid.

16. Patricia Murphy, "Donald Trump Could Make Stacey Abrams the Next Governor of Georgia," *Atlanta Journal Constitution*, December 3, 2021, https://www.ajc.com/politics/opinion-donald-trump-could-make-stacey-abrams-the-next-governor-of-georgia/OFCHN7YV3JCJLPNPMPI5YVV634/.

17. James Salzer and Greg Bluestein, "Final Price Tag on Georgia Governor's Race Exceeds $100 Million," *Atlanta Journal Constitution*, January 9, 2019, https://www.ajc.com/news/state—regional-govt—politics/final-price-tag-georgia-governor-race-exceeds-100-million/RobrqTrDaxwkAXq4mLMHuK/.

18. Nick Corasaniti, "Georgia G.O.P. Passes Major Law to Limit Voting Amid Nationwide Push," *The New York Times*, March 25, 2021, https://www.nytimes.com/2021/03/25/us/politics/georgia-voting-law-republicans.html.

Index

NOTE: Page numbers for maps and figures appear in *italics*.

affordable housing *(continued)*
157–58, 175, 223–24; Gentrification
Task Force recommendations for
protection of, 63–64, 222; the "Gulch"
redevelopment and, 114, 116; high-
wage job growth and destruction of
low-cost rental stock, 97, 134; homeownership units, 126, 247n51; House
ATL (policy coalition), and recommendations, 121–23; as issue in
mayoral election of 2017, 99, 117,
120–21, 122, 134; loss of lower-cost
rental stock and need for action on,
118; Mayor Bottoms' pledge of
funding for, 120–21, 123–24; Mayor
Dickens' commitment to, 232; media
attention to, generally (2010–2020),
117–18; multifamily development
requirement for (inclusionary zoning,
IZ) (2017), 118–20; multifamily
developments receiving subsidies,
requirement for (2016), 118, 119; One
Atlanta Affordable Housing Action
Plan (2019 city plan), 123; Ponce City
Market, 92; private-sector proposal to
serve those with 50 to 120 percent of
area median income, 122–23; rents
allowable, generally, 119–20; Turner
Field redevelopment and, 113–14;
zoning reform as no panacea for, 131.
See also affordable housing, lower-
income qualified by percentage of
metro area median income (AMI);
AHA (Atlanta Housing Authority);
Beltline TAD and affordable housing;
community advocacy for affordable
housing; community land trusts
(CLTs), and shared-equity housing;

rental stock, loss of lower-cost;
subsidized housing; suburban
affordable housing
affordable housing, lower-income
qualified by percentage of metro area
median income (AMI): advocacy
organizations calling for focus on
household incomes below fifty
percent, 120, 122; the Beltline and
increase of percentage from agreement, 86, 247nn51–52; given a choice,
developers choose the higher-percent-
age option, 118, 119; as higher than the
surrounding community, 114, 126, 195;
inclusionary zoning (IZ) and higher
percentage, 119; LIHTC program
rents set to, 128; suburban affordable
housing and, 195
Africa, immigrants from, 190–91, 194
AHA (Atlanta Housing Authority):
"Atlanta Model" of public housing
redevelopment and demolition, 124,
125–26; Beltline (ABI) counting
subsidized housing as their own, 86;
ceding ownership and control to
private-sector partners, 124, 126–27;
federal HOPE VI funding secured by,
45–47, 90, 221–22; gentrification
process aided by, 48, 127, 222; Rene
Glover as CEO, 46–48, 124–26; as
ill-prepared to develop new affordable
housing, 47–48, 127; Integral Group
partnership with, 46, 125–27, 255n62;
"neoliberal turn" away from owning
and managing public housing, 47–48,
222; "Olympic Legacy Program," 47;
problems faced by, 44–45; reduction of
public housing units (1996–2010), 47;

Black institutions of higher education, overview, 14, 118–19; Atlanta as center of Black enterprise and, 22

Black intellectual history, Atlanta's critical place in, 14, 89–90

Black leadership: and the Beltline, 67; Black radicals and progressives as unable to effectively contest the dominant urban regime, 55; and civil rights movement, Atlanta as the seat of, 54, 55; clergy and politicians as basis of, 54; as "junior partners" in the urban regime, 25, 27, 54, 228; as middle class, 54; and the Old Fourth Ward, 89–90; open housing, calls for, 26; public accommodations, demands for access to, 26, 54; and reform within the confines of Jim Crow, 55; "voluntary agreements" for segregation, 27; voting rights, demands for, 26, 54, 55; white violence and the choice to expand segregated Black neighborhoods, 21, 22, 25–26, 27. *See also* urban regime politics of Atlanta

Black-majority city, prevention of, as goal of the Atlanta urban regime, 62–63, 95

Black Mecca, Atlanta as: overview, 1; as region more than the city, 100; as suburban, 36

Black middle class: Black leadership rising from, 54; class-based zoning and exclusion of, 20; influx to the city (1990–2007), 62; in-migration directly to the suburbs, 36–37; in segregated Black-majority DeKalb County, 33; SFR firms as targeting, 187–88, 224; size of, and disproportionate impact of tight mortgage market during and

after the foreclosure crisis, 171; underwater mortgages predominately made to, 143, 174. *See also* Black homeownership; Black neighborhoods; Black suburbanization

Black neighborhoods: the Beltline and gentrification of, 79–81, 93; Black model home, 23; Black radical and progressive community work for, 45, 55; desire of residents to remain in their communities, 47, 85, *85*; early development of, 16, 23; eviction rates as much higher than in white-majority neighborhoods, 128–29; FHA programs financing, 23; land value increases (2013–2021), 102–3, *103*; and segregation, the Atlanta urban regime's racialized negotiation for expansion of, 24–27, 54; and segregation, white violence and Black leadership's choice for expansion of, 21, 22, 25–26, 27; Turner Field redevelopment controversy of gentrification, 111, 113–14; wealth extraction and disinvestment in, 30, 62, 67–68, 225. *See also* Black homeownership; Black neighborhoods, removal of; Black suburbanization; foreclosure crisis (2007–2012); lower-income neighborhoods; public housing; segregation

Black neighborhoods, removal of: overview, 225–26; Black residential clusters as target, 31–32; as enforcing segregation, 20; federal urban renewal projects, 30, 90, 203; highway construction, 31, 90; the Olympics and redevelopment of, 43; public housing

111–12; suburban displace-and-replace redevelopments projects and, 203, 204, 207, 208, 209. *See also* public finance system

Borders, Lisa, 66

Borders, Reverend William, 90

Bottoms, Keisha Lance: and affordable housing, 120–21, 123–24, 232; and the "Gulch" redevelopment, 114, 115; and zoning reform, 132

Bradbury, J. C., 116

Brewer, Brent, 157–58

Brookhaven: Affordable Housing Task Force, 195; affordable housing units, loss of, 195, 196; Asian population, 194; Black population, 194; Buford Highway corridor and, 191; gentrification and displacement pressures in, 194–96; homeownership rate, 193; immigrant population, 194; inclusionary zoning ordinance (2018), 195, 196; Latinx population, 194; as majority-white suburb, 194; median home value, 193; median household income, 192–93; secession (cityhood) and, 198; and suburban displace-and-replace redevelopment, 206–7. *See also* Buford Highway corridor (DeKalb County)

Brown, Karen, 150

Brown-Nagin, Tomiko, 11, 25, 55

Brown vs. Board of Education, 31

Buckhead (neighborhood): and affluent census tracts, concentration of, 186; annexation of, 26, 198; the Beltline and, 70; jobs shifting to, 37; median household income, 202; multifamily housing construction in, 97, 104, 117,

218; opposition to zoning reform proposal to end single-family zoning, 132; population of, 202; and property tax limitations (2018), 111; secession (cityhood) movement in, 201–3; tax base of, 201–2

Buckhead City Committee, 201, 202

Buford, 191

Buford Highway corridor (DeKalb County): affordable housing units, losses of low-cost, 194–97, 213; Asian population cluster, 33, 52, 182–83, 191, 194; Black population, 194; "Chinatown" and "ethnoburbs" as misnomers for, 191, 193; community advocacy for affordable housing, 195–96; as dangerous road for walking or cycling, 191, 194; gentrification and displacement pressures in, 193, 194–97; geographic location of, 191, 192; as "global neighborhoods," 193; immigrant population, 194; immigrant residents of, 191–92, 193, 194, 197; Latinx population cluster, 33, 52, 181, 190–91, 193–94; multiethnic- and immigrant-owned mix of restaurants, retail, and service businesses (1,000+), 191–92, 193, 196; multiple families cohabiting together, 196; relative affluence of suburbs in, 192–93; white population, 193–94. *See also* immigrants; multiethnic metropolis, Atlanta as

building codes, exclusion of rental housing via, 199–200, 205, 268n33

building permits, expedited review of, 119

Chicago, Illinois: and Black enterprise, 22; contract-for-deed (CFD) home sales, 159; foreclosure crisis (late 1990s), 136–37; immigrants to, 52; stigmatizing references to, 200
Chick-fil-A, 99
children. *See* families with children; schools
China, immigrants from, 191, 194
Christophers, Bret, 166
CIM Group, 114
Citizens Trust Company, 22, 26
City Beautiful movement, 15
City Council: Atlanta Beltline and, 66; Atlanta Beltline ordinance (2005), 67, 71, 77; "backalley dwelling law" (1955), 31–32; election of 2021 and new members of, 232; Gentrification Task Force, 63–64, 222; homeless people forced out of the city prior to the Olympics, 42–43; mandatory inclusionary zoning for multifamily developments (2017), 118–20, 232; multifamily developments with subsidies require affordable units (2016), 118, 119; white members increased in annexation of white suburbs, 29, *29*. *See also* inclusionary zoning (IZ) (2017); zoning; zoning reform
City for All (grassroots affordable housing advocacy group), 120–21, 122
city of Atlanta: annexation of affluent white suburbs (1952), 27–29, *28*, 62, 198; annexation of Black suburbs, 178; annexation of Emory and CDC (2017), 101, 250n11, 272n3; as "city too busy to hate," 52–53; establishment of, 13–14; as "Gate City," 13; and House ATL (affordable housing policy coalition), 121–23; income inequality in, 118, 177; industrialization of, 14, 15; inferiority complex and need to focus on image, 52–53; institutional SFR investors as avoiding, 164; jobs and commercial tax base moving to northern suburbs and neighborhoods, 37, 48–49, 56; jobs and commercial tax base shifting back to the city, 62, 96–97, 133–34; naming of, 13, 236n1; "park-neighborhood" as model for, 15; secession (cityhood) movement in Buckhead, 201–3; segregation as racialized negotiation of Black neighborhood expansion, 24–27, 54; the state as constraining self-governance of, 98; as state capital, 14; subprime loan prevalence in Black neighborhoods, 140, 141; "turnaround" of, 10, 59, 60, 61, 62, 94; white flight and white avoidance of, 32–33, 36–37. *See also* City Council; gentrification; mayoral elections; metropolitan Atlanta; multiethnic metropolis, Atlanta as; population of city of Atlanta; public finance system, dysfunctional; segregation; state of Georgia; urban regime politics of Atlanta; "world-class, global city" vision for Atlanta
City Springs redevelopment, 204
civil rights movement, 54–55. *See also* Black electoral power; public accommodations, segregation of; voting rights for Black citizens

public housing tenants (Black-woman led), 45, 55; the suburbs and need for greater focus of, 213, 214; tenants' rights, 55. *See also* Atlanta Legal Aid; community advocacy for affordable housing; community benefits agreements; neighborhood planning units; *specific organizations and individuals*

community advocacy for affordable housing: and AHA conflict with Integral Group, 125; the Beltline and mobilization of lower-income residents, 80; and Buford Highway corridor, 195–96; call for focus on household incomes below fifty percent, 120, 122; City for All recommendations, 120–21, 122; the city of Atlanta as primary focus of, vs. the suburbs, 210, 213, 215; the foreclosure crisis and call for conversion of vacant properties to, 152, 157; share of renter households who are cost-burdened, and need for, 118; and state government, the need for help from, 210, 213, 214, 215, 230–31; the suburbs and need for, 195–96, 210–14, 215; Turner Field controversy, 113–14

community benefits agreements (CBA): the Beltline and, 71, 77, 80; Turner Field redevelopment's refusal to engage in, 113–14

Community Foundation of Greater Atlanta, 98, 227–28

community land trusts (CLTs), and shared-equity housing, 155–57, 260–61n38

Confederacy, and inferiority complex of cities, 52–53

Consumer Financial Protection Bureau, 160

Contract Buyers' League, 159

contract-for-deed (CFD) home sales, 158–60

corporate-led white-Black governing regime. *See* urban regime politics of Atlanta

Corporation for Olympic Development in Atlanta (CODA), 43–44, 221

Couchman, David, 211–13, 269–70n49

Council for Quality Growth, 227

Cousins, Tom, 66–67

COVID-19 pandemic: Black homeownership shut out due to, 188–89; bond issue for affordable housing following, 124

Coweta County, 179

Cox Enterprises, 99

crime: claims justifying suburban racial and economic exclusion, 199, 201, 207; public housing problems, 44, 45

DAFC. *See* Development Authority of Fulton County

Davis, Charles, 38

Davis, John, 156

Decatur, 210

DeKalb County: affordable housing advocacy in, 210; Asian population, 33, 52, 182, 220; Black suburbanization and, 33–36, 179; foreclosure crisis and, 141, 142, 154, 155; foreclosure crisis proposal to register vacant properties, 230; governed by Black leadership, 33,

foreclosure crisis (continued)

for affordable housing, 7–8, 11–12, 152–55, 157–58, 175, 223–24; federal funds used to buy and rehabilitate homes sold to Black homebuyers, 154–55, 173–74, 175, 223, 264n80; investor-owner foreclosures as exacerbating decline, 141, 152; investors receiving a large transfer of ownership from Black homeowners, 116, 136, 153, 157–58, 172, 186–87; nonprofit Black and low-income home ownership initiative, 173–74, 264n80; recovery from, as uneven, 144–46, 171–73; underwater mortgages of Black homeowners, 135–36, 137; underwater mortgages, as disproportionately affecting (middle-class suburban) Black homeowners, 143, 174; vacant homes as exacerbating decline, 136, 143, 146, 152. See also institutional investors in single-family rental (SFR) market (2012 and later); investors in single-family rentals (SFRs)

foreclosure crisis, federal response: overview, 135; funds for local government acquisition of vacant homes for affordable housing, 152–55, 157–58; HAMP (Home Affordable Modification Program), 142, 148–49; Hardest Hit Fund (HHF), inefficient state administration of, 150–51; Home Affordable Refinance Program, 142; HOPE NOW Alliance, 147, 148; Housing and Economic Recovery Act (2008), 152; institutional investors in SFR market, policy establishing, 136,

164–67, 169–70, 172, 224; institutional investors in SFR market, policy for Fannie Mae and Freddie Mac to sell foreclosed properties to, 161–62, 164–65, 167; institutional investors in SFR market, policy providing low-cost financing to, 170; investors, FDIC policy of bulk-sale of foreclosed homes to, 157–58; modification of loans inadequate and forcing re-default, 148–49; Neighborhood Stabilization Program (NSP), 152–55, 157–58, 173, 175, 223; proposed bankruptcy reform to allow reduction of loan balances, failure of, 147–48; quantitative easing programs, 142; refinancing into lower-cost loans, 142

foreclosure crisis, local response: cancellation of loans, 147; community-based foreclosure prevention activities, 147; Home Defense Project (HDP), 147; purchase and rehabilitation of single-family homes for sale to lower-wealth and Black homeowners, 154–55, 223; purchase of multifamily housing for rent, 154; restructuring of loans, 147; slow deployment of NSP money, 153–57, 223; state legislators making phone calls to lenders, 147

foreclosure crisis, state of Georgia response: overview, 135, 149; "deserving vs. undeserving" candidates, focus on, 151, 175; federal funds, ineffectiveness of state administration of, 150–51, 174–75; other states' activism compared to, 150; refusal to change lender-friendly foreclosure laws, 149–50, 174, 230; refusal to

gentrification *(continued)*

for existing residents, 80; eviction rate increases and, 129–30; exclusion of lower-income families, 48, 61–62, 93; "fifth wave," 100, 105, 217–18, 249–50n10; foreclosure crisis and pause of, 100, 101; foreclosure crisis outcomes as supporting, 175; Gentrification Task Force policy recommendations ignored, 63–64, 222; job growth and, 62, 96–97, 133–34, 217–18; land values and rents boom, 102–3, *103*, 219; median household income city-to-metro ratio, as exceeding the suburbs, 9, 101–2, *102*, 218; median household income, increases in, 61, 93, 101–2, *102*, 218; multifamily housing, increase of, 93, 97, 104, 117; non-college-educated population, decrease in, 9, 61; the Olympics and growing problem following, 48, 63, 133; other metros compared to Atlanta, 9–10; poverty decreases as statistic of, 61–62, 101, 102, 218–19; private equity capital accelerating, 100, 249–50n10; public housing demolition/redevelopment as aiding, 48, 127, 222; segregation reproduced by, 5; the suburbs and, 193, 194–97, 206, 212; Turner Field redevelopment controversy, 111, 113–14; upper-income homebuyers, increases in lower-income neighborhoods, 79–80, 245n38; white population, increase in, 88–89, *88. See also* college-educated population, increase in; suburbanization of poverty; white-majority suburbs, planned efforts to maintain racial and economic exclusivity

Gentrification Task Force and "A City for All" report, 63–64, 222

Georgia. *See* state of Georgia; state of Georgia elections

Georgia Advancing Communities Together (Georgia ACT), 120

Georgia Department of Community Affairs, 86, 92, 151; Hardest Hit Fund/"HomeSafe Georgia" program, 150–51

Georgia Dome, replacement of, 111–12

Georgia Fair Lending Act (2001, GFLA), 137; opposition to and overturning of, 137–38, 149

Georgia Poverty Rights Organization, 55

Georgia Regional Transportation Authority (GRTA), 58

Georgia Stand-Up (community benefits advocacy group): opposition to the "Gulch" redevelopment, 115–16; study of Beltline effects on land values and homeownership, 78–80, 81, 156, 245nn36,38

Georgia State University (GSU): and corporate relocations to the city, 96, 133–34; Turner Field controversy, 111, 113–14, 158

Georgia Tech, 46, 64, 74–75; and corporate relocations to the city, 96, 133–34

Gingrich, Newt, 49

Giornelli, Greg, 66

global capital: as focus of the Atlanta urban regime, 42, 53, 95–96; foreclosure crisis and speculation in single- and multifamily rental housing, 100, 116, 161. *See also* institutional investors in single-family rental (SFR) market; private equity capital

global city, 53; defined as foreign-born persons, 266n20; factors in growth of population, 190; metros as emerging immigrant gateways, 52, 190; moving directly to the suburbs, 52, 190; origins of, 190–92; population of (1950–2019), 190, 194. *See also* Buford Highway corridor (DeKalb County); multiethnic metropolis, Atlanta as

inclusionary zoning (Brookhaven suburb, 2018), 195

inclusionary zoning (IZ) (2017): citywide ordinance, call for, 120; commitment of City Council to pass, 117, 232; compensation to developers for meeting requirements, 119; limited geographical extent of, 118–19; lower-income definition, developer choice in, 119; rent formula higher than typical affordable housing, 119–20; state laws feared to nullify, 119

income inequality, 118, 177

incorporation of suburbs. *See* secession (cityhood) as racial and economic exclusion

India, immigrants from, 191

in-fill development: and dampened segregation in working-class communities, 16; early rentals, 15

inflection points furthering racial and economic exclusion: overview, 6–8, 221–24; affordable housing as, 134; the Beltline as, 7, 60, 94, 222–23; definition of, 6–7; the foreclosure crisis as, 7–8, 175, 223–24; the Olympic Games (1996) as, 7, 60, 94, 221–22. *See also* gentrification; policy choices, development and redevelopment processes as con-

structed by; urban regime politics of Atlanta

Inman Park (neighborhood), 15, 20

installment land contracts. *See* contract-for-deed (CFD) home sales

institutional investors in multifamily housing: Atlanta as prime market for, 129; eviction rate increases and displacement of Black residents, 130; gentrification as sought by, 129; multifamily properties as target of, 129–30; and the post-crisis period, 129; private equity markets moving into, 97, 100, 129, 134; unregulated ("landlord-friendly") rental markets sought by, 129, 130

institutional investors in single-family rental (SFR) market (2012 and later): overview, 136, 161–64; Atlanta metro as ideal "strike zone" for, 136, 163, 175, 224; compensation of CEOs, 167; cutting operating costs as focus of, 169; diverse suburban neighborhoods as target of, 162; eviction practices of, 167–68; federal policy and establishment of, 136, 164–67, 169–70, 172, 224; federal policy for Fannie Mae and Freddie Mac to sell foreclosed properties to, 161–62, 164–65, 167; federal policy providing low-cost financing to, 170; foreclosure auctions and mortgage services as sources of homes, 161, 167, 168; growth of SFR industry, 162–63, 164; high property value neighborhoods not target of, 162–63, 164; homeownership declining due to, 187–88; as landlords, significant problems with, 167–69; lawsuits

institutional investors *(continued)*
against, 167; market power of, 163;
media investigations and advocacy
research on, 167–68, 170; moderate-
and middle-value neighborhoods as
target of, 162, 175; ownership patterns
across the Atlanta metro, 163–64;
policy failures as facilitating, 164;
tenant charge-backs and, 169; tight
mortgage credit policy as facilitating,
164, 170; unregulated ("landlord-
friendly") markets sought by, 136, 161,
170, 175, 264n72. *See also* investors in
single-family rentals (SFRs)
insurance companies, Black-owned, 22,
26, 90
Integral Group: developer relationship
with AHA, 46, 125–27, 255n62; as
subsidized housing firm, 127
internationalization. *See* "world-class,
global city" vision for Atlanta
Interstate 20, as racial boundary, 31, 179,
219
Interstate Highway Act (1956), and
system, 41, 50
Invest Atlanta (formerly Atlanta
Development Authority): ACP
members as recipients of tax breaks
and subsidies, 99; affordable housing
requirement for subsidized multifamily developments (2016), 118; and
Beltline affordable housing, 70–71, 84,
86, 87; the Beltline facilitated by, 66,
69; cash grants by, 106; the "Gulch"
redevelopment, 114–16; property tax
breaks given to large properties, 98,
106–8, 113, 114–15; stadium project for
Arthur Blank's teams, 112

investors in single-family rentals (SFRs):
bankruptcy-court ordered loan
reductions, 147–48; "dumping" least
attractive properties, 158; eviction
practices of, compared to institutional
investors, 167–68; federal policy for
Fannie Mae and Freddie Mac to sell
foreclosed properties to, 158, 159, 160,
161–62; federal policy for FDIC to sell
foreclosed properties to, 157–58;
foreclosure crisis and large transfer
of home ownership to, 116, 136, 153,
157–58, 165, 172, 175, 186–87, 224;
growth of SFR industry, 162; homeownership declining due to, 187–88,
224; loan-servicer preference to
quickly sell foreclosed properties
to, 153; lower- to middle-income
neighborhoods as target of, 155, 161,
162–63; "mom and pop" landlords, 161,
167–68; as quicker to let their homes
fall into foreclosure, 141, 152; with
subprime and Alt-A loans, 139, 141. *See
also* institutional investors in
multifamily housing; institutional
investors in single-family rental
(SFR) market
Invitation Homes, 163, 164, 166–67,
169, 170
Isakson, Johnny, 207

Jackson, Maynard, Jr.: as first Black
mayor, 37–38; Shirley Franklin and,
66; and perpetuation of the Atlanta
urban regime, 38, 55; resistance to the
Atlanta urban regime, 37–38, 55, 62–63
Jamaica, immigrants from, 191
Jamestown Properties, 90–92, 99

in non-Hispanic white population
share in the city of Atlanta (2008 to
2017), 88; Latinx and Asian populations
(2017), 182; MARTA plans and the
realities of anti-transit suburbia, 40; Old
Fourth War/Sweet Auburn, 91; The
racialized fall of home values during
the crash, 144; The racialized nature of
subprime home lending during the
2000s, 138; The segregation of Black
Atlantans (1940), 24; The suburbanization of poverty (1990 to 2017), 184; The
urbanization of the Atlanta region
(1950 to 2010), 3
Marietta: Latinx population, 52; and
suburban displace-and-replace
redevelopment, 206, 207–8, 209, 227
"market-inevitability" fatalism, avoidance of, 12, 233–34
Markley, Scott, 206–7, 269–70n49
MARTA (Metropolitan Atlanta Rapid
Transit Authority): anti-transit
suburbia and, 40–42; and Beltline
light-rail transit as controversy, 74,
75–76; and desire to internationalize
the city's image, 53; map, 40; planning
for, 39–41. See also public transit
Marthasville (early name of Atlanta), 13,
236n1
Martin, C. T., 69
Martinez, Matthew, 16–17
Mason, Keith, 72–74
Mason, Wayne, 72–74
Massell, Sam, 37–38
mayoral elections (city of Atlanta): 1973,
37–38; 2017, 99, 117, 120–21, 122, 134;
2021, 132, 232; ACP involvement in, 99

media: affordable housing coverage
generally (2010–2020), 117–18;
affordable housing inattention in the
suburbs, 209–10, 213; affordable
housing in the Beltline, 77, 83–84, 87;
AHA vacant-parcel options conflict
with Integral Group (developer),
125–26; Atlanta Daily World (historic
Black-owned newspaper), 90; DAFC
per-diem fees covered by, 108; false
reports of assaults on white women
by Black men, and 1906 anti-Black
massacre, 18; and the foreclosure
crisis, 147; institutional SFR investors,
investigation of, 167; and public
subsidies to development in hot
neighborhoods, 106, 108
median home value, in the Buford
Highway area, 193
median household income: of Buckhead
neighborhood, 202; in the Buford
Highway corridor suburbs, 193;
gentrification and increases in, 61, 93,
101–2, 102, 218
median household income, city-to-metro
ratio: city median increasing to exceed
the suburbs, 9, 101–2, 102, 218; decreases
in (1970–1990), 36; other metro
increases compared to Atlanta, 9
median income of metropolitan area,
and definition of affluent and very
affluent neighborhoods, 186, 265n6.
See also affordable housing, lower-
income qualified by percentage of
metro area median income (AMI)
median sales price of homes, the Beltline
and increases in, 78–79, 245n36

Mercedes-Benz Stadium, inclusionary zoning (IZ) in area of, 118–19

Metro Atlanta Chamber of Commerce, 98, 121, 122, 227–28

metropolitan Atlanta: Black population as second only to New York metro, 10; five core counties, 2–3, 4; as ideal "strike zone" for institutional SFR investors, 136, 163, 175, 224; as inverting the poor-in-the-core urban model, 2, 76–77, 101–2, 133, 218; low municipal fragmentation of, 197–98; map of region, 2; metropolitan statistical area (U.S. Census Bureau), as not geographically constant, 235–36n1, 264–65n1; nonprofit Black and low-income home ownership initiative, 173–74, 264n80; size ranked with other metros, 3; urban form of, 1; urbanization patterns of, 3, 4. *See also* foreclosure crisis (2007–2012); growth-above-all development ethos; multiethnic metropolis, Atlanta as; population of metro Atlanta; sprawl; suburb(s); suburban increases in racial and economic diversity; suburbanization of poverty

Metropolitan North Georgia Water Planning District, 235–36n1

Metropolitan Planning Commission (MPC): established as a research and planning operation, 49–50; recommendations for limits on growth ("Up Ahead"), 50; recommendations for unlimited growth ("Now . . . for Tomorrow"), 50; and segregation of Black residential development, 26–27

metropolitan regions: Atlanta as paradigmatic case for, 8–10; Black and Latinx borrowers disproportionately given subprime loans, 140; Black suburbanization occurring earlier in Atlanta, 4; as emerging immigrant gateways, 52, 190; eviction rates, 128; gentrification driven by job growth as national problem, 217–18; growth of SFR industry, 162; non-college educated population, decrease in, 9; size of Atlanta ranked among, 3; top ten fastest gentrifying cities, 105; underwater mortgages as disproportionately Black homeowners, 143. *See also* metropolitan Atlanta; Sunbelt metros

Mexico, immigrants from, 191, 194

middle-income households: the city's intention to attract, 43–44, 98, 134, 221; "workforce" housing meant for, 211. *See also* Black middle class; white middle class

middle-income neighborhoods: the foreclosure crisis and transfer of homeownership to investors, 224; multifamily housing in, 97, 104, 117, 134, 161, 218; rental housing as scarce, 161; as target of SFR investors, 155, 161, 162–63

Midtown (neighborhood): Black residential expulsion from, 32–33; jobs shifting to, 37; multifamily housing construction in, 97, 104, 117, 134, 218; property tax breaks awarded to developments in, 107, 108

Milton, 49, 198

mixed-income housing developments: developer control and ownership of, 124, 126–27; failure to protect residents of neighborhoods surrounding, 222; Gentrification Task Force recommendations for, 63; and loss of public housing units, 46–47, 90, 124, 222; Low-Income Housing Tax Credit financing, 46–47; profit-sharing arrangements with AHA, 126, 255n62; as "revitalization," 61; Techwood/Centennial Place, 46–47, 125, 222. *See also* AHA (Atlanta Housing Authority); public housing redevelopment; public-private partnerships

mixed-use developments: the "Gulch" redevelopment, 114–16; New Urbanist design, 208–9; sale of Fort McPherson and loss of, 112; suburban displace-and-replace redevelopment, 204–5, 206, 208–9; Turner Field controversy, 113–14. *See also* commercial tax base

Molotch, Harvey, 225

Morehouse College, 14

Morgan County, 235–36n1

Morningside (neighborhood), 70

Morris Brown College, 14

mortgage lending: Black enterprise as supporting Black homeownership, 22–23, 26, 54, 178; Fannie Mae and Freddie Mac selling foreclosed homes to investors, 158, 159, 160, 161–62, 164–65, 167; FHA and discriminatory practices in, 22–23; foreclosure crisis diffusing to prime market, 141, 142, 161–62; private lenders and racial discrimination in, 22; redlining, 22,

24–25, 140. *See also* foreclosure crisis (2007–2012); mortgage lending as tight market during and after the foreclosure crisis; predatory housing market activity targeting the Black community; subprime lending and crisis

mortgage lending as tight market during and after the foreclosure crisis: Black households as disproportionately shut out by, 136, 171–72, 172, 186; CFD (contract-for-deed) sales due to, 159; as facilitating institutional-investor SFR industry, 164, 170; growth of rental market and, 162, 170; higher-wealth households and continued access to mortgage credit, 163; lower-wealth households as disproportionately affected by, 163; as policy choice, 170. *See also* post–foreclosure-crisis period (2012 onward)

MPC. *See* Metropolitan Planning Commission

MSA (Atlanta metropolitan statistical area), as not geographically constant, 235–36n1, 264–65n1

multiethnic metropolis, Atlanta as: overview, 1; factors contributing to, 58; immigrants as moving directly to the suburbs, 52, 190; multiracial dynamic vs. Black-white dichotomy in, 52, 178, 191; population changes 1980–2000, 51–52; population changes 2000–2019, 177–78, 219; segregation in, geography of, 52; as threat to anti-planning ideology, 58; underestimation of the power of, 58. *See also* Asian/AAPI residents; Buford

metro ratio of, 62; decline of, as gentrification statistic, 61–62, 101, 102, 218–19; increase of (1970–1990), 36. *See also* capital as favored by the Atlanta urban regime system; suburbanization of poverty

predatory housing market activity targeting the Black community: overview, 158; contract-for-deed (CFD) home sales, 158–60; devastation of neighborhoods and, 67–68; "rent-to-own" schemes, 158. *See also* foreclosure crisis (2007–2012); subprime lending and crisis

press. *See* media

presumptive veracity of ARC projections, 51

prisoners, forced-labor camps of, 15

private clubs, 32

private equity capital: gentrification accelerating due to, 100, 249–50n10; and the Midtown and Beltline areas, 134; and the multifamily housing market, 97, 100, 129, 134; reselling foreclosed homes through contract-for-deed sales, 158–59. *See also* global capital; institutional investors in multifamily housing; institutional investors in single-family rental (SFR) market

private schools, 32

private-sector initiatives: and affordable housing at 50 to 120 percent of area median income, 122–23; Beltline TAD allowing, 71

Project Homeward Bound, 43

property taxes: appeals of, and attempts to reform, 109, 110, 230; failure of assessments to keep up with real market values, as stifling TAD revenues, 82; failure to protect existing residents from rises due to the Beltline, 60–61, 63–64, 82, 94; failure to protect existing residents in neighborhoods surrounding mixed-income housing projects, 222; limitations imposed on (2018), 105, 110–11; proposals to ease the burden on lower-income homeowners, 63–64; speculators buying tax liens, 63; structural problems with, resulting in failure of the city to capture revenue from massive growth in land values, 5, 8–9, 11, 98, 105–6, 107, 109–10, 123, 134; suburban displace-and-replace redevelopment and expected increases in, 208, 209; TADs as funded by, 70; tax breaks given to large commercial properties, 82, 92, 98, 105, 106–8, 110–11, 113, 114–15; tax breaks given to large properties, as stifling TAD revenues, 82, 92, 106–7; underappraisal and under-taxation of large commercial properties, 105, 108–10, 123, 230. *See also* commercial tax base

property values. *See* foreclosure crisis, decline in home values and rise in vacant homes; land value increases

public accommodations, segregation of, 17–18; Black leadership demands for access to, 26, 54; desegregation of, 32; school desegregation, 31, 54

public finance system: overview, 6–7; affordable housing recommendations for, 120, 122–23; affordable housing requirements for multifamily

City Market (PCM), 90–92; public financing tools and power used in, 7, 225; stadium project for Arthur Blank's teams, 111–12; "structural speculators," private parties as, 225; suburban displace-and-replace redevelopments, 177, 209, 225; Techwood Homes redevelopment as key venture in, 46, 125; Turner Field controversy, 113–14. *See also* mixed-income housing developments; mixed-use developments; public finance system

public transit: anti-bus stigma, 76; anti-transit attitudes, 40–42, 58; and the automobile, dependence on, 41, 42; the Beltline and, 64–65, 74–76; Buford Highway corridor (DeKalb County) and, 194; bus-based system, 41, 75–76; equity and justice in, 74, 76. *See also* MARTA (Metropolitan Atlanta Rapid Transit Authority); streetcars

Purpose Built Communities, 67

racial and economic exclusion. *See* Black neighborhoods; gentrification; inflection points furthering racial and economic exclusion; policy choices, development and redevelopment processes as constructed by; segregation; white-majority suburbs, planned efforts to maintain racial and economic exclusivity

racial and social equity, failure to pursue, 50–51, 57, 208–9, 226. *See also* inflection points furthering racial and economic exclusion

racial intermarriage, and segregation laws, 19

racially restrictive covenants, 20

racially restrictive housing laws. *See* segregation

racial wealth gap, foreclosure crisis as exacerbating, 171–73, 175

racial zoning laws (overturned), 19, 20, 21, 25, 130. *See also* zoning

racism: in first Black mayor's election campaign (1973), 37–38; governor's election race baiting (1906), 18; hegemonic whiteness and, 14, 227; in housing markets, exclusionary white suburb boom as driven by, 36; suburban displace-and-replace redevelopment dynamic of, 207–8, 227. *See also* housing discrimination; segregation; white-majority suburbs, planned efforts to maintain racial and economic exclusivity; white supremacy; white violence against Black population; xenophobia

railroads: and Atlanta as name, 236n1; the Atlanta Beltline path following right-of-way, 64, 66, 72; city as developing at nexus of, 13; and land speculation, 14; segregation of, 18; state aid to, 14. *See also* public transit

Raymond, Elora, 129–30, 144, 167–68

Reagan administration, 18

real estate development: Black enterprise and, 22–23, 26, 27, 54, 178; FHA and focus on white owners and renters, 23; in-fill, 15–16; land speculators holding parcels hostage in the Beltline, 72–74; park-neighborhood model, 13; post-crisis controversial

rent control: SFR (single-family rental) firms seeking markets without, 161, 170; state law preempting local ordinances for, 6, 119, 161, 212, 226, 230

renter households: the foreclosure crisis and increase of, 162, 164; lower-income, percentage who are cost-burdened, 118; property tax limitations as shifting the tax burden to, 111; state law providing few protections for tenants, 6, 123, 129, 161, 170, 175. *See also* affordable housing; evictions; institutional investors in single-family rental (SFR) market; investors in single-family rentals (SFRs); multi-family housing; public housing; rent increases; subsidized housing; suburban multifamily housing; suburban redevelopment projects (displace-and-replace); white–majority suburbs, planned efforts to maintain racial and economic exclusivity

rent formulas. *See* subsidized housing, rent formulas

rent gaps, 44, 48

rent increases: failure to protect tenants in neighborhoods surrounding mixed-income housing projects, 222; failure to protect tenants in the Beltline area, 60–61, 76–77, 82, 84, 88, 94; and gentrification acceleration (2010–2021), 102, 103, 219; and suburban displace-and-replace redevelopment, 206, 212

"rent-to-own" schemes, 158

"REO-to-rental," Federal Reserve white paper (2012), 165–67, 170

Republican Party: constraint of regional planning, 57–58, 98, 226–27; control of state government, 6, 58, 98, 149, 228; gerrymandering legislative boundaries, 228; northern suburbs and, 49; and secession of suburbs as tool of racial and economic exclusion, 198, 202–3; voter suppression efforts by, 231–32

Research/Action Cooperative, 85

restrictive covenants, 20

"revitalization," suburban displace-and-replace redevelopment projects portrayed as, 176–77, 204–5, 208

Reynoldstown (neighborhood), 89, 107

Right to the City Alliance, 167

Roark, Randall, 64

Rockdale County, 179

Rodriguez, Akira Drake, 38, 45, 47, 55

Rosen, Sam, 198–99

Roswell, 37, 206

Roswell Road, 204

Rutheiser, Charles, 13, 53

sales tax revenues, diverted as development subsidy, 114

Sandy Springs: affordable housing advocacy in, 210–13; as annexation target of city of Atlanta, 198; Black and Latinx population, 199; displace-and-replace redevelopment projects, 204–7, 210–13, 269–70n49; diversity as increasing in, 205; homeownership rate, 204; homeowner vs. renter population of, 205; jobs and the commercial tax base shifting from the city to, 48; multifamily housing stock, exclusion of, 198–200, 204, 268n33;

Sandy Springs (continued)
multifamily housing stock of, 204;
replacement of low-cost housing with
luxury apartments and single-family
homes, 205–6, 212, 213; secession
(cityhood) and increased power to
exclude, 198–200, 204, 205, 268n33
Sandy Springs Gateway redevelopment,
204–5, 269–70n49
Sandy Springs Together, 210, 213
Saporta, Maria, 125–26, 214
Satter, Beryl, Family Properties, 159
Schneggenburger, Andy, 71
schools: Beltline TAD and recovery of
lost revenues by, 82; desegregation of,
31, 54; displace-and-replace suburban
redevelopment and, 203, 205, 207, 213;
funding frozen in TAD districts, 70,
71–72; lawsuit against Beltline TAD
for depriving schools of revenue,
71–72, 78; private, and segregation of
upper-income whites, 32; property tax
breaks, objections to, 107; property
tax underappraisals costing funding
to, 109–10; secession (cityhood)
movement and, 176, 177, 199, 202;
Superintendent Carstarphen's
contract not renewed, 115; TADs,
objections to, 115, 116
Seamster, Louise, 227
Sears Roebuck building, 90
secession (cityhood) as racial and
economic exclusion: overview, 197;
defined as legal incorporation of
previously unincorporated suburb,
197; as increasing municipal power to
exclude, 133, 199–200, 203–4; less-affluent Black suburbs incorporating,

267n30; previously low fragmentation
of Atlanta metro, 197–98; race as
factor, denial by supporters, 199,
200–201; rental housing exclusion as
motivation, 198–201, 203–4, 268n33;
Republican Party and movement for,
198, 202–3; state involvement in, 198,
200, 202–3, 268n33; tax base segregated
via, 198, 201–2. See also suburban
redevelopment projects (displace-and-
replace); white-majority suburbs,
planned efforts to maintain racial and
economic exclusivity
segregation: Atlanta anti-Black massacre
(1906) as accelerating, 18; the Atlanta
urban regime's racialized negotiation
of Black neighborhood expansion,
24–27, 54; Black boycott of streetcars
(1891), 18; in Black-majority DeKalb
County (2000), 33; checkerboard,
street-by-street, and building-by-
building, 16, 17; claim that southern
cities weren't as residentially
segregated as northern cities, 16, 17;
dissimilarity index as measure of, as
sensitive to geographic unit (neighborhood vs. streets or buildings),
16–17, 237n16; enforcement of, 20–21;
gentrification as reproducing, 5; in-fill
development as dampening, 16;
neighborhood-level increases in (1940),
23–24, 24; racially restrictive covenants as tool of, 20; racial steering by
the real estate industry, 32; removal of
Black neighborhoods as enforcement
of, 20; secondary pattern of small
Black enclaves in white-majority
areas, 23–24, 24; in the suburbs, 33, 36,

sprawl *(continued)*
    job sprawl as accelerating residential
        sprawl, 37; northward shift in wealth
        and, 49; as "Sprawl City," 58
stadium project (for Arthur Blank), 111–12
Standard Life Insurance Company, 22
state of Georgia: overview of constraints
        placed on local governments, 230–31;
        affordable housing advocacy and the
        need for help from, 210, 213, 214, 215,
        230–31; AMRPC established by, 50;
        anti-homeless laws, 43; anti-public-
        planning ideology, 57–58, 226; Atlanta
        Regional Commission established by,
        50, 226; banks and legislators, cozy
        relationship of, 149–50; critical role in
        whether the interests of those
        vulnerable to exclusion are given
        consideration, 5–6; foreclosure law, as
        nonjudicial and lender-friendly, 149;
        foreclosure law, refusal to change
        during foreclosure crisis, 149–50, 174,
        230; highway construction through
        Black neighborhoods, 31; historic tax
        credits, 92; landlord-friendly eviction
        laws, 129, 130, 230; landlords may
        refuse housing vouchers, 48, 230;
        Metropolitan Planning Commission
        established by, 49–50; as preempting
        ban of lumber construction in
        apartment buildings, 200, 268n33; as
        preempting rent control by local
        governments, 6, 119, 161, 212, 226, 230;
        as preempting vacant property
        registration in foreclosure crisis, 230;
        as property-rights state, 6; property
        tax appeals, refusal to reform, 110, 230;

property tax limitations (2018), 110–11;
        regional planning constrained by,
        57–58, 98; secession movement and,
        198, 200, 202–3, 268n33; segregation of
        streetcars and railroads, 18; self-gov-
        ernance of the city constrained by, 98;
        subprime lending, failure to regulate,
        135, 137–38, 142, 149, 174; suburbaniza-
        tion of business and development and,
        56; tenant protections constrained by,
        6, 123, 129, 161, 170, 175; and underap-
        praisal and under-taxation of large
        commercial properties, 108, 110. *See
        also* Democratic Party; foreclosure
        crisis, state of Georgia response;
        Republican Party; state of Georgia
        elections; Supreme Court of Georgia
state of Georgia elections: demographic
        changes and, 228–30, 231; elections of
        2018, 228, 229, 231; elections of 2020, 1,
        228–30, 231; elections of 2022, 228,
        231–32; strength of political organiz-
        ing and, 229–30, 231. *See also* state of
        Georgia
Stone, Clarence, 11, 25, 39, 55–56
streetcars, 14, 15; Black boycott following
        segregation of, 18
student debt, and growth in rental
        market, 162
subprime lending and crisis: overview,
        135–36, 174–75; Black homebuyers
        disproportionately targeted for, 140,
        141, 143–45; Black neighborhoods
        targeted for, 135, 138–39, 140, 141, 186;
        boom of, as crisis (2007) beginning in
        Black neighborhoods, 11–12, 135–36,
        141; boom of, as earlier crisis (late

suburban affordable housing (continued)
194–97, 267n22; building codes written
to exclude, 199–200, 268n33; denial of
issue, 206; displace-and-replace
redevelopment and loss of, 203, 204,
205–7, 211–12, 213, 269–70n49; inclusionary zoning setting income limits
higher than surrounding community,
195; luxury housing replacing, 206,
212, 213; media inattention to, 209–10,
213; performative measures vs.
substantive action for, 196–97. See also
suburban redevelopment projects
(displace-and-replace)

suburban increases in racial and
economic diversity: overview, 176–77,
216–17; deliberate efforts to maintain
racial and economic exclusivity as
mobilized by, 4, 176–77, 203, 205,
214–15, 217; not spatially uniform, 176;
population changes 2000–2019,
177–78, 181. See also Asian/AAPI
residents; Black suburbanization;
Buford Highway corridor (DeKalb
County); immigrants; Latinx
residents; multiethnic metropolis,
Atlanta as; suburbanization of
poverty; white-majority suburbs,
planned efforts to maintain racial and
economic exclusivity

suburbanization of poverty: overview,
9–10; the Beltline and, 76–77; as
inverting the poor-in-the-core urban
model, 2, 76–77, 101–2, 133, 218;
isolation from critical services, 5;
map, 184–85; other metros compared
to Atlanta, 9–10; percentage of all
poor individuals living in the suburbs,

220; rates of (1990–2019), 183–85, 184–85,
220; as spatially concentrated, 184–85,
186, 220. See also suburban affordable
housing; suburban increases in racial
and economic diversity; suburban
multifamily housing; suburban
redevelopment projects (displace-and-
replace); white-majority suburbs,
planned efforts to maintain racial and
economic exclusivity

suburban multifamily housing: county
refusal to limit, as motivation for
secession, 198–99, 204; "favored
quarter" developments of, 187;
homeownership declines due to
construction of, 204; low-cost rental
stock, loss of, 194–95, 206, 212, 267n22;
secession movement and exclusion of
rental housing, 198–201, 203–4, 268n33.
See also secession (cityhood) as racial
and economic exclusion; suburban
redevelopment projects
(displace-and-replace)

suburban redevelopment machines, 7, 227

suburban redevelopment projects
(displace-and-replace), 203–14;
overview, 176–77, 197, 203–4, 226–27;
and advocacy for affordable housing,
need for, 195–96, 210–14, 215; in Buford
Highway corridor, 194, 196; families
with children and, 205, 208; gentrification and, 193, 194–97, 206, 212;
government power as "doing the
dirty work" of physical displacement,
209; Latinx and Black families
displaced by, 203–4, 205, 206–7, 208–9,
215, 269–70n49; media inattention as
facilitating, 209–10, 213; multifamily

low-cost rental housing as target of, 203, 204, 205–7, 211–12, 213, 269–70n49; New Urbanist rhetoric and, 208–9; portrayed as "revitalization" into modern "live-work-play" environments, 176–77, 204–5, 208; property tax base as factor in, 208, 209; public financing of, 177, 203, 204, 205, 207, 208, 209, 215; public-private partnerships for, 177, 209, 225; racialized dynamic of, 207–8, 227; replacement of low-cost housing with luxury apartments and single-family homes, 205–6, 212, 213; and schools, 203, 205, 207, 213; secession (cityhood) as increasing power to employ, 203–4. *See also* white-majority suburbs, planned efforts to maintain racial and economic exclusivity

Sunbelt metros: gentrification and, 105; institutional investors entering the single-family rental (SFR) industry, 136, 161, 162, 163, 170. *See also* metropolitan regions

Supreme Court of Georgia: racial zoning ordinance (1922) struck down, 19; ruling against foreclosure reform (2013), 150; ruling in favor of challenging TADs, 71–72; segregation ordinance (1915) struck down, 19

sustainability. *See* environmental sustainability

Sweet Auburn area, 89

TADs (tax allocation districts): overview, 69–70; constitutional amendment allowing, 72; the "Gulch" redevelopment, 114, 115–16; lawsuit challenging the right to divert property tax revenues from schools, 71–72, 78; property taxes as funding, 70; schools objecting to, 115, 116. *See also* Beltline TAD

tax allocation districts. *See* TADS

taxes. *See* commercial tax base; property taxes; public finance system

tax-increment financing districts (TIFs), 69–70. *See also* TADs (tax allocation districts)

Taylor, Keeanga-Yamahtta, 135

Techwood Flats demolition as "slum clearance," 30–31

Techwood Homes (public housing), 31, 44, 45–47, 125, 221

Temporary Coordinating Committee on Housing, 26

Tenants United for Fairness, 55

Terminus (original settlement), 13

transit. *See* public transit

Troubled Asset Relief Program (TARP), SIGTARP criticism of Georgia's HHF program, 151

Trump administration, suspends investigations by Consumer Financial Protection Bureau, 160

Trump, Donald, and election of 2016, 202

Trust for Public Land, 68

"turnaround" of Atlanta, 10, 59, 60, 61, 62, 94

Turner Field Community Benefits Coalition (TFCBC), 113–14

Turner Field controversy, 111, 113–14, 158

Union Depot, 15

United Way, 98, 227–28

U.S. Department of Housing and Urban Development (HUD), 46, 147, 152, 154

U.S. Securities and Exchange Commission, 169

U.S. Supreme Court: Brown vs. Board of Education, 31; Louisville's racial zoning ordinance struck down, 19; Smith vs. Allright (1944), 27; white Democratic primary struck down, 21, 27

U.S. Treasury Department, 150

vacant home crisis. *See* foreclosure crisis, decline in home values and rise in vacant homes

Vietnam, immigrants from, 191, 194

Vinings, 199

violence. *See* white violence against Black population

voter registration organizing, 229, 231

voter suppression, Republican efforts toward, 231–32

voter turnout and organizing, 229

voting rights for Black citizens: Atlanta urban regime's support for, in view of federal lack of, 29; increasing demands for, 26, 54, 55; racist propaganda against, 18; as threat to white political hegemony, 21, 23, 27, 29; voter registration campaigns, 21, 55; white Democratic primary struck down, 21, 27. *See also* Black electoral power

vouchers for housing: in addition to LIHTC program, 128; AHA dependence on, 47–48, 127, 222; for displaced residents in public housing demolitions, 46, 124; landlords not required

to accept, 48, 222, 230; rent formula, 128; vulnerability of rental stock in, 48, 222. *See also* AHA (Atlanta Housing Authority); subsidized housing

Walcott, Susan, 191–92, 193

Wall Street capital. *See* private equity capital

Wang, Kyungsoon, 144

Washington Park, first Black suburb, 22

wealth inequality, 171–73, 175

Weeks, Ray, 67

We Love Buford Highway, 191, 195

West Cobb, secession moves of, 199

West End (neighborhood), 30, 63

West End Cooperative Corporation (WECC), 21

Westside Mutual Development Committee, 27

Wheatley, Thomas, 83

White, Bill, 202

white-majority neighborhoods: Black residential clusters eliminated from, 31–32; eviction rates as much lower than for Black-majority neighborhoods, 128–29; the foreclosure crisis as mostly sparing, 142–43, 144–45; as insulated from desegregation, 32; located on higher ground north of downtown, 15; the "park-neighborhood" model for, 15; school desegregation and panic about Black residents, 31; secession (cityhood) movement in Buckhead, 201–3; zoning codes excluding lower-income families, 49, 130; zoning reform

public accommodations, 32; the foreclosure crisis as mostly sparing, 142–43, 144–45; and segregation within Black-majority DeKalb County, 33. *See also* white-majority suburbs, planned efforts to maintain racial and economic exclusivity

white violence against Black population: Atlanta anti-Black massacre (1906), 18; Atlanta urban regime and discussions of how to avoid, 54; and Black leadership's choice for expansion of segregated Black neighborhoods, 21, 22, 25–26, 27; as ever-present threat, 20–21; fear of, as enforcing segregation, 16, 18, 20, 21, 22, 27; white and Black flight from neighborhoods in wake of, 18

white working class, loss of legal supremacy and flight to the suburbs, 32

Whitten, Robert, 19–20

Woodham, John, 71, 78

Woodruff Foundation, 99–100

Woodruff, Robert, 38

Woolard, Cathy, and the Beltline, 66

"workforce housing," 200–201, 211, 247n51

working-class neighborhoods: the foreclosure crisis and transfer of homeownership to investors, 224; housing discrimination methods used to enforce segregation in, 20; in-fill development as dampening racial segregation in, 16; in-fill development for renters, 15; as relegated to lower-lying, flood-prone areas, 15; in segregated Black-majority DeKalb County, 33. *See also* Black working class; white working class

"world-class, global city" vision for Atlanta: Beltline light-rail transit advocates and, 66, 74, 75–76; as failure, 53; and focus on attracting global capital, 42, 53, 95–96; MARTA system and, 53; the Olympics (1996) and, 42, 53, 221; and public relations, 52–53

xenophobia, anti-immigrant, as confounding Atlanta's desire to be a global city, 53

Young, Andrew: and the Atlanta urban regime, 38–39, 98; and Bankhead Courts (public housing), 45; federal aid to the city slashed during tenure of, 38; foreign investment as focus of, 38–39; Shirley Franklin and, 66; lack of attention to problems of everyday residents, 39; the Olympics and, 42; "world-class city" vision of, 42, 53, 76

Youngblood, Mtamanika, 84

zoning: affluent neighborhoods excluding lower-income families, 49, 130; class-based zoning, 19–20; "homevoter" power and, 7, 225; minimum lot sizes, 20, 49; racial zoning ordinances, struck down, 19, 20, 21, 25, 130; and secession of suburbs as tool for racial and economic exclusion, 197, 198–99, 201, 203–4, 215; as tool for racial exclusion, 19, 130, 225; updates and incremental changes in, 131. *See also* inclusionary zoning; zoning reform

Founded in 1893,
UNIVERSITY OF CALIFORNIA PRESS
publishes bold, progressive books and journals
on topics in the arts, humanities, social sciences,
and natural sciences—with a focus on social
justice issues—that inspire thought and action
among readers worldwide.

The UC PRESS FOUNDATION
raises funds to uphold the press's vital role
as an independent, nonprofit publisher, and
receives philanthropic support from a wide
range of individuals and institutions—and from
committed readers like you. To learn more, visit
ucpress.edu/supportus.